George Augustus Sala

A Journey due South

Travels in Search of Sunshine

George Augustus Sala

A Journey due South
Travels in Search of Sunshine

ISBN/EAN: 9783744743860

Printed in Europe, USA, Canada, Australia, Japan

Cover: Foto ©Andreas Hilbeck / pixelio.de

More available books at **www.hansebooks.com**

THE CORRICOLO.

JOURNEY DUE SOUTH:

TRAVELS IN SEARCH OF SUNSHINE.

BY

GEORGE AUGUSTUS SALA,

AUTHOR OF "AMERICA REVISITED," "PARIS HERSELF AGAIN," "DUTCH PICTURES," ETC.

ILLUSTRATED WITH 16 PAGE ENGRAVINGS.

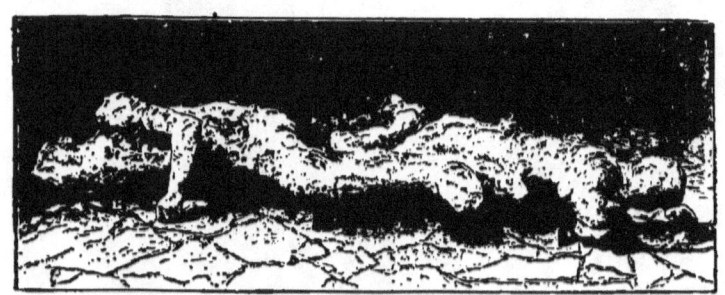

Human bodies preserved in ashes at Pompeii.

LONDON:
VIZETELLY & CO., 42, CATHERINE STREET, STRAND.
1885.

PREFACE.

Sait-on où l'on va? The question has been asked innumerable times; and, on this side the grave, will never have an answer. The mad fellow in Plutarch whom the captain of the watch asked whither he was going, when he met him wandering up and down the town in the night season, replied that he did not know. "Ha!" cried the haughty captain of the watch. "Is it so? We shall see. March me this impudent vagabond off to prison, and lay him by the heels." "Yet made I a proper answer," quoth Pillgarlic as the soldiers haled him away. "I said that I knew not whither I was going. Did I know that I was going to gaol?"

This hackneyed apologue must, in the main, serve as an introduction to this little volume of sketches of Continental Travel. The essays of which the volume chiefly consists were the result of a few weeks' holiday enjoyed two or three years ago, and were originally published in the columns of the *Daily Telegraph* newspaper. They were laid by for careful correction and revision and possible reproduction in book-form when I should have a little leisure; but the little leisure never came, and I continued to labour under the burden of invincible ignorance as to whither I was going, and of finding myself in places where I never expected to be.

I had at the outset of these papers one definite object in view, and one definite bourne to reach. I meant to go to Ajaccio to see the house in which Napoleon the Great was born, and thence to proceed to Porto Ferrajo, and endeavour to conjure up some mind-pictures of the Escape from Elba. Those journeys, I thought, would absorb the bulk of my autumnal outing. The Ironical Fates decreed that I should not visit Elba, this time; that I should be driven by stress of weather into Bastia (which detestable hole I had not the slightest intention of exploring), and that when I did get to Ajaccio I should be attacked by a fit of sickness so sore that so soon as I was convalescent I made haste to scuttle out of the island of Corsica. Bronchitis had brought me to Death's door, and my life was saved by a wise and kind German physician resident at the Hotel Germania, who told me that he too was on a holiday, and resolutely refused to take any fee, so that I was compelled just before I departed to slip a hundred-franc note, with "for the poor" inscribed on the envelope, underneath his bedroom door.

I travelled as swiftly as I could to Rome (whither I had not thought of going that year) to recruit. The chemists and druggists of the Eternal City keep, to my thinking, the nicest apothecaries' shops in Europe. I have the highest esteem for the Roman doctors; the Roman climate, in the hot and in the cold season, suits me admirably. I am always as much at home at the Albergo d'Inghilterra on the Via Bocca di Leone as I am in my own house in London; my wife is as fond of Rome as I am. We like the Roman speech, the manners, and the people; and I should like (*sait-on où l'on va?*) to die in Rome, or to be carried there, dead, and laid in the Protestant Cemetery hard by the Pyramid of Caius Sestius, and the wall of Rome. It is the greenest and most beautiful and happiest-looking graveyard that I have ever seen.

But we do not know whither we are going—here below. There is a country called Russia, the climate, the institutions, and the governing classes of which—

from the highest of Excellencies to the lowest of police-agents—I very cordially hate. When in January, 1877, I left Odessa (having come down from Petersburg to see the Russian army in the process of mobilisation at Kischeneff) and crossed the Black Sea to Constantinople, I did not precisely "register a vow" that I would never visit Russia again. It is about the most foolish thing that anybody can do to register vows. But I cherished the earnest hope that I might never have to visit the big, ugly, enslaved empire of the Tsar again. As it chanced I had to go to St. Petersburg again in 1881, to record the funeral of the murdered Alexander II., and to Moscow again in 1883, to record the coronation of the not yet assassinated Alexander III. To Tsars the Ides of March are sadly elastic.

From a strictly geographical point of view, this unpretentious little book is no more descriptive of a "Journey due South" than my first journal of Russian travel, published more than a quarter of a century ago, was descriptive of a "Journey due North." Publishers, however, have their whims; and mine thought that it might be as well to adhere in these republished papers to their original title. For the rest and in conclusion (*sait-on où l'on và?*) I venture to hope that I am slightly more geographically accurate in stating that at this present time of writing I am beginning a journey South West':—that is to say, I am bound from the South of Ireland to North America; thence to the Great West, and so from California to Melbourne. But I had always a fine natural capacity for blundering, and (setting aside the inevitable contingencies of not knowing whither you are going,) my course, during the next two months may not turn out to be a South-Westerly one, after all. Good bye, Ladies and Gentlemen. A Merry Christmas and a Happy New Year.

GEORGE AUGUSTUS SALA.

On Board the Cunard s.s. "Gallia,"
    Queenstown, Ireland,
        Sunday, December 28, 1884.

CONTENTS.

A JOURNEY DUE SOUTH.

		PAGE
I.	A Few Hours in the Delightful City	13
II.	Life at Marseilles	28
III.	Southern Fare and Bouillabaisse	40
IV.	Nice and its Nefarious Neighbour	51
V.	Quite Another Nice	67
VI.	From Nice to Bastia	80
VII.	On Shore at Bastia	95
VIII.	The Diligence come to Life Again	108
IX.	Sunday at Ajaccio	121
X.	The Hotel Too Soon	134
XI.	The House in St. Charles Street, Ajaccio	147
XII.	A Winter City	160
XIII.	Genoa, the Superb.—The City of the Leaning Tower	172
XIV.	Austere Bologna	185
XV.	A Day of the Dead	196

CONTENTS.

		PAGE
XVI.	VENICE PRESERVED	211
XVII.	THE TWO ROMES.—THE OLD	225
XVIII.	THE TWO ROMES.—THE NEW	233
XIX.	THE TWO ROMES—THE NEW—(*continued*)	246
XX.	THE ROMAN SEASON	254
XXI.	IN THE VATICAN	268
XXII.	WITH THE TRAPPISTS IN THE CAMPAGNA	283
XXIII.	FROM NAPLES TO POMPEII	296
XXIV.	THE SHOW OF A LONG-BURIED PAST	312
XXV.	THE "MOVIMENTO" OF NAPLES	331
XXVI.	IN THE SHADE	347

SPRING-TIME IN PARIS.

I.	A CONTINENTAL SUNDAY	361
II.	"TO ALL THE GLORIES OF FRANCE."	377
III.	LE ROI SOLEIL AND LA BELLE BOURBONNAISE	390
IV.	A QUEEN'S PLAYTHING	404

LIST OF ILLUSTRATIONS.

	PAGE
THE CORRICOLO	*Frontispiece*
HUMAN BODIES PRESERVED IN ASHES AT POMPEII	*Title Page*
THE PORT OF MARSEILLES	17
MONTE CARLO	57
A CORSICAN FOREST	98
THE FORTIFICATIONS OF BASTIA	101
ON THE BEACH AT AJACCIO	128
A PRICKLY PEAR TREE	168
ST. MARK'S PLACE, VENICE	223
ARRIVAL OF THE CARDINALS AT THE QUIRINAL	231
THE POPE IN THE SEDIA AT ST. PETER'S	232
A CARDINAL ENTERING THE VATICAN	277
WOMEN OF THE CAMPAGNA	283
THE HOUSE OF PANZA AT POMPEII, RESTORED	312
DISCOVERY OF LOAVES IN A BAKER'S OVEN AT POMPEII	318
A NEAPOLITAN MACARONI SELLER	349
A WATER VENDOR'S STALL AT NAPLES	354

A JOURNEY DUE SOUTH.

I.

A FEW HOURS IN THE DELIGHTFUL CITY.

PARIS, *September* 22.

I JUST looked in upon Paris, that Great City, on my way down South; and I am not in the least ashamed to confess that—it may be for the fiftieth, or, for the matter of that, the hundredth time in my life—the aspect, manners, and humours of the metropolis of France have fairly astonished me. Nay, so hardened have I grown in sincerity and completeness of "owning up" that I aver the Paris of to-day to be, in many respects, a much more astonishing capital than the Paris of August, 1839, in which last-named month and year I first alighted from the Boulogne diligence at the offices of the Messageries of MM. Laffite et Caillard, in the Rue Notre Dame des Victoires; and, pretty much as a newly-born duckling takes to the water, I found myself, not many minutes afterwards, "en plein Palais-Royal."

Paris was astounding enough under Louis Philippe; and a very wonderful city was it during the Republic which sprouted up, gourd-like, in February, 1848, and collapsed, very much after the manner of a soap-bubble, in December, 1851. Throughout the duration of the Second Empire Paris never ceased to present a spectacle of continuously recurring marvels. It was as though you were beholding a gala display of fireworks; and each new shower of golden rain, each new ascent of coruscating rockets, elicited from the cosmopolitan crowd below a more prolonged and more wonder-stricken cry of "O-o-o-oh!" At last came the "bouquet"—a wind-up which occurred on the 4th of September, 1870; and was truly astonishing after its kind, but which scarcely came to the culmination expected by the Imperial pyrotechnists, who contrived to set not only their remaining stock of squibs and crackers, Catherine wheels and Roman candles, but also the Empire and all France to boot, in a blaze.

It were unnecessary to dwell upon the astonishing features presented by Lutetia throughout the successive vicissitudes of the Siege, the Commune, the Versailles Terror, and the Clericalist and Legitimist intrigues which marked the dictatorship of M. Thiers and the uncompleted Septennate of Marshal MacMahon. Our friend the "merest schoolboy" is old enough to have taken his holiday trips to Paris—I hope under the guardianship of a fond female relation or of a discreet tutor —and to have seen for himself how astonishingly Paris, after enduring almost unprecedented suffering, convulsion, and devastation, has progressed in the path of restoration and recuperation. It was in the Exhibition year, 1878, that she triumphantly proclaimed herself completely convalescent, and cast the nightcap of the invalid and the crutches of the cripple "par-dessus les moulins"; still, although it chanced that I abode in the very heart of Paris during the entire summer and autumn of the Exposition year, and found in the daily unrolling panorama of manners much to excite wonder and admiration, the Paris of 1878 did not astonish me half so much as that of a few years afterwards has done.

In the Government of the former year a phantom of aristocratic, or at least of oligarchic, rule yet lingered. The Marshal was yet in power. The amnesty was scarcely an accomplished fact. M. Gambetta was yet regarded as a Radical of the reddest dye. The Jesuits were everywhere, and devout persons still hoped to see the coping-stone laid to the Propitiatory Church on the summit of Montmartre. Bonapartism still went about, its head arrogantly lifted, and muttering in tones not by any means inarticulate that its turn was coming again, and that at no distant date; and, finally, it was not quite a prudent nor quite a safe thing to talk German too loudly in a café or in a railway carriage. Travellers of Teutonic nationality visiting Paris to see the Great Show in the Champ de Mars were apt preferentially to patronise hotels kept by and frequented almost exclusively by Germans; and politic children of the Fatherland who were obliged by their business engagements to have a permanent domicile in the French capital, were more inclined, on the whole, to be taken for Austrians, and especially for Alsatians, than for Prussians, Bavarians, or Saxons pure and simple.

Whether there are any Legitimists, Bonapartists, or Orleanists left in French society, it is not my present purpose to inquire. I suppose that there are politicians of many different shades of opinion who hate the Democratic Republic which is at present predominant, and who would like to see it destroyed in blood and fire to-morrow; but these enemies of Liberty, Equality, and Fraternity—as at present understood and practised—make few, if any, public protestations of their anti-Republicanism. The *Gaulois* has, with one of the most amusing *volte-faces* ever witnessed, become an " independent and liberal paper," and announces its intention of remodelling its foreign intelligence after the fashion of ".the great English newspapers, which frequently have a staff of six special correspondents in a single metropolis, and even maintain flotillas which go out to meet news-bearing ships, and, when necessary, penetrate to the North Pole and the interior of Africa." This is, indeed, "approbation from Sir Hubert Stanley." May the *Gaulois* build a flotilla which shall penetrate to the moon! Such, at least, should be the devout wish of wandering Englishmen, who, for all intellectual sustenance, have to peruse those French daily papers which, as a brilliant English *chroniqueur* deceased used to say, "bear the date of to-morrow and contain the intelligence of last week."

The conversion of the *Gaulois* is not the only curious sign of the times just now. The Bonapartist organs have, as a rule, taken down the well-known sign of the Grey Great Coat and the Little Cocked Hat from their shop fronts. Imperialism evidently rules very low in the book market, for an obliging bibliopole on the Boulevard des Italiens offered me the entire set of the "Correspondence du Roi Joseph"—ten octavo volumes—for seven francs fifty centimes. Literary taste at present in Paris sets more strongly in favour of "raw head

THE PORT OF MARSEILLES.

and bloody bones" stories in disparagement of the Second Empire, related in the so-called "Memoirs of Monsieur Claude," sometime Chief of the Police de Sûreté, which is perhaps the most audacious collection of ribald Munchausenisms ever published since the "Memoirs of Jacques Casanova" achieved their scandalous notoriety.

As a memoir-writer Claude beats his predecessor, Canler, who rarely overstepped the bounds of probability in his narrations, and was consequently very often dull. The merit and charm of M. Claude's performance consist in the ingenuity with which an arabesque of fibs has been embroidered on the plain tissue of the diary of a not exceptionally shrewd detective. Take, for instance, the wondrous cock-and-bull stories related by the ex-Alguazil-in-Chief of the Rue de Jérusalem concerning the Emperor Napoleon III. We learn from this veracious chronicler that about the year 1831 Prince Louis Napoleon, disguised in a blouse and sabots, was in the habit of associating with the bandits and the lost creatures of the Cité; and that, under the name of "Le Charmeur," he was a well-known *habitué* of that notorious *tapis franc*, the "Lapin Blanc," in the Rue aux Fèves. It was in the midst of the scum of the crime and profligacy in Paris that, if this ex-Sbirro of the Second Empire is to be believed, the nephew of Napoleon the Great "organised Bonapartist conspiracies." Alack, Cæsar is very dead indeed; and the slaves who licked his boots are grumbling at the nasty flavour of the blacking which, "dans le temps," they swallowed so greedily.

M. Claude has not the slightest doubt that Prince Louis Napoleon, the pseudo-associate of the "Chourineurs" and

"Goualeuses" of 1831, was the prototype of Eugène Sue's Prince Rodolphe, Grand Duke of Gérolstein, who made his first bow to the public in "Les Mystères de Paris" about 1842. M. Eugène Sue, the ex-detective cogently remarks, was a son of one of the surgeons of Napoleon I. Hence his reticence as to the identity of Prince Rodolphe with the "Charmeur." Now, M. Eugène Sue was the son of a naval surgeon, and the grandson of the famous Sue "le Fils," who was surgeon to Louis XVI., who wrote one of the best treatises on graphic anatomy that has ever been published, and who, in a memorable essay, strenuously denied the painlessness of decollation by the guillotine.

The author of the "Mysteries of Paris" and the "Wandering Jew" was an irreconcilable Republican and Socialist. He hated Louis Napoleon and the Second Empire as bitterly as Armand Barbès, as Félix Pyat, as Blanqui, or as Raspail ever did; he died in exile in Savoy in 1857, five years after the Coup d'État, and it is literally inconceivable that, had he known anything in the remotest manner disparaging the character of the Man of December, he would have held his peace. Red Republicans did not write in rose-water between 1852 and 1857.

The Rue aux Fèves and the surrounding labyrinth of foul and criminal streets over against the Palais de Justice have long since been demolished; but I preserve a lively remembrance of the horrible old locality. It was on the Thursday of the Coup d'État week that, having passed the merry season of the bombardment of Paris in a cellar of the Hôtel de Lille et d'Albion, Rue St. Honoré, I determined, in company with a young English friend, to explore the *penetralia* of the Cité. The porter of the hotel warned us against the attempt; but we were just two young English fools, with our heads full of Prince Rodolphe and Fleur de Marie, Bras Rouge and Tortillard, the Maître d'École and the Chouette. So we took a *fiacre* on the Thursday night, looking in on our way at the Salle Valentino, where the officers, " en tenue de campagne," were dancing with the sweethearts of the *blouses* whom they had been shooting down the day before, and made for the Cité. It was about the period when silly young Englishmen were in the habit of wearing overcoats of a monstrously rough and hairy texture—the overcoats caricatured by John Leech in *Punch*, when he makes an Oxford Proctor say to a youth arrayed in the fashionable garb of the day, "I beg pardon, sir; *but are you a member of the University, or a Scotch terrier?*" Muffled up in these hirsute wrap-rascals, and with wideawake hats slouched over our eyes, we thought ourselves very picturesquely disguised indeed.

The *tapis franc* of the "Lapin Blanc" was a bitter disappointment. Behind the counter, instead of an "Ogress" there was a fat man in a blue apron. There was at one of the tables a little old woman in a mob cap and a blue checked bedgown, who was excessively tipsy, and vehemently implored to be treated to more *cassis* on the score of her being the old original Fleur de Marie of Eugène Sue. Beyond this elderly Bacchante there was little worth mentioning. The few men in blouses scattered about the dark and dirty room were probably thieves, and possibly, on occasion, murderers; but they did not molest us. In all likelihood they arrived at the very natural conclusion that we were foreigners who had come there "to see the show," and that we had a sufficient escort of police outside ready to make their appearance at a given signal. As it happened, we were quite unarmed and unattended; and we certainly deserved to have gotten our heads broken for our pains.

I have little doubt the critics will tear to shreds the monstrous fables which M. Claude has invented about the Orsini-Pieri plot of 1858—I was dining at the Café Riche at the moment when the explosion took place, and I remember Count Félice Orsini very well;—about Louis Napoleon's interview "dans le Waping, vieux quartier de Londres" with "Miss Howard;" and especially about M. Claude being robbed during the Exhibition year, 1867, by a "Miss Palmer," a "Blonde Venus" of the English refreshment bar, and an English pickpocket who passed himself off as "Inspector Clarskovich," of the English Detective Force, Scotland Yard. The imperfectly-informed Claude had apparently heard in some misty manner about two English police-officers, named respectively Clarke and Druscovich, and had so " combined his information," as the gentleman did in the well-known case of " Chinese Metaphysics."

One of the most astonishing phases of the existing condition of society in France is, perhaps, the apparently implicit faith placed by young France in the melodramatic fables of Monsieur Claude on the one hand, and the "realistic" revelations of M. Emile Zola on the other. The press, as a rule, seems to be gravely convinced of the veracity of the ex-thief-taker's "blood-and-thunder" stories about the Emperor Napoleon III. and the leading personages of the Imperial Court, and to look upon the revolting state of French manners as depicted in "Nana" and novels of a similar character as inherent to and inseparable from the "corruption, venality, and profligacy of the Second Empire," and as representing a state of things which has passed away, never to return.

Whatever was ignoble, whatever was scandalous, whatever was wicked a dozen years ago, was all, according to the believers in MM. Claude and Zola, the fault of the Second Empire and Napoleon III. "Who filled the butchers' shops with large blue flies?" Clearly the Second Empire. "Who made the quartern loaf and Luddites rise?" Manifestly, Napoleon III.; or, to come nearer home, in the French sense, what student of Béranger does not remember—

> Si Borgia, jadis au public
>   Vendait indulgences et bulles ;
> S'il aurait à ce trafic
>   Vendu jusqu'à sa mule ;
> S'il fût marchand de chapeaux,
> *C'est la faute de Rousseau ;*
> En Dieu s'il ne crût guère,
> *C'est la faute de Voltaire.*

Meanwhile an édition de luxe of "Nana," illustrated by the first draughtsmen of the day, is selling by the thousand ; and in almost every print-shop window may be seen photographic reproductions of "Le Signe de Nana." In this respect let me call attention to another thing which has mightily astonished me in this Paris, which, since the "corruption, venality, and profligacy" of the Second Empire have been swept away, is supposed to be, from a moral as well as a political point of view, "regenerated." If I remember aright, in one of the curiously minute studies of the First Revolution, which we owe to the industry and research of the brothers de Goncourt, it is incidentally mentioned that to so great an extent, when the Reign of Terror was at its height, had the bonds of moral restraint and even of common decorum become loosened that the scandalous pictures illustrative of the mad Marquis de Sade's "Justine" were openly exposed for sale in the shop-windows of the Palais Royal. Well, I have been intimately acquainted with Paris for the last forty-two years, and wayfarers of equal seniority with myself may agree with me that at no time during the period which I have named have the printsellers of the gay capital been very straightlaced. Indeed, French and English ideas as to propriety in matters of literature, the drama, and art may be said to run in parallel lines which have never met, and happily—at least, so I hope—will never converge. But I do most unhesitatingly declare that at no time during my acquaintance with Paris have the shop-windows presented such an astounding exhibition of pictorial and plastic, but chiefly photographic indecency, as they do at the present moment.

The normally indelicate illustrations which embellish the French so-called "comic" papers—the *Journal Amusant*, the *Vie Parisienne*, the *Petit Journal pour Rire*, and so forth—which are sold at the Boulevard kiosques, mainly concern the French themselves. English people are apt to find the eternal allusions to the inability of *cocottes* to pay their rent, and their desperate attempts to extort money from the other sex, in order to make things pleasant with the *concierge* and the *crémière*, rather trite and unamusing. It is the same with the professedly "funny" anecdotes which one finds in the *Triboulet* and the *Tintamarre*, the *Voltaire* and the *Gil Blas*. The bulk of these laboured witticisms read like long-since exploded Joe Millers garnished with *doubles entendres* in Boulevard *argot;* but the unseemly productions of which I speak, and which have nothing whatever to do with fine art properly so called, abound in the thoroughfares most frequented by English and American visitors. Under the arcades of the Rue de Rivoli they literally swarm, and they are nearly as numerous in the Boulevard des Capucines and in the Rue Vivienne.

One is tolerably sure to be wrong in flying into a passion about anything, and the older a public writer grows the more sedulously—if he be a sagacious writer—should he endeavour to subdue any tendency towards enthusiasm in his views of things, and to bear in mind Talleyrand's sapient caveat against zeal. For example, a French gentleman, to whom I was recently talking about things in general, and about Liberty as contradistinguished from Licence in particular, shrugged his shoulders, folded his arms, knitted his brows, and, with a concentrated expression of disapproval of the existing "ordre de choses," said "Que voulez vous, monsieur? Ces voyous triomphent."

Now, it would be very unmannerly in me, a stranger in the land, to say that in the France of the existing dispensation "les voyous," or "the Gavroche party," or "the gentlemen of the pavement" are triumphant. Much more to my mind was the ostensibly philosophical dictum I heard the other day, to the effect that France is governed under a system of leases varying in duration between four and eighteen years. As a rule they are never renewed, although the contracts are generally in the strictest sense repairing ones. But when the lease has expired out goes the tenant, not only without the slightest compensation for improvements made, but the luckless wight is very often sued by the owner of the freehold for waste. "Révolution pour cause de fin de bail" is an inscription which, at divers periods in French history, has been appropriately placed side by side with "Vive la République!" "Vive l'Empire!" and "Vive le Roi!" I have heard all three cries in Paris yelled with thunderous unanimity and enthusiasm—while it lasted. Perhaps the *enseigne* put up by the Paris hairdresser on the restoration of the Bourbons in 1814 was in its broad philosophy and its widely embracing common sense the best of all. "Vive le Roi!" wrote the unprejudiced coiffeur—"Vive le Roi, ma Femme et Moi!"

But there is another way out of the difficulty, and that is to be simply and submissively astonished. It will all come right —or wrong—in time. All is for the best or for the worst. "Toutes choses se meuvent vers leur fin," wrote Rabelais; but what is to be the end, or, rather, the next act in this marvellous French masquerade, who shall say? It is the opinion of the Clericalist journals that the destruction of Paris by showers of burning brimstone and marl is merely a question of time, and that the time in question is an extremely brief one. It is the opinion of the *Figaro* that France is politically wholly demoralised and disorganised, and that the ship of State is rapidly drifting on a combination of Scylla and Charybdis, the Rapids of Niagara, the Bell Rock, and the Goodwin Sands, hitherto undreamt of by the hydrographer to the Admiralty. It is the opinion of the *Intransigeant* and the *Rappel* that MM. Jules Ferry and Barthélemy de St. Hilaire, in conjunction with General Farre, are rapidly ruining the country; that the French army in North Africa is melting away like wax before a fire; and that national cataclysm will be precipitated by the accession to power of M. Léon Gambetta.

At the same time, if you enter a shop on the Boulevards to buy a pair of gloves, or one of the countless nicknacks which French art workmen are never tired of producing, French shopkeepers of selling, or English simpletons of purchasing, the lady behind the counter will, in answer to your inquiries as to how things are going, rub her hands cheerfully, smile one of her sweetest smiles, and reply that things are going charmingly. The weather has been rather rainy lately; still "les affaires marchent et tout le monde est content." The cafés are crammed by night and by day, and at the fashionable Boulevard restaurants the good old Exposition prices of 1867 and 1878 seem to be established *en permanence*.

At a very fashionable restaurant last Sunday night a French gentleman who, with his wife, was dining at the next table to mine, was so ill-advised as to grumble because, forsooth, he was charged the sum of four francs and fifty centimes for the slender "portion" of grapes at which I had seen him and his lady pensively pecking. It is with the extremest difficulty that your Frenchman can keep his hands off small delicacies at which he can peck, grapes, nuts, radishes, prawns, and such like. That is why artful head waiters place platefuls of the pretty tiny kickshaws before him, in order that he may peck and pay the more. The shrewder Englishman with a motion of the hand bluffly waves the dangerous delicacies away. The Frenchman who was charged nearly four shillings for perhaps four-pennyworth of grapes was fairly infuriated. It was scandalous, it was monstrous, he declared. The urbane proprietor, in a voice soft and sweet as neatsfoot oil, explained to the exasperated client that between " lui et sa dame, un raisin et demi "—grapes for one and a half—had been consumed. The exasperated client " s'en moquait pas mal." He would write to the newspapers, he asseverated; a scathing newspaper article should be published to expose such brigandage. Again the urbane proprietor sweetly smiled. Such an article, with light sarcasm, he opined, would be an excellent advertisement for his establishment.

This observation, I could not help thinking, bordered slightly on the unblushingly impudent. But there was no remedy. The urbane proprietor knew it. The Frenchman paid eventually, and went away swearing as only a Frenchman can swear when he is fairly roused; nor did his fair companion—she wore a Gainsborough hat with black ostrich plumes, and looked like Mrs. Haller in " The Stranger "—omit to give the *dame de comptoir* " a piece of her mind " as she swept out of the expensive and extortionate precincts. The landlord, who is a very ancient ally of mine, whispered to me gaily that *ces gens* were evidently " Sunday folk " who did not understand " le vie comme il faut." The urbane creature had just charged me three francs for a tiny ration of haricot beans and eight francs for a partridge, which at the first glance I took to be a conceited quail. But the cooking was admirable, the service perfect, the Pontet-Canet very ambrosial, and—what would you have? It is so many years since I was first fleeced at that urbane establishment. Astonishing city, where one likes to be fleeced, and where one even with willing nod invites the shearer! Astonishing city, where no one thinks of to-morrow until to-morrow comes with a roar and a rush, such as those that whelmed the cities of the plain!

II.

LIFE AT MARSEILLES.

MARSEILLES, *September* 27.

I KNOW very few populous and affluent cities which have been so systematically ignored and maltreated—if there be ill-usage in indifference—by tourists as it has been the lot of Marseilles to be; and, since the substitution of the Brindisian for the Massilian point of departure of the Indian mail, Marseilles has fallen, among ordinary British travellers, into even sorer disparagement than of yore. In the days fondly regretted by all good Marseillais of "La Malle des Indes," each incoming P. and O. steamer from Alexandria brought a host of British officers, civilians, ladies and children to the three colossal hotels of the Phocœan city; and although the sojourn therein of these home-returning Anglo-Indians was, as a rule, of the briefest, they contrived to spend a good deal of money during the few hours of their stay.

The hotel and restaurant keepers, the cab-drivers, and the tradespeople of the Cannebière profited largely by the periodical influx of the lieges of Queen Victoria; and it also happened that the home-returners, fatigued with the sea voyage, frequently "laid over" at Marseilles for a whole day and night, in order to "repair the tissues," and that, in the course of such a four-and-twenty hours' delay, English ladies discovered that in the *magasins de modes* of the Rue St. Ferréol, bonnets, costumes, lace, and embroidery, quite as tasteful as and much cheaper than those to be found in the Rue Vivienne or the Chaussée d'Antin, were purchaseable; while English gentlemen became aware of the fact that in the Cannebière are some of the largest and most splendid cafés to be found in the whole of Europe; that the Grand Théâtre is a sumptuous edifice, wherein such an opera as "L'Africaine" can be given with the fullest lyric, choregraphic, and spectacular *éclat;* that the Théâtre des Nations rivals the gigantic theatres of Barcelona in area and magnificence; that in the Museum of the Palais de Longchamps there is a collection of more than five hundred excellent oil paintings, including, among works by French masters alone, pictures by Ary Scheffer, Corot, Gerard, Granet, Bougereau, Mignard, and Rigaud: and, finally, that on the Chemin de la Corniche there are numerous "restaurants à reserve"—each one proclaims itself to be *the* Reserve, the term meaning only a fish-pond—where the traditional Provençal dish called "Bouillabaisse" is procurable at prices, now sweetly moderate and now simply extortionate.

Marseilles is a city alike for large and small portemonnaies. I showed lately to my guide, philosopher, and friend a dinner bill of the Maison Dorée, in the Cannebière—a dinner bill for one person. Not much in the way of gastronomy. A slice of melon, a potage St. Germain, a fish "loup de mer," a "cotelette de mouton, sauce Béarnaise," a "salade à la Romaine," and a pint of Ernest Irroy. Total eighteen francs. "Nothing can be said to be overcharged," quoth Figaro; "but if Monsieur had ordered the *dîner du jour*, he would have enjoyed as much, and more, including the *vin fin*, for nine francs." I knew nothing about the "dîner du jour." Marseilles in the halcyon times of the Malle des Indes exulted in the weekly patronage of hundreds of travelling Britons who knew nothing about the "dîner du jour."

The withdrawal of the Anglo-Indian transit service from Marseilles administered a staggering, but not a knock-down, blow to the city. The three giant hotels were the greatest sufferers, for chief among the things which you cannot by any possibility succeed in persuading the ordinary Frenchman to do is to induce him to stay in a first-class, and consequently expensive, hotel, either in his own country or abroad. "Pas si bête" is his usual reply when he is asked why he has not alighted at the Grand Hôtel. He adds that "on est très bien" at the Cheval Blanc, or the Hôtel du Commerce, or the Petit Luxembourg. Why there should be all over the Continent, from Cambrai to Constantinople, so many hostelries by the sign of the province concerning which France and Germany so nearly fell to loggerheads in the summer of 1867—it was one of the false starts which preceded the real contest of 1870—passes my comprehension. What does the ordinary Frenchman want with an hotel, in which there are ladies' drawing-rooms, reading and smoking-rooms? Very little. An hotel is to him only an *auberge*—a place where one can eat and sleep. All that he requires in the way of smoking, reading, conversation, and conviviality he obtains at the nearest café. At a watering-place, "à la bonne heure," as much company and conversation as you like; but Marseilles, although on the sea, is not a watering-place. In nine cases out of ten the typical Frenchman travels—his annual excursion "aux eaux" excepted—not from inclination but from necessity; and old Bishop Hall, who wrote his vehement tractate, "Quo Vadis?" in the hope of dissuading young English gentlemen of the Elizabethan age from travelling on the Continent, is amusingly reflected in a protest against "tourism" which I lately read in a *feuilleton* by one of the most brilliant of living French essayists. "Why should I expatriate myself," asked the lively writer, "when I can travel every morning from the Café de la Madeleine to the Café de Foy—when I can travel every evening from the Boulevard des Italiens to the Boulevard Montmartre? Why should I wander over an indefinite number of kilometres in order to pay one franc fifty centimes each for fabulous *bougies*, and make the acquaintance of hitherto unknown fleas?"

Thus the surcease of the *clientèle* of La Malle des Indes produced for a season a far from agreeable vacuum in the *caisses* of the grand hotels of Marseilles. Ere long, however, they recuperated, and at present they may be said to be fairly prosperous. The middle-class hotels are, on the other hand, continuously crowded with commercial travellers and persons taking passage in the innumerable lines of steamers which leave this port for most parts of the world. The Grand Hôtel, in the Rue de Noailles, where I am for the present residing, and which I have "used" these fifteen or sixteen years past, is not by any means full. Indeed, during the summer heats, only the rooms on the ground and the first floors are kept open for the accommodation of visitors. Imagine the Adelphi or the London and North-Western, or the Washington at Liverpool, shutting up three-fourths of their bed-rooms between the beginning of June and the end of September! Yet Marseilles is not, any more than Liverpool, a fashionable watering-place. The city of the Bouches-du-Rhône is, like the city on the Mersey, a vast commercial entrepôt, and a bourn at which countless travellers by sea and land embark and disembark: but it is the inns of the Cheval Blanc, the Hôtel du Commerce, and the Petit Luxembourg class—pray bear in mind that I am speaking generally, and am not particularising in hotel nomenclature— which absorb the vast majority of the strangers who come to Marseilles.

During the winter months the grand hotels do better, being often the halting-place of families who like easy travelling, and of invalids on their way to Cannes or Nice, or the lovely health resorts in the Riviera di Levanti. There is also, from November to March, a tolerably shady contingent of Britons of a speculative and sporting turn who have thrown down the gauntlet to Fortune in the way of backing the red or "plunging" on the "pair et impair" at Monte Carlo, and who, having been, with more or less promptitude, satisfactorily "cleaned out" at that pleasant Inferno, "wash up," so to speak, in dire stress for ready cash, at Marseilles. The name of the city has a mercantile and moneyed sound; and it seems more respectable to write home thence for remittances than from the Albergo dei Bancherotti at Monaco, or the

Hôtel des Grands Dégommés on the Boulevard de la Condamine.

At our Grand Hôtel in the Rue de Noailles we have a most imposing *salle-à-manger*, where, in days gone by, I have been, at tables-d'hôte yet more imposing, a deferentially observant guest. Such grandees we used to meet with! Senators and prefects, Imperial chamberlains and equerries, masters of requests and auditors of the Court of Cassation; sunburnt Anglo-Indian generals, coming home on leave; dashing young English soldier officers; solid Dutch millionnaires from Java; English and American tea and silk kings, from Canton or Shanghai, in snowy suits of white duck; cadaverous French Governors from Mauritius or Pondicherry; now and again a real Hindoo Rajah, or a sham Chinese Mandarin; and any number of ladies more or less exhausted by the burning sun of Ind. Those days are fled, not to return again, perchance. Our *salle-à-manger*, be it understood, has lost nothing of its pristine splendour. Its windows are yet draped with gorgeous curtains of many hues, stiff with brocade and bullion-tasselled. So deeply coved, so richly corniced is its ceiling that the Saints of Verrio and Laguerre might appropriately sprawl there. In their stead are an azure sky, and roseate clouds, and festoons of brilliant flowers. From the centre depends a crystal chandelier which Wardour-street or High Holborn might prize and Indian begums adore. But that crystal chandelier is not to be lighted yet awhile. The salle is not yet to be decked with the monstrous epergnes and bowls of *faïence* full of flowers and sub-tropical plants. The stately chairs, covered with maroon-coloured morocco, are not yet to be occupied by the mighty and the proud. The winter tables-d'hôte have not yet commenced. They had one as a *coup d'essai* yesterday, but only six sat down to the all too ample board. I am glad, somehow, that I did not make one of the pioneer half-dozen, but that I was refecting at the Maison Dorée opposite. I should have fancied that the remainder of the maroon-coloured morocco chairs were occupied by so many Banquos, some of them blood-boltered and shaking their gory locks at me. I peeped furtively into the palatial *salle-à-manger* this morning while it was temporarily opened for dusting purposes, and it seemed to me that the place was haunted. Not by the spectre of La Malle des Indes, but by an entirely different species of phantom.

Let me explain a little. Marseilles, they tell me, is at present, next to Paris and Lyons, the most Radical and the most anti-clerical city in fair France; and Madame Veuve Gaston Crémieux—the poor lady's husband was a distinguished Marseilles advocate of advanced Democratic opinions, whom a reactionary general of the Galliffet type caused to be shot by sentence of drum-head court-martial in 1871—is more venerated than ever. Some years since, when I was here last, coming from Constantinople, the old lady at the newsvendor's stall at the railway station, who sold me a paper called *Le Petit Caporal*, hinted, with an approving nod, that "la gare était encore Bonapartiste;" and, indeed, it was notorious that the majority of the inferior employés were Corsicans; but all that is changed. The railway station has apparently been entirely purged of Imperialism; the working classes are described as Intransigeant Socialists of the reddest hue, and the shopkeepers are Opportunist Republicans, gaily content with the existing order of things, principally for the reason that trade is flourishing, and that Marseilles is making a great deal of money. The local gentry are sulkily and prudently silent. No religious processions are visible, nor, I believe, are such manifestations tolerated any more by the Municipal Council; the monks have altogether vanished; and it is very seldom even that you meet a Sister of Charity or a Petite Sœur des Pauvres. The Intransigeant deputies, Citizens Tony Revillon and Clovis Hugues, are the heroes of the hour. They have been giving *conférences* on Voltaire and Condorcet; they have been entertained at a "Fraternal Punch" by the "Free-thinking Cabdrivers' Association—Réunion des Cochers de Voitures de Place Libres Penseurs." "Civil interments" are the fashion; and the "Marseillaise" is yelled late at night by bacchanalian hopes of their country returning from the innumerable *bastringues* of this city of dram-shops, with an enthusiasm equally patriotic and distressing to the nerves of unsound sleepers.

Yes; Marseilles has grown to be terribly Radical: it is Red to the very finger tips. Not the less is it to me, from the Meilhan to the Joliette, from L'Estacque to Roquefavour, from the Chateau d'If to Notre Dame de la Garde, haunted by the ghost of the Second Empire—father, among other less beneficent things, of grand hotels, well-built carriages, and municipal and residential cleanliness. Augustus found Rome of brick and left it of marble. At least Napoleon III. and his satraps found Paris, Lyons, and Marseilles structurally and sanitarily filthy, and left them clean. The Rue de Noailles or " Cannebière Prolongée" cost in its construction the enormous sum of twelve millions eight hundred thousand francs. The Rue Impériale, now called the Rue de la République, pierced through the mountain, on the summit of which is old Marseilles, was a Titanic enterprise. The street is more than three thousand feet long, and seventy-five feet wide. Its ostensible "mission" was to open up a communication between the old and the new ports of Marseilles; its real purport was to pour splendid dividends into the cash-box of some association of financiers of the Crédit Mobilier order, who fondly hoped to see all the flats of the stately six-storeyed mansions of the Rue Impériale occupied at rents ranging between three and six hundred pounds a year, and all the ground floors tenanted by banks, assurance offices, steamboat agencies, jewellers, goldsmiths, milliners, porcelain warehouses, and so forth, all cheerfully paying *loyers* based on the tariff of the Boulevard Haussmann or the Avenue de l'Opéra.

Both the Cannebière Prolongée and the Rue de Noailles are the direct and deliberate creations of the Second Empire, and reflect its lust for speculation and "town-lot" jobbing, its pomp and vanity and ostentation, but at the same time its reforming, embellishing, and luxuriously civilising tendency. The Rue de Noailles contrives to hold its head up, and that, too, somewhat defiantly, simply and solely because it is only separated from the Cannebière itself by the Cours St. Louis, and is virtually part and parcel of a thoroughfare of which the Marseillais are traditionally and divertingly proud. So long as Regent Street flourishes Waterloo Place will not, I take it, be in danger of falling into evil case; and Piccadilly Circus may be accepted as the Cours St. Louis which divides the two Regent Streets. But, on the other hand the Rue Impériale, now Rue de la République, has turned out a most disastrous failure, and presents at most hours of the day and night the wofullest of aspects.

Imagine Regent Street and Waterloo Place—the parallel is not by any means inapplicable—with two or three more storeys added to Mr. Nash's somewhat stunted edifices, but with more than two thirds of the grandiose structures to let. On the ground floors a minimum of banks, offices of insurance companies, steamboat agencies, jewellers, goldsmiths, milliners, china shops, and other inflated rent-paying *magasins*. In lieu of such fat-dividend promising premises, imagine a maximum of wood, coke, and charcoal sheds, petty groceries and dramshops galore, cheap slop-shops, "bazars à bon marché, entrée libre," dealing chiefly in sixpenny watches and twopenny-halfpenny corkscrews, *charcutiers*, tripe-dressers, and "débits de tabac." These are the interests of retail commerce principally represented in the quondam Rue Impériale. No fashionably attired loungers, no joyous groups of Provençal grisettes, such as you may see in the Rue St. Ferréol (the Bond Street of Marseilles), are visible on the almost deserted flags of the Rue de la République. Only a sprinkling of snuffy, chocolate-faced old women, with red or yellow turbans, reminding you strangely of the "gumbo" mulatto women who sell fruit under the piazzas of New Orleans; only a few Southern "Gavroches" in tattered blouses, and with bare feet, and, late at night only, a few "esclaves ivres"—possibly members of the Free-Thinking Cabdrivers' Association—staggering homewards and bawling their eternal "Marseillaise;" and in the spacious road-way a few toiling wains, drawn now by oxen and now by mules, their collars adorned with monstrous horny protuberances, and the vehicles heaped high with cotton bags and cotton bales, with hogsheads of wine and oil.

"Vive la République!" with all my heart; but at the same time I fancy that I see the ghost of the Imperial eagle sitting with ruffled plumes and crushed talons on the chimney-pot of a "House to Let," while between the hoarse chaunts of the "Marseillaise" I seem to hear a low and dismal wail, as low and sad as the voice which is said to haunt the Taurida Palace of St. Petersburg. It is the moan, the superstitious Russians whisper, of the Last Khan of the Crimea mourning for the Chersonese. But the phantom voice of the Rue Impériale, at Marseilles, is that of the late M. Mirès, bewailing a Lost Cause and a bursten bubble.

There is even a more palpable and audible apparition of the Second Empire in the huge and pretentious pile known as the Château Impérial, which stands on a cape overlooking the Mediterranean between the Great Reserve and the Lighthouse. The compilers of the local guide books content themselves with reciting the dimensions of this notable structure, and dwelling on the admirable view obtainable from the English garden which surrounds it. The guide-books omit to mention, or, perhaps—so short is political memory—have forgotten the fact that the Château Impérial was built about sixteen years ago, in a tremendous outburst of Imperialist enthusiasm and adulation, and presented by the City of Marseilles to the Emperor Napoleon III., shortly after the return of that ruler from his second expedition to Algeria. The guide-books do not repeat the fulsome address in which the Municipal Council laid their offering at the feet of Cæsar, nor Cæsar's affable answer, in the course of which he remarked that one of his dearest wishes had ever been to possess at Marseilles a marine residence, where he would have "his feet in the sea." It was not his lot to enjoy for any length of time this stately palace perched high, with its English garden, on a rocky cape. Yet he managed to find a Tarpeian rock, over which he tumbled very completely. The Château Impérial these ten years past has been wholly and entirely empty; and it is understood that the Municipal Council of Marseilles and the Ministry of Public Works in Paris are squabbling as to the authority in which the fee-simple of this disestablished Pleasure Dome of an evanished Kubla Khan is legally vested. The common people in Marseilles whisper ominously that the Château Impérial is mined, from end to end, with dynamite. For my part, I firmly believe it to be haunted.

III.

SOUTHERN FARE AND BOUILLABAISSE.

MARSEILLES, *October* 1.

THE table-d'hôte at the Grand Hôtel Noailles not being yet ready, or rather the daily average of guests not being thought a sufficient one for the setting forth of the banquet in the imposing Second Empire *salle-à-manger*, we breakfast and dine for the present, in the garden. That is an arrangement which suits at least one guest at the Grand Hôtel admirably. To take one's meals *al fresco* is not an English practice. Our climate is, in general, against it, to begin with; yet I doubt whether, in an abnormally hot June or July, the manager of the Ship Hotel, Greenwich, would feel justified in acceding to the wishes of a visitor who expressed a desire to be served with his salmon zoutchje and his whitebait at a neat little table on the lawn which slopes to the river. It would be so very "un-English," the manager might opine.

Common people, it is true, in their now lamentably diminishing tea-gardens, have been accustomed time out of mind to devour in the open those crustacea and those bivalves, that bread and butter, and that hot water in which are infused the leaves of some mysterious plant ostensibly of Oriental derivation, the whole of which symposium may be summed up in generic term of "tea and s'rimps, ninepence;" but between the commonalty and the Brahminical classes in my beloved country there is still a gulf, the practicability of the bridging over of which has not even as yet been thought worthy of being made a subject of study on the part of social inquirers. What, I should like to think, would Society say if the committee of a fashionable West-end club which was so fortunate as to possess a garden in rear of its premises were to cause breakfasts and dinners during an unusually sultry summer season to be served on the green sward overlooked by the coffee-room window instead of in the coffee-room itself? Stay; on reflection it must be admitted that there is little fear of the governing bodies of London clubland acceding to such a monstrous proposal. We will be content with imagining the horror and indignation of the committee on the proposal being made to them.

Yet old Colonel Polloddle, of the Senior Spartan, thinks out-of-door breakfasting and dining a capital thing at Marseilles. The three big boys of Alderman Hoddington loudly proclaim the garden refection system to be an "out-and-out jolly one," and the two Miss Hoddingtons, of course too refined to echo their rude brothers' slang, still simper and blush their acquiescence in an arrangement which in their "for intérieur" they doubtless think exceedingly nice. The travelling clergyman, mindful of pulpit exigencies and the contingencies of bronchitis or catarrh, wears his felt wideawake; and Aunt Mehitabel, from New England, comes down to breakfast with her head surmounted by a wondrous covering of some knitted fabric of bright azure hue. She may, with tolerable certainty, be expected to foregather with Mrs. Brownjohn,. from the Potteries, who is not yet free from the thraldom of prejudice, and cannot be brought to look upon the *al fresco* breakfast or dinner table in any other light than that of the innumerable and normally reprehensible "carryings-on" of foreigners. Apart from the possibility of frogs making their appearance in the table-napkins, snails in the butter-dish, spiders in the milk-jug, and a daddy-long-legs in the sugar-basin, I am convinced that, were Mrs. Brownjohn from the Potteries put through the whole of her paces in the way of prejudices, she would make no secret of her conviction that, between the Continental custom of eating and drinking in the open air in fine weather, the Continental code of morality, and the Continental Sunday, there was, from the point of view of wickedness, not much to choose.

Those who dread the "grand air," the "totality of the sky" —to paraphrase the French lady's remark to Sir Walter Scott about the pavement of the streets of Paris—may take their repasts in alcoves or recesses somewhat resembling the well-remembered supper-boxes of old Vauxhall Gardens. For the rest, when the noonday sun is at its hottest, a great awning of linen is stretched from terrace to terrace across the hotel garden. Nobody asks for this "velarium" to be rigged at dinner-time, albeit it is just past Michaelmas. The weather has been magnificently hot at Marseilles, and the evening sea-breeze—"la fresca"—is anxiously looked for and intensely enjoyed. I wish that I had come here sooner, to have had more of the sun. I was for three weeks in Brussels, and out of twenty-one days it rained pitilessly during just eighteen.

One began to feel like so much barley that was being "sprinkled" on the maltster's "couch," and to think that germination must necessarily follow so much external moisture. At all events it was worth coming down to Marseilles to be duly roasted, by the Southern sun, into malt.

The Phocæan City is the Gate of the Levant, and its cookery is as cosmopolitan as are the manners and customs of its people. Thus, in the garden *salle-à-manger* you may have, if you choose, the ham and eggs, the broiled fish and kidneys, the mutton cutlets, the cold meat, the tea, coffee, and toast of a traditional British breakfast. This meal may be modified to suit the more exigent Anglo-American palate by the addition of tender loin steak, eggs in omelettes or "scrambled," and any quantity of potatoes, fried, stewed, or *sautés*. Then there is the regular French "déjeûner à la fourchette"—see, there is Monsieur le Commandant Bonmorceau revelling in it even now; already has he taken off his sword-belt and unloosened three buttons of his undress uniform. The "déjeûner à la fourchette" is pretty much the same all France over, from Nancy to Nîmes, and from Brest to Bordeaux. A big slice of melon—at the proper time and season—a few pretty tiny kickshaws in the way of *hors d'œuvres*—it is good to see M. le Commandant make play with the olives and the radishes, the sardines, and the thin disk of Lyons sausage—then come the eggs "on the plate," or with "black butter," the unchanging cutlets consisting of two little knobs of tough meat and gristle adhering to two highly-blanched shank-bones tastefully frilled at the opposite extremities "à la pantalette." If it be not cutlets, it must be "bifteck," or else haply "tête de veau à la vinaigrette." The duc and allowed vegetable, French beans, cauliflower, artichoke, or salsifis, must follow, or M. le Commandant's collation would be incomplete, and the dejeûner must wind up with a cheese and a fruit. At Marseilles, as in other Southern cities, the dessert is varied and bounteous— including pears, walnuts, black and white grapes, black figs from the Var, and green figs from the Bouches du Rhône. Walnuts have just come in; and oranges are promised for the week after next. Where shall I be, the week after next?

But, if you leave the "déjeûner à la fourchette" to the discretion of the head waiter, and hint to that functionary that you like the "cuisine du Midi"—that is, the cookery of the Langue d'Oc, which is based on oil, in contradistinction to the cookery of the Langue d'Oil, which is based on butter—and especially if you tell him that you have no very rooted antipathy to garlic, he will introduce you to some very characteristic dishes of a cosmopolitan kind. Those who are fond of fish that do not eat as such, but have the taste of veal or of pork, may enjoy the "thon" or tunny of the Mediterranean, and even the highly meaty sturgeon. There is a kind of Phocæan zoutchje likewise, a " bouillon de poissons," made of whitings, moraine, tafel, loup, and, in particular, of the popular rascasse. Indulgence in these local dishes, into the preparation of all of which a good deal of oil and garlic enters, will by degrees prepare you for the consumption of the world-famous "Bouillabaisse," or, as it should be more correctly spelt, "Bouil-Abaïsse," or fish-stew.

A prodigious amount of nonsense has been put in print about this dish, which, in England, at least, owes its celebrity to its having furnished a theme for a very beautiful lyric by Mr. Thackeray. We have all read about the restaurant in the "New Street of the Little Fields," "the Chambertin with yellow seal," and the touching reflections, memories, and associations evoked by the genius of the poet from the not very promising font of a bill at an eating-house. The "Ballad of Bouillabaisse" will be read and applauded, I take it, as long as good English letters endure and are appreciated; but, in a strictly culinary sense, the smoking dish of which Mr. Thackeray partook was not bouillabaisse. It was more of the nature of a "matelote," which may be compounded of carp, roach, dace, eels, and crawfish, stewed with fine herbs and red wine, and garnished with mushrooms.

In days gone by, ere the Thames became a "society" stream, there were numbers of unpretending little hostelries on river bank, frequented by the brethren of the angle, where "matelotes" of freshwater fish used to be prepared quite as appetisingly as, and were by some gastronomic judges esteemed to be, a great deal more wholesome than bouillabaisse. The greatest drawback to a "matelote" is that it is apt to be "bony." In a genuine bouillabaisse there should be no fresh-water fish; and it is worthy of remark that many years after Mr. Thackeray had immortalised the restaurant in the Rue Neuve des Petits Champs, he admitted that the very best bouillabaisse he had ever tasted had been at a French Creole tavern at New Orleans, on the road to Lake Pontchartrain. And the reason why the Louisanian bouillabaisse was necessarily and largely superior to the Paris preparation, and in all respects equal to the Marseilles one, will be at once obvious when it is remembered, first that the Creole crookery of New Orleans is fully on a par with that of Provence, and, next, that the Gulf of Mexico yields equally with the Gulf of Lyons, a surprising variety of fish, important in size, firm in flesh, and delicious in flavour.

To come to the technics of bouillabaisse, it is necessary to point out that the highest authority as to the proper confection of this dish is the famous Provençal *chef* Durand, the author of " Le Cuisinier du Midi et du Nord." M. Durand's observations on the vital question of garlic may be quoted with advantage here, since the " rank and guilty" bulb plays a most important part in the compounding of bouillabaisse. Writing during the Restoration, Durand, with calmly justifiable self-consciousness, remarks: " I have illuminated the kitchen for more than seventy years; and I have always maintained that it is practicable to suppress the employment of garlic in the preparation of sea-fish. I have never used it without having in the first instance ascertained whether garlic was in the slightest degree offensive to the persons who were about to partake of my production, nor can I give too strong an expression of my sentiments of indignation towards those cooks who chop their garlic without having subjected the esculent to a thorough preliminary scraping. Garlic is full of grumous particles; and it is sufficient for one of those granules to get between the teeth to produce the direst complications, aberrations, and depravations of taste."

The weighty Durand only admits two kinds of Bouillabaisse, or Bouil-Abaïse, that " à la Marseillaise" and that " à la Nîmoise." Touching the Marseillaise one, the following is the recipe: In the bottom of a stewpan a small quantity of chopped onion should be placed. This, with a little good oil, should be passed for a moment over the fire. Then your assortment of sea-fish must be cut in slices, notably your loup, your moraine, your whiting, your rascasse, and your langouste, or cray-fish; but of this last only the tail of him. The slices of fish are then to be placed in the stewpan together with some well-chopped parsley and garlic, a slice of lemon, a tomato from which the water and the seeds have been expressed: the whole seasoned with salt, pepper, and a little powdered saffron. The whole mass is then to be sprinkled, and that liberally, with good olive oil, and it is then to be thoroughly " wetted" with a glass of dry white wine and some fish bouillon, zoutche, or broth made from fishes' head and "trimmings," carefully boiled down and strained through a tamis. When the fish is entirely covered by the liquid the stewpan is to be set to the "double-quick boil," until, by means of such heroic coction, the contents are reduced to three-quarters of their original volume. The reduced sauce—" Bouil-Abaïse "— is then to be poured into a deep dish, in which slices of the crumb of fine white bread—what we term French roll—have been symmetrically arranged. The slices of fish are served separately.

"Bouillabaisse à la Nîmoise" differs from that "à la Marseillaise" in the particulars that among the fish red mullet, soles, and eels are admitted, and that when the fish is cooked it is served up with a sauce made from the boiled and pounded liver of a fish called a "baudroie," mingled with the yolks of three eggs, some good oil, and a glass of Madeira. Instead of the sauce of the "Bouil-Abaïse" being poured over slices of bread in that of Nîmes, the sauce and the fish are served together, and the whole dish is encircled by "croûtons" of bread fried in butter. Altogether, there would appear to be a minimum of garlic in the Nîmes recipe; nor is there any mention made of saffron as an ingredient. In the Marseilles bouillabaisse saffron is almost unpleasantly prominent.

Of course the Marseillais asseverate that the Nîmois know nothing whatever about bouillabaisse, and that the only true, genuine, and legitimate stew of sea-fish, oil, and garlic is that which is dispensed at Marseilles and at the restaurants on the Chemin de la Corniche. How, they ask, should Nîmes dare to put forward any pretensions to knowledge in the matter? Is she on the sea-coast? Has she a Chemin de la Corniche? Has she—let Nîmes answer that—got a Cannebière? To which Nîmes, with infinite disdain, replies that she could have any number of Cannebières if she chose, but that she is quite content with her Maison Carrée, her Triumphal Arches, her Arena, and her other peerless Roman remains; whereas Marseilles, which brags so much about her antiquities, possesses not a solitary monument of the classic past beyond a grimy little bas-relief encrusted in a wall of a house of the Rue Radeau, and which bas-relief is impudently asserted by the Marseillaise to have been a votive tablet erst suspended in the temple of the Masilio-Delphic Apollo, because, forsooth, the sculpture presents the dim outline of a person in a toga, a man habited as a sailor, a ship's prow, and a dog wagging his tail; the whole with the inscription " VALISINIUS MARCARII ANEONVSID," which some antiquaries take as meaning

"Valisinius, son of Marcus Caris, having fulfilled his vow of distributing provisions, of his own free will dedicated this monument;" while another section of archæologists maintain that the tablet simply announces the trade and origin of "Valisinius, general grocer, from the Carian Sea." Analogously there is an inscription extant at Cahors, "Bazar Génois. Gambetta, Marchand de Denrées Coloniales."

The critic who endeavours to steer a middle course between the fiercely recriminative pretensions of Nîmes and Marseilles on the subject of bouillabaisse, or bouil-abaïse, should not lose sight of the fact that although Durand, who entered the service of the Bishop of Alais, in 1779, as "gâte-sauce," or scullion, acquired most of his subsequent renown at Nîmes, he practised for a considerable period at Marseilles, and that there, as well as at Toulon, Arles, Montpelier, Narbonne, and other cities of the Midi, he was for more than half a century recognised as the King of Languedocian cookery. It is probable that he found bouillabaisse in its savage garlic-reeking state on the coast of Provence, and that in his Nîmes recipe he improved on the Phocæan original. Thus Alexis Soyer, visiting Marseilles on his way to his culinary mission in the Crimea, in 1855, partook of bouillabaisse at the Original Réserve, and was fraternally furnished with a recipe for making it by the *chef* of the establishment. It at once struck the astute mind of Soyer that bouillabaisse might be vastly improved by the addition to the seasoning either of cayenne pepper, of whole chillis, or of taragon vinegar, or by the larger admixture among the components of red mullet, which, being a "game" fish, warrants the introduction of a more liberal quantity of chopped eschalot in the seasoning. Touching garlic, Soyer was of the same opinion with the discreet Durand. To many palates it is utterly abhorrent and abominable. With regard to oil, the case is entirely different. Many English people profess to prefer the "cuisine au beurre" to the "cuisine à l'huile;" yet they are quite unconscious of the number of things which, even in the Northern kitchen, are prepared with oil; and I have rarely found them decline to partake of "poulet à la Marengo," which is not "à la Marengo" at all unless the basic fowl be fried in oil.

In conclusion, let me point out that genuine bouillabaisse is a fisherman's dish—a rough and ready one, and with a flavour so high as to require the stomach of a fisherman—or of a horse—to appreciate it thoroughly. The finest bouillabaisse is not to be had at a restaurant. It is best cooked in an iron pot over a furnace in a hole in a rock under the lee of the sail of a speronare. Most appropriate dinner costume—a red woollen nightcap or a sou'-wester, a well-knitted jersey, and bucket boots. As it is with bouillabaisse on the coast of Provence so it is with "clam-bake" on the New England shore.

IV.

NICE AND ITS NEFARIOUS NEIGHBOUR.

NICE, *October* 4.

UNTIL only the other day I flattered myself that I knew Nice, in the Département des Alpes Maritimes, tolerably well. Certainly a sufficient number of years have passed, during which I have been a periodical visitor to the City of Sunshine and the "Mistral," of palm-trees, oranges, and baccarat, to entitle me to claim graduation as an Anglo-Nizzard. Indeed, if my memory do not play me false, I was acquainted with Nice before it was in the Department of the Maritime Alps at all, and when its suzerain was Charles Albert of Savoy, King of Sardinia, Cyprus, and Jerusalem, high-sounding albeit somewhat empty dignities, long since merged by his son and grandson in the shorter but more significant title King of Italy.

The Sardinian Nice was—well, you know what an Italian watering-place usually is—delightful, but somewhat dirty. The feathery palms waved, the sub-tropical vegetation glowed, the white marble villas dazzled the eye as they do now; but the smells of the city were manifold, and far from aromatic; and the Promenade des Anglais abounded with ugly holes and fissures, which made walking home to the hotel, on a moonless night, after a whist party, rather a perilous expedition. The hotels were fairly good, the mosquitoes were many, and the hackney carriages few; the cigars were very few and very nasty; and if you wished to travel from Nice to Genoa along the Cornice-road—one of the most exciting and most picturesque drives in Europe—you were fain to have a *berline*, or else to book a place in the lumbering old diligence of the period. One used to stop half-way, I think, at Savona. A few miles out of the city a road branched off skirting the side of a mountain called La Tucha, and then you came upon a little romantic-looking town, perched upon a rock overhanging the deep blue Mediterranean. There was a great lumbering pile of white stone, half-castellated and half palatial in appearance, and a tiny Piazza d'Armi, the ramparts of which were garnished with sundry rusty and quaintly-fashioned pieces of artillery, as old, so it was said, as the days of Francis I. From the Piazza d'Armi, fronting the castellated palace, wound a narrow, shadowy little street, on the jagged pavement of which you met, in the daytime, only a few monks and nuns, fishermen, fruitwomen, and ragged, bare-legged *ragazzi;* but with these, strangely enough, towards afternoon and evening, would be mingled groups of ladies and gentlemen, arrayed in the first style of fashion, and many of whom you might recognise as table d'hôte acquaintances from Nice.

For the little half Italian, half Saracenic town, perched on the rock, was Monaco, capital of the principality of that name, and his Highness the Prince of Monaco, Duke of Valentinois, Lord of Mentone and Rochebrune, had condescended to lease to a speculative Frenchman—who had been, they say, in the old Parisian *tripot* days which came to an end early in the reign of Louis Philippe, a croupier at Frascati's—a commodious mansion, to be used as a common gambling-house. The highly mathematical "trente et quarante" and the fascinating roulette were the two authorised games; but the play was not by any means high, and was carried on by means of *jetons*, or counters, which you purchased at the door of the casino, and which were, indeed, a convertible circulating medium in the shops and cafés of the town. The *jetons* were worth only two francs apiece, and ruin, when it did overtake the inveterate gamester—which ruin generally did after the first run of luck—was of a very modest kind.

I never heard of any bankrupt suitors of fickle Fortune flinging themselves from the Saracenic battlements into the Mediterranean; and the most serious "burst up" that I remember was that of a young chocolate manufacturer from Marseilles, who had driven from Nice to Monaco in his own barouche and pair, and towards ten of the clock at night, having lost all his ready cash through a heavy run on the red, was compelled to pawn his carriage and horses, the attributes of Mine Uncle being for the nonce assumed by a veteran member of his Highness's bodyguard, which numbered eleven in all. This brave advanced the formidable sum of eight hundred francs on the security of the barouche and pair. Of course the chocolate manufacturer lost the thirty-two pounds sterling before eleven o'clock, which was the hour at which the "établissement" closed. On the following morning he had to undergo the humiliation of being driven back to Nice in his own vehicle, but with Mine Uncle's father-in-law sitting by the side of the coachman, on the box. It was the relative by marriage of his Highness's bodyguard who had undertaken to see after the delicate little matter of the four-wheeled and eight-footed pledge being redeemed when the barouche and pair and their mortified occupant reached Nice.

Thus has life its ups and downs. "Fortuna de la guerra, Señor Moro," cried Don John of Austria, laughingly, to a great Moorish Emir, whom he recognised toiling as a galley-slave on the quay at Barcelona. The Moorish Emir did not laugh; yet, probably, he consoled himself with the thought that one is bound to take the rough and the smooth alike, and, with the hope that the day might come for the accursed and insolent Giaour to be chained to the bench and made to tug at the oar while he, the enfranchised True Believer, or haply a vicarious boatswain, strode up and down the gangway, and whacked the Christian dogs with a rope's end, well tarred.

This was the Nice of days gone by, before what Garibaldi termed an illicit "mercimonio" between the French and Italian Governments handed over the fair land of Savoy and the loveliest of Italian watering-places to France. With the Nice of the Second Empire you are, no doubt, as familiarly acquainted as I am. It was very gay, very beautiful, and very dissipated. I remember descending upon it unawares, so to speak, one evening in the late autumn of 1866. We had come from Coni by Turin, in the vilest of diligences, over the Col di Tenda. A fearsome journey of some six-and-twenty hours, through some of the most splendid scenery in the world, and through a number of villages resembling nothing more or less than so many pigsties. Cramped and bruised in the vile diligence, dizzy with the continual jolting, and half fainting with hunger and thirst, what a relief, what a luxury it was to reach Nice at last, and to be in a mood to condone all its wickedness for the sake of its bustle and brilliancy, its life and gaiety, and the capital supper it proffered to the wearied traveller: As Nice was then so is it, to most intents and purposes, at present.

Quite apart from any political associations, Nice is a town which, with all due deference to Garibaldi, naturally pertains to France. I mean the Nice of the Promenade des Anglais, of the Quai Massena, of the Cercle de la Méditerranée: of arcades full of fans, corals, flowers, old china, photographs, and other knicknacks of the "article de Paris" order, dispensed at extortionate prices by the most affable and the most rapacious of shopkeepers. The Italians scarcely understand the art of plundering the tourist in an artistic and elegant manner. Brigandage, of course, they thoroughly understand—they are to the manner born—but as banditti they are ordinarily of a rough-and-ready type, who think that everything can be done with a stiletto and a blunderbuss. With greater completeness, but with a grace and delicacy of execution seemingly unattainable by the Peninsular professor of rapine, does the French shopkeeper victimise you. He was made for Nice, and Nice for him, or rather for her; for I think that as an accomplished lightener of the traveller's purse the palm should be awarded, not to Claude, but to Claudine Du Val. Surely it is better to be plundered by such a skilled and refined depredator than to be brutally bidden to "put your nose in the sand" while Fra Diavolo rifles your pockets, and Beppo, his lieutenant, ransacks your portmanteau.

Old *habitués* of Nice not unfrequently complain that since the shutting up of Hombourg, Wiesbaden, and the other gambling dens of the Rhineland, or rather the conversion of those disestablished Inferni into peaceable Assembly Rooms, where people who have really come to drink the waters can enjoy themselves with the innocent relaxation of playing chess and draughts instead of rouge-et-noir and roulette, the general aspect and tone of society in Nice have been appreciably changed, and not for the better. It is not pleasant to hear an expression which is very current at present, "the scum of Monte Carlo," or to be told that not only the purlieus of that sumptuous and nefarious establishment, but the railway station and cafés of Nice, are infested by downright thieves, "loafing around" in the hope of being able to steal something from the unwary. The "reduced gentlewoman," too often, I am sorry to say, of British extraction, who suffers under a chronic delusion that your winnings are hers, and furtively stretches forth a lean paw to seize the coins which belong to you, was quite as well known at Hombourg as she is now at Monte Carlo; but the administration, for its own sake, as well as for that of the public, did its very best to keep manifest rogues and swindlers out of the place.

Not the less, however, have I heard some very disagreeable stories of the outsiders of both sexes who, unable to obtain admission to the gambling-rooms, hang about Monaco and Nice—predatory Mr. and Mrs. Micawbers—waiting for "some-

MONTE CARLO.

thing to turn up." In good society, also, murmurs may be heard that not only do French, Italian, and Russian swindlers abound in Nice, but Captain Cashless, the Hon. Claude Neverpay, the O'Doo, and the MacBilk are far more plentiful than they used to be in the old times, and that private card-playing scandals are deplorably rife. Meanwhile the hotel and shopkeepers of Nice are in a chronic state of fury, caused by the competition of Monte Carlo; while reputable people, who have something wrong at the chest, and who regard Nice merely as a health resort, bitterly complain that it has become the mere ante-chamber to a common gaming-house.

At least people were thus murmuring and complaining some few years ago, when I came to Nice from Constantinople. I heard similar lamentations at Marseilles only the day before yesterday. I was told that even at Cannes and Antibes, at Nîmes and Arles, and far-off Montpelier, the maleficent influence of the Monte Carlo plague was felt; and that the roulette wheels and *tapis verts* of the Mediterranean *tripot* were beginning to be denounced as " la désolation des familles " throughout the south of France. If such be the fact, it will probably lead, sooner and more efficaciously than any other cause can do, to the interference of the French Government with the Prince of Monaco's "little game." France cannot be expected to trouble herself very seriously about the tourists from England or the United States, from Mexico or from Brazil, who are foolish enough to lose their money at Monte Carlo, and occasionally to blow out their brains or hang themselves afterwards; but the case materially alters its aspect when it is found that a very large proportion of the victims of the gaming-house in

which his Highness is a sleeping partner are French citizens.
A passion for gambling is one of the normal vices of the Provençal Frenchman. Marseilles is literally honeycombed with sham clubs, which are in reality gaming-houses, and into one or more of which the police make an irruption about twice a week on the average; and, in the end, the pressure of the Southern French municipalities and Councils-General on the Government may be sufficient to bring about the much-wished-for protest on the part of France against the iniquities of Monte Carlo. How long it would be ere such a protest would be followed by practical action it is rather difficult to tell. His Highness of Monaco is in the curiously exceptional position of a person between two stools who does not fall to the ground. Italy, as well as France, must be scandalised at the enormities of Monte Carlo before the Prince can be internationally coerced into putting his house in order; and, for the nonce, Italy appears to be wholly indifferent to the wickedness of roulette and rouge-et-noir on the Mediterranean littoral.

The galled jade, so I thought, might wince when I heard at Marseilles the last batch of equivocal stories from the naughty Riviera. My withers should be unwrung, so far as Nice was concerned. On that point I had very firmly made up my mind. Nice in no wise entered into my scheme of travelling this autumn. The mysterious Russian financier's musical parties—he has a travelling orchestra, they say, of sixty performers, and tenors and high sopranos are being trained, exclusively for him all over Europe—excited in me no envy of participation; the pleasant réunions at Mr. Gambart's marble villa, embosomed in palms and orange groves, brought me no longing;

the table d'hôte at the Hôtel d'Angleterre, one of the very pleasantest of its kind, troubled me not; nor did I even feel a furtive and illicit hankering to "have a gallop" over the familiar green cloth sward at Monte Carlo, and ascertain, for positively the last and I know not how many times, that, when you have backed almost every number on the roulette table, Zero will probably turn up, and that when—to make quite sure —you have backed Zero and almost every other number except four, four will be the number so proclaimed as the winner. Not for me these immoral sports and pastimes. "Sat me lusistis: ludite nunc alios." No; I would not go to Nice. My goal was Leghorn, *viâ* the land of Corsica.

But the ironical Fates decided otherwise. The ironical Fates, while permitting me to moralise over the heinousness of Monte Carlo, have kindly refrained from landing me in that detestable and delightful Temple of Plutus; yet has a sardonic Destiny brought me, entirely against my wish and my will, to Nice. It has fallen in this wise. On the day after I reached Marseilles I engaged a passage by one of the Fraissinet line of steamers direct for Bastia in Corsica, whence I thought I could journey to Ajaccio, and so reach the Italian mainland. But I changed my mind, wishing to pass a day or two longer in Marseilles in the interest of letter-writing and of bouillabaisse. I directed the commissionaire at the hotel to get my passage ticket changed for the next departure of a steamer for Bastia; and this he did, telling me, however, that he had been called upon to pay a "supplément" of eight francs for "additional restoration." Why was I to be "additionally restored" on my voyage to Bastia? Did they feed the passengers more bountifully on board the *Marie Louise* by which I was going, than on board the *Spahis*, by which I should have gone? The mystery, however, was unravelled when I came to examine my ticket. I found that it was good from Marseilles to Bastia, *touching at Nice*. Beshrew Nice! It was precisely the place where I had not the slightest intention of touching, and where I did not wish to touch. There was something exasperating in being called upon to pay eight francs for "additional restoration" at a haven where you objected to being restored.

It was eight o'clock in the morning when I joined the *Marie Louise*, which was lying in the new port at the extremity of that Rue de la République, once Impériale, about which I had recently something to say. It would be an abuse of terms to speak of the Fraissinet steamer *Marie Louise* as a "gallant craft," or to say that "she walked the waters like a thing of life." She jogged along pretty well with a full cargo of a miscellaneous nature, including a good deal of salt fish, and an unpleasantly conspicuous deck-loading of petroleum in casks. I say unpleasant, for the reason that most of the deck hands were smoking, and that they were apt when they had enjoyed a sufficient number of whiffs to fling away the smouldering ends of their cigarettes "promiscuously." The crew were the usual Levantine and piratical-looking mariners, who all appeared to have been trained by the late Mr. Augustus Harris, and to be ready at a moment's notice to "go on" in "Masaniello."

Two things on board the *Marie Louise* struck me as somewhat droll, and as eminently French. A tolerable breakfast was served at ten o'clock, and a passable dinner at five. "Cuisine du Midi." Rather too much oil over the haricots, and slightly too much garlic in the attendant steward. The wine, an acid memory of many lands. Catalonia? Perhaps. Val de Peñas? It is possible. Cette? It may be. The Beaujolais? Why not? Bordeaux? No; certainly not Bordeaux. As far I should say from the Garonne as from the Yang-tsi-Kiang was that dark and dubious vintage. Altogether there was not much to grumble at in the commissariat of the *Marie Louise*. The drollery was in this, that, although we had half a score of saloon passengers, the captain, his little son, a certain Monsieur Chose, and your humble servant were the only guests at breakfast and dinner. The blue Mediterranean was as calm as a millpond. The steamer ploughed her way along the coast, sullenly but steadily; but, wise in their generation, the half score saloon passengers, who were all French people, had declined to pay in advance for that "restoration" of which they feared the elements might decline to allow them to partake. One gentleman told me, with quite pathetic candour, the story of a friend of his who had been so rash as to pay for his "nourriture" in advance. He partook at breakfast of some "civet de lièvre," "a dish which he adored." Five minutes afterwards he had the *mal de mer*; and "bang went," not only his peace of body and mind, but also eight francs. For he was not able to eat anything else that day; and one of the strictest maxims of maritime economy in the Mediterranean is "No money returned."

I have rarely met with a band of such rigid total abstainers as those who were my fellow-passengers on board the *Marie*

Louise. They ate not, nor drank, neither did they smoke. Stay, one in a corner by the funnel was chewing green apples. The fruit in that condition was good, he was told, for the *mal de mer*. He was a second-class passenger, and swiftly, having turned nearly as green as the apples he had munched, he disappeared down a hole somewhere among the petroleum casks. Another, in the little glazed caboose by the companion-ladder, drank from time to time, and with a guilty expression of countenance, something from a little bottle. It was not brandy, I think; people do not make such wry faces when imbibing cognac. I fancy it was some medicament compounded by some cunning *pharmacien* of Marseilles as a preventive against the *mal de mer*. Bless the poor gentleman! how he groaned in his state-room all through the dinner-hour! And yet the sun shone brightly; there was never a cloud in the sky, and scarcely a ripple on the sea.

There was another gentleman with a red beard, and in a remarkably cut suit of what he told me was real "Twiddelle Ecossaise," but which more resembled buff baize, who, according to the Bunyanian system of nomenclature, might be described as "Mr. Overweening Confidence." This gentleman —he was from Dijon, and travelled in "conserves alimentaires"—was good enough to give me a lesson in what he called "The Art of Not Being Seasick." All that was required, according to his showing, was to have "le pied marin." I told him that we had an English colloquialism having reference to "one's sea-legs." He smiled with superb superciliousness, and remarked that "le pied marin" was quite another thing. How was it to be acquired? Simply thus. If you wish to avoid sea-sickness never keep your knees stiff. Look at the professional mariner. He stiffens not his knees; he hinges them, loosely. Thus the whole of his frame is in repose, and the movement of the vessel does not beat against the movement of his stomach. On the other hand, if you hold yourself like a Prussian grenadier, the rigidity of your limbs is in opposition to the oscillations of the ship, and the result—the sure and deplorable result—is the *mal de mer*. It is thus that you practise "le pied marin," the proper execution of which, you will observe, is not without a kind of grace.

And my red-bearded adviser proceeded to give a practical illustration of the acquisition of "sea-legs à la Française." Unfortunately, the Fates were in an unusually ironical mood that morning. One of his marine feet stumbled over a hawser, and he fell upon his nose. I am sure that I did my best not to laugh at his mishap, but he spoke to me no more that day, and glowered at me from afar off, as though I had been his bitterest enemy or a rival traveller in the "conserves alimentaires" line. He had only his overweening confidence to thank for his disaster.

There was yet another droll feature in our voyage, and thereto I would specially direct the attention of MM. Fraissinet and Co. There were on the poop of the *Marie Louise* two benches providing sitting accommodation for precisely eight passengers. Seats along the bulwarks there were none. Even before the steamer started the two benches were taken possession of by two parties of four—women, old and young, a squalling child, and a hoary patriarch with a snow-white beard and a straw hat. These people, who were second-class passengers, held with resolute tenacity the eight available first-class deck seats throughout the whole of the voyage to Nice. They should have been at Rorke's Drift. They should have been at Thermopylæ. They, honest folks, were not in the least afraid of the *mal de mer*, for towards four o'clock the party to starboard produced a great basket of provisions, including sausage, a melon, leeks, tomatoes, cheese, and hard-boiled eggs. The mingled odour of these comestibles may have been scarcely conducive to the comfort of the most qualmish among the passengers. The party to port were not quite such Sybarites as their neighbours. They were content with a collation of *charcuterie*, garlic, and grapes; while the patriarch in the straw hat indulged in potations pottle-deep from a wicker-covered bottle, like an exaggerated Florence flask, and containing, I will warrant, something stronger than water. He afterwards smoked a briarwood pipe, well filled with tobacco of amazing strength and acridity of aroma.

Meanwhile we who had paid for first-class accommodation were free to pace the deck, or to rest our wearied frames against the bulwarks, or to practise the "pied marin" precisely as we chose. It was impossible to be angry with these good people. They found the places vacant at early morn; they retained them until dewy eve; and I dare say they found things much more comfortable, high and dry there on the poop, and shielded from the rays of the sun by an awning, than they would have found them on the main deck, among the petroleum casks and the coopsful of noisy poultry and the piratical-looking crew. Wishing to read a book during the golden afternoon, and growing rather weary of walking about, I brought a bundle of railway rugs on deck, and built up quite a nice little ottoman under the lee of the companion hatch. But I had occasion to return to my state-room for a paper-knife, and when I came up aft again, I found that part of my pile of rugs had been quickly annexed by one of the party to starboard, and converted into a pillow for the squalling child. I grudged it not my wraps. At last the intolerable little brat went to sleep, which was something to the good.

But the humours of the *Marie Louise* were not yet exhausted; and the crowning piece of drollery was reserved for the conclusion of our voyage. We should have reached Nice by half-past six p.m. As a matter of fact, we did make the entrance to the port by about a quarter to seven; but then came the fun of the thing. It transpired that the captain—he was a "capitaine au long cours," who had duly served his time in the French Navy—had just been taken off the Black Sea and Constantinople line, and transferred to that between Marseilles, Nice, and Bastia, and that of the bearings of the ports of Nice and Bastia he was altogether ignorant. The first mate, or "capitaine en second," had never made the Nice-Bastia voyage, and his boatswain, a hairy little man whose light blue canvas vestments were covered by a perfect mosaic of dark blue patches, was quite as unenlightened as his superior officers as to the navigation of the port of Nice. The result of this charming state of things was that we were a whole hour feeling our way into the port, and another hour-and-half taking up a berth in the port itself. Even then we could not make a gangway close to the shore, but were fain to anchor a good two longboats' length from the wharf, so that the health officer had to board us by means of an aerial viaduct of quivering planks, uncomfortably suggestive of the bridge in the Vision of Mirza.

V.

QUITE ANOTHER NICE.

NICE, *October* 6.

THE captain of the *Marie Louise*—a very worthy fellow, as most of the Provençal "capitaines au long cours" that I have known have been—expressed his opinion to the health officer who boarded us that the port of Nice might have proved a highly convenient anchorage for the caravels of Christopher Columbus, but that for heavily-laden vessels having a considerable draught of water the harbour was slightly behind the age and the requirements of steam navigation. He said so also, in stronger terms, to the supercargo, qualifying the port as a "vilain trou," a "scie," and other opprobrious things. He would make haste, he added, to get out of the detestable place as early as he could next morning, after unloading what cargo he had to the consignation of Nice. But, to his wrath and astonishment, he now learned that orders had been received by telegraph from the company at Marseilles, that he was to remain at Nice until five o'clock the next afternoon, taking in more cargo.

This certainly seemed slightly "rough" on the passengers, who could have had no interest in the *Marie Louise* as a commercial venture; but Mediterranean steamboat companies are not in the habit of consulting the wants or wishes of their passengers, who may grumble as much as ever they please, but for whom there is no redress. Nor will there be any such redress until the conductors of foreign newspapers discover that one of the most legitimate and most beneficent functions of journalism is that of making "the newspaper" a vehicle for the expression of the demands and the grievances of the public at large—demands and grievances reiterated, re-endorsed by other correspondents, and editorially commented upon, until at length the scandal denounced or the shortcoming protested against is forced upon the attention of the Legislature and the Government. One vigorous newspaper, sternly adopting the English system of battering breaches, by means of continual and indignant correspondence, in the walls of malfeasance, extortion, and mismanagement, and one resolute Senator or Deputy as strongly bent on worrying the Ministers' life out until a remedy was provided for the evil complained of would, I venture to think, bring about in the course not of a few years, but of a few months, such a social revolution in France as would equally astonish and delight Monsieur Joseph Prudhomme.

At present Monsieur Prudhomme, representing the patient and paying public, is bullied, maltreated, tyrannised over, and imposed upon in a hundred different ways, while the evening newspaper press of Paris has scarcely even a word to say enforcing the necessity of social reform. It is left for the "Intransigeants" to point out that the English public would never tolerate the extortion and maltreatment to which Frenchmen, with a patient shrug, submit. As for the gentlemen of the press, they are far too busily occupied in fighting with each other to be able to find time even to discuss the bearings of a social reform, more imperatively needed in the France of the present day than any other—I mean the reform which should bring about the entire abolition of the absurd, barbarous, and bloodthirsty practice of duelling.

In the meantime we were booked at Nice for the night, and throughout the next day. With grim courtesy did the captain apologise for having arrived so late. An hour earlier we might have been in time to catch a train for Monte Carlo, pass a couple of hours in that "Abode of Pleasure," and return to Nice and the *Marie Louise*. Never mind. There would be plenty of time next day. Confound Monte Carlo! In vain did I endeavour to persuade the captain that I had not the slightest intention of being slain on the Board of Green Cloth or broken on the roulette wheel. He shook his head sadly. "I hear the louis jingling in your pocket," he said. "I see the five-franc pieces waltzing from your hand, now pirouetting on the *pair* or the *impair*, now placing themselves à *cheval* between the Thirty-five and the Thirty-six, and now coquetting between Zero and the *quatre premiers*. They all do it."

This was the captain's first visit to Nice; but old Monsieur Chose had told him all about Monaco and Monte Carlo. Monsieur Chose was a retired "capitaine au long cours"—one of the oldest on the list. He had been long on the Nice and Marseilles line, and had appalling stories to tell about passengers who had gone up to Monte Carlo "just to have a look at things," and had returned looking very ghastly, and minus many hundreds of francs. One Child of Misfortune he had brought back from the Abode of Pleasure who had, in the course of three hours, lost the sum of eleven thousand francs —"imaginez-vous, Monsieur!"—which he had just received for the stock, goodwill, and fixtures of his business as a perfumer, and which constituted every sou which he possessed in the world. He had lost it all, and he had a wife and five children. There was no remedy for it. They all did it. The sage Ulysses himself would have fallen a ready victim to the wiles of the Circe of Monte Carlo. Thus the captain of the *Marie Louise*, on the authority of that very ancient mariner, Monsieur Chose.

There is to me a peculiar and not wholly comfortable sensation attendant on sleeping aboard ship in harbour. It is an odd feeling of having somehow defrauded the sea. It is scarcely " i' the bond" which Neptune, through the intermediary of steam navigation companies, enters into with passengers that there should be a period of entire repose, when the floor and the ceiling of your state-room are in a perfectly horizontal and the walls thereof in an unimpeachably perpendicular position, and when there is no creaking, straining, grinding, rasping, grunting, growling, or whistling of the vessel or the machinery whatsoever. Almost painful was the stillness which prevailed on board the *Marie Louise* when midnight chimed, in rather a cracked and discordant manner, from the churches of Nice. The gossip of the steward had come to an end. This worthy had been my sole companion in the saloon since the captain and his little son and old Monsieur Chose had gone on shore. I trust that they were not bound for Monte Carlo. The rest of the first-class passengers had mysteriously disappeared, and at length there was sitting room on the poop.

The steward, excited by the promise of a handsome *pourboire* if he refrained, when passengers for Bastia came on board, from putting anybody else in the berths in my cabin—there were four to a single washstand in the sofaless little den—proceeded to make startling statements and to reveal dark secrets. He spoke his mind about the boilers, and made no attempt to conceal his scorn for the supercargo and his aversion for old Monsieur Chose. He, the steward, hated the Mediterranean. He loathed the Riviera. "C'était un fichu pays." He was not a Frenchman, but a Swiss, from the Canton of Berne. Did Monsieur ever stay in a Swiss hotel? What *luxe!* What politeness! What moderate charges! Monsieur did not think so. It must in any case be admitted that the hotels of London were the most luxurious, the most politely managed, and the cheapest in the entire universe. Monsieur did not think so, again? Well, one was master of his opinion. For himself, he preferred the Black Sea—Odessa, Yalta, Sebastopol, Galatz, Ibraila, Kustendji, the Iron Gates of the Danube. Speak to him of that—of anything in preference to "cette maudite Méditerranée."

So I let him babble on in his tiny caboose of a pantry, polishing my boots, and puffing away at a cigarette, with the lightest of possible hearts. Always with the hope of a *pourboire* in the morning. I scarcely think that in our modern system of social economics we properly appreciate the value of the *pourboire*, of backshish, of the "tip." The idea has been, within these latter days, steadily gaining ground, that for a fair day's work a man is entitled to a fair day's wage, and to nothing more. There are those who think that the worker deserves a great deal more. The Norman knights who helped William to beat Harold at Hastings only did a fair day's work in the throat-cutting line; yet they received in guerdon a great deal more than a fair day's wage. They had half the land of England for their fee. In the days when war was properly and logically conducted—that is to say without pity or remorse or hypocritical prattling about "civilized warfare" —as though there could be anything "civilized" in blowing out the brains or ripping up the stomach of a person a perfect stranger to you, who had never done you any harm—in those times of straightforward warfare the soldier's backshish was pillage; the sailor's bonus was prize-money. If you made an enemy the captive of your bow and spear, and he turned out to be worth anything, you held him to ransom.

Is it not a pity that nearly all the fine old practices of war —practices as profitable as they were picturesque—should have drifted from the hands of princes and barons and knights into the coarse palms of "gasthaus" keepers and tavern waiters, of steamboat companies, and roadside lodging-house and fancy warehouse keepers? Musings of such a kind came over me as I watched the steward of the *Marie Louise* building up the edifice of to-morrow's backshish. I sought at last the narrow cot on which the architect of MM. Fraissinet's line of Mediterranean steamers had fondly imagined that the body of an Englishman of considerable inches might be bestowed, and as I slept there seemed from time to time to be mingled with the shrill chimes of the Nice churches the impassibly strident chants of the priests of the Temple of Plutus *là-bas*. "Rouge gagne, et couleur." "Rien ne va plus." In a dream one has just flung the last rouleau upon the red. "Rouge perd." Of course.

I was up betimes in the morning, for tonsorial purposes, to purchase some stationery and postage-stamps, and "just to have a look at Nice." I may as well confess that rarely in the course of my wanderings have I been so completely bewildered and astounded as I was when I went ashore, and gazed upon a city with whose almost every aspect I thought that I had been familiar for ever so many years. The port, to begin with, certainly looked far more adapted as a place of embarkation for a Columbus or a Cortes than for "capitaines au long cours" in the nineteenth century. We had contrived to take up, as I have already mentioned, a scrambling and uncomfortable kind of berth, which left us a good fifteen feet from the quay side; but later in the night had come in a huge Italian freight steamer from Palermo—the *Muffato* was, as well as I could make out, the name painted on her bows—which lay right athwart the port, inside the two moles. How we were to get out again at five o'clock in the afternoon, and how a little flotilla of speronari waiting to sail outward, and another and larger flotilla of fishing smacks waiting for entrance, were to go about their several businesses, unless the *Muffato* could by means yet unknown be swung into some less obstructive position, were primarily of the nature of mysteries; but was not the Wise Man as sorely troubled in his mind to account for the way of a ship upon the sea as he was to understand the way of a serpent on a rock, and a fowl in the air? To the ordinary and unwise who occasionally "goes down to the docks," and muses upon things maritime, there are two things perennially and inscrutably marvellous and phenomenal. First, that, even with the assistance of any number of tugs and pilots, a ship should be able to get into a crowded dock, and next, that she should be able to get out again without doing herself or her neighbours some dire injury. There is not the slightest reason why we should feel ashamed of our ignorance in the matter. Did it not baffle all Solomon's sapience to make it out?

The quaint forms and gay colours of the barks at anchor; the sails reefed into a thousand-fold variety of festoons; the rigging of the different craft interlacing in inextricably labyrinthic tracery; the yards bent into strange arcs and angles; the patches—now blue, now orange, now blood-colour—on the white sails that were bent; the half-decked hulls; the tiny spirals of blue smoke creeping from dim cabooses where darkskinned, grizzly-bearded men were cooking strange messes under a continuity of awnings amicably knotted together from vessel to vessel; the cheery laugh of a black cook hurrying forward to "dump" a skid of tomato and potato peelings overboard; the inquiring bark of a coasting-vessel dog— inquiring in the sense of his being also interested in the question of breakfast, and wishful to know when the *rascasse* or the *frittura* would be ready; the plashing of the boat's oars in the still waters of the port as some skipper was being rowed on shore; and, in strange contradistinction to these Levantine sights and sounds, the metallic voice of an unknown mariner, seemingly a chief mate of Scottish descent, apostrophising, in terms of bitter reprehension, an irascible Sandy—all these made up a picture that one longed for the pencil of a Beverley or an Oswald Brierley to depict, or the pen of a William Black to describe. I had to tear myself from the view of these trumpery little skiffs in the port of Nice, so enchanting were they to the sight.

Perhaps, from a commercial and maritime point of view, it would be better if the stone wall encircling three sides of the port were not, in many places, broken down, thickly masked by creeping plants, and in a general condition of neglect and disrepair. It may be also held as a moot point whether the advantages of trade and navigation would not be more fully served if one of the portals of ingress and egress did not lead to nowhere in particular save to a kind of howling little wilderness choked with shards and pebbles and decaying vegetation, which may have been at some remote period a vineyard, but which, incurably attacked by phylloxera, had been given up as a bad job by its proprietor. As to the expediency of expelling numerous varieties of stray animals—pigs, poultry, goats, and donkeys—from the premises, I am loth to express a decided opinion, seeing that they might haply form part of the live stock which the *Marie Louise* or some other coasting steamer might carry away that very afternoon; and, under those circumstances, there was little harm in the poor creatures trying to pick up a light breakfast on the edible odds and ends lying about. The goats, I observed, had a good time over some very toothsome-looking vine-stalks; and it is to be presumed that the pigs did not find a brown canvas bag, full of prickly pears, offensive to their taste.

If they were doomed to go on board ship, they would not get much there, poor beasts, in the way of sustenance. Almost every Mediterranean coasting steamer is, after its kind, a Noah's ark in miniature, and I have very seldom undertaken a Mediterranean voyage without seeing the most abominable cruelties wreaked on the dumb creatures among the cargo. It was Constantine the Great who abolished the gladiatorial sports in the amphitheatre. Just study the episodes of the cattle transit system in the Mediterranean—ay, and from far-off Odessa, and through the Straits, and you will at once be in a position to admit—without troubling yourself about Spanish bullfights or the *lutteurs* of Nîmes and Arles—how very easy it is for the wonted fires of the brutalities of the arena to live in their ashes, in the holds and on the decks of steamers laden with live stock.

We are not immaculate ourselves, you may urge, in this respect. I reply that we have done much, and that we are continuing to do our best, to mitigate the horrors of a system at once scandalous and revolting to humanity and to civilisation. In the Mediterranean and in the Levant I have not, on the other hand, in the course of a quarter of a century's recurrent visits to those regions, noted one single symptom of amelioration in the treatment of dumb animals conveyed as cargo. I am afraid that the Southerner of the Latin race is inherently incapable of the feeling of compassion towards the brute creation.

By dint of trying, and much trying—in the course of which

I nearly tumbled down a sand-bank and into a deep gully—I managed to effect an entrance into a back garden, where a nut-brown and bare-legged maid was, like her sister in the nursery rhyme, "hanging out the clothes." This damsel, however, seemed so despitefully bent on assuming, in addition to her own part, the *rôle* of the blackbird in the story in question, and, as far as opprobrious epithets went, manifested so lively a resolution to bite off what remains of my nose, that, still in quest of the city of Nice, I beat a precipitate retreat from the inhospitable drying ground—may her ironing be disastrous and her clear-starching end in contempt!—and, traversing successively what appeared to be a deserted tanner's yard, a disused brickfield, and the site of an extensive conflagration, I came at last on a dusty road, bordered by sparse tufts of cactus.

The port of Nice was still irritatingly close by, and I had fetched a uselessly wrong compass in endeavouring to find a short cut to the town. I marked a lamp-post. That looked like civilisation; and by and by I discovered that in the dusty road there was a tram. Presently came trudging along the most primitive kind of tram-car that I had seen since I gazed upon the "trolleys" in the streets of San Francisco. The Nice tram-car is only a board or platform on wheels, what in the United States is termed a "float," and at right angles to which are rows of wooden benches. It is, in fact, a *char-à-bancs*, without front, back, or sides; but, covered with a canvas awning, and easy to jump into and easy to jump out of, it is not to be despised as a vehicular convenience. I asked the conductor of this lengthened chariot where Nice was. "Monsieur," he replied, "vous y êtes."

Perplexed, I continued to wander until I found myself in the midst of a labyrinth of streets in an idle, sleepy, and dirty Italian town without the slightest pretensions to grandeur or even picturesqueness in architecture. The names over the shop-doors were almost exclusively Italian. Most of the shop-fronts were unglazed, and the wares sold within generally of the paltriest description. I marked a brawny girl with a "touzled" head of hair, and barefooted of course, emerging from a corner grocery, and bearing 'twixt her finger and her thumb a farthing rushlight. Many years had passed since I had seen a farthing rushlight! It did me good. I went into a *débit de tabac* and purchased a halfpenny cigar. I began to feel that my foot was on my native heath, and that my name was—say, Leatherlani. Very soft, when they were not sour, came from the recesses of tortuous by-lanes the odours of maccaroni and stuffato, of the comforting polenta, of the stimulating minestra, of the exhilarating frittura.

The only things which I had some difficulty in finding were a barber's, a newsvendor's, and a post-office; but, fortunately, I met the captain of the *Marie Louise*, who, with his little son, had been taking, like myself, his walks abroad. "It is a strange town," he remarked; "I should have thought that Nice, of which we have all heard so much, would have been a somewhat gayer and livelier place. Can Monte Carlo be as dull as it is here? What *blagues*—what lies people tell, to be sure!" This excellent captain informed me that I should find a tolerable barber's some five-and-twenty yards up the street, next to a dealer in charcoal, and that I could procure *Le Petit Marseillais* from an old woman who sold fruit a few doors higher; but that for a post-office he was afraid that I should have to walk as far as the Place Garibaldi. He bade me, in conclusion, not forget that breakfast would be ready on board the *Marie Louise* at nine a.m., punctually, and so walked away, with his little son, cheerily. The Place—La Piazza Garibaldi! Why, of course, I should have known that there was Quite Another Nice—Nizza, the maritime, the fishing, the salt-smelling—Nice, that had nothing whatever in common with the curled and oiled and perfumed Nice, with which most of us are so well acquainted. Yet I am glad, nevertheless, to have had a peep at that Other Nice.

VI.

FROM NICE TO BASTIA.

BASTIA, *October* 9.

THE *Marie Louise* experienced quite as much difficulty in emerging from the port of Nice as it had been her fate to undergo in effecting an entrance into that exiguous harbour. She began to take in additional cargo shortly after breakfast, and, with the seemingly insatiable voracity characteristic of a ship, she continued to devour, so to speak, all kinds of merchandise throughout the afternoon. I had some work to do, and having done it, went on deck, and for an hour or two watched, in the company of old Monsieur Chose and the captain's little boy, the to me always interesting—nay, almost fascinating—spectacle of a vessel that is being laden.

What a microcosm of commodities! Socrates, in the market-place, expressed his astonishment at beholding around him so many things that he did not want; but all the multifarious things which the mariners were stowing away in the hold and on the deck of the *Marie Louise* were destined to serve some definitely-expressed demand. Somebody, for instance, needed that very extensive consignment of waterproof coats and leggings loosely packed in sail-cloth. Somebody had written for the despatch of several crates full of bottles of absinthe, vermouth, and bitters. Some Corsican *pharmacien* needed to have his stock of drugs replenished, since on many packing cases, with the address of Bastia upon them, I took note of ginger and senna, of camphor and of orris root. Behind some watercasks by the forecastle there was a tall heap of fir-cones. Who wanted fir-cones, and where? At Bastia, or at Leghorn? The Tuscan port was to be the ultimate bourn of the *Marie Louise's* voyage; and the sacks of wool and hemp, the bags of rice and arrowroot, the tubs of butter, the boxes full of cheeses, the kegs of turpentine and varnish, and the innumerable baskets, bundles, and packages holding no end of wholly dissimilar articles, were all wanted by somebody — the somebody unknown to or voluntarily ignored by the son of Sophroniscus.

Old Monsieur Chose was very talkative. He had been a cabin-boy on board a French frigate at the Battle of Navarino; he had been a master-at-arms in the expedition to the Morea. He rose to the rank of gunner, and had served at the bombardment of Vera Cruz. Then he had entered the commercial marine, and for more than thirty years had been ploughing the blue waters of the Mediterranean. Some years had passed since he had retired on a well-earned pension; but he was not tired of the sea yet; and the companies often favoured him with a trip to some port or another—now to Leghorn, now to Barcelona, now to Valencia or Carthagena, or even to Algiers and Tunis.

"I like to look at the vessel lading," remarked old Monsieur Chose; "it is a pleasure that never palls upon me; and when I am at home at Marseilles there is scarcely an afternoon that I do not stroll down to the quay of the Joliette to see the vessels lading and unlading, and to listen to the talk and raillery of the sailors and the boatmen and wharf labourers. They are an original race. They have always something fresh and racy to say, whether in wrath or in merriment, and have been saying it I know not how many thousands of years." Thus old Monsieur Chose. He was of the same mind, probably quite unconsciously, with that "little wearish old man," Democritus of Abdera, who, after a day spent in abstruse studies and deep philosophic musings, could find no more soothing recreation at noontide than to stroll down to the haven, and watch the going and coming of the craft, and listen to the noisy traffic and rough jokes of the waterside folk.

I think that it must have been about twenty minutes past four when the sight of a victoria, driven right down to the quay-side, and in which were two lady passengers for Leghorn, having with them no less than twelve canaries in a cage, filled me with a sudden and burning desire to behold, if only for five minutes, not the maritime Nice—the species of Mediterranean Wapping, which I had perambulated in the morning, but the Nice of Other Days. Besides, I remembered that I had no cigars, and that there was a shop on the Quai Massena, where, of an austere widow, "weeds" really bearing some resemblance to genuine havanas were procurable at a moderate price. Forthwith I hailed the victoria which had brought down the lady passengers and the twelve canaries, and I asked the captain if he thought there was sufficient time to accomplish the journey to the

Nice of Other Days and back. "Parfaitement," he replied. There was still much *marchandises* to find room for ; "although," added the worthy commander of the *Marie Louise*, "where I am to find room for them all I scarcely know. These supercargoes seem to think that a litre can be put into a bottle that only holds four *petits verres*."

Fortified with the consent of the captain, I did not precisely "leap" on shore, such an exercitation being wholly foreign to my age and habits; but I made as much haste to reach the quay as the slippery planks of the aerial bridge would allow me to do; and I bade the driver conduct me to a designated *débit de tabac*, on the Quai Massena, promising him what I fondly hoped he would esteem as a munificently generous *pourboire* if he did his errand swiftly. Fortunately for me, he was a young cabdriver, comparatively inexperienced in the arts of extortion. A veteran Nice *cocher*, used to conveying impatient gamblers to the railway station for Monte Carlo, would have seen his way to a demand for at least five francs, while my youthful charioteer was entirely satisfied with the promise of twenty sous above his fare.

He thoroughly understood the emergency of the occasion— that is to say, that the *Marie Louise* was to start at five p.m.— and to the height of that occasion he rose at once. Standing up on his box, he cracked his whip with a savagery of sound appalling to listen to, and apostrophised the meek animal between the shafts as "Tête d'éléphant," "Tête de chameau," and "Tête de phoque." Away we went, clattering and dust and pebble scattering, out of the port, over the tramway, and through the devious lanes of that Nice which I have likened to a Mediterranean Wapping. "Hue là, sale rosse!" shrieked the youthful driver. "Hue là, Khroumir, Bedouin, Bou-Amema!" The last epithet "fetched" the horse, and he went at a tremendous pace through the quaint and sleepy-looking Place Garibaldi, along the Boulevard du Pont Neuf, and so by the Place Charles Albert.

Then I began to recognise the Nice that erst I knew—the Nice of Other Days. Watched not too amicably by a couple of sergents de ville, we crossed the Pont Neuf, and found ourselves in full Quai Massena. Yes, there was the dear old river, or torrent, or watercourse—call it what you will—of the Paglione, its bed as dry as ever, with the exception of two or three tiny streamlets, which have trickled down from the Col di Tenda, and in which the *blanchisseuses* of Nice are busily employed in washing. There they are, the familiar forms, away down on their knees on the stony bed of the Paglione, sousing and wringing their linen, or thwacking away for dear life at the clothes with wooden pallets. Their voices, laughing, gibing, wrangling, sound as fresh and sonorous as of yore. And how they bang away at the linen!

> Pan! Pan! Margot au lavoir,
> Pan! Pan! à coups de battoir,
> Pan! Pan! va laver son cœur
> Pan! Pan! tout noir de douleur.

The savage refrain in the "Assommoir" rings in your ears as you regard the washerwomen down on their knees scrubbing and banging away at the linen.

I found the *débit de tabac* of which I stood in need, and the well-remembered tobacconist, an old lady of vast dimensions, broad of brow, with large, black, flashing eyes, once superbly handsome in profile, but now with many superadded chins, complacent but dignified of mien, meditative of aspect when not engaged in sweeping the francs and centimes into the till—a memorable old lady, somewhat injured by time, it is true, somewhat shored up and underpinned it may be, but on the whole grand and majestic as a Roman ruin. She was so glad to see me. Where had I been so long? The same cigars—the "paquets de quatre foncés." Naturally she had them. Did she not always keep the "foncés" in stock for monsieur, awaiting his return? She knew he would return. "Angélique, he has returned." This last piece of information, conveyed in a deep contralto whisper, sheltered by the grand old lady's dexter palm, to an invisible and perhaps non-existent niece in the back parlour, crowned the edifice of her diplomacy. I purchased four "paquets de quatre foncés" from her, instead of two, as I had originally intended.

Adding to his vocabulary of abusive epithets addressed to the patient horse the names of "Troppmann," of "Billoir," and of "Si-Sliman," my youthful driver—I was glad to note that the abuse was only "his fun," and that he did not strike his willing steed—brought me back to the port of Nice in excellent time. Indeed, there was, if anything, slightly too much time to spare; for five and half-past five, and even a quarter to six, came and went without any apparent signs of the approaching departure of the *Marie Louise*. She had got her steam up; of that we were informed at least half-a-dozen times; but the circumstance did not prevent her taking in more and more miscellaneous items of cargo—a formidable array of empty wine casks among the number. These, I was told, would return from Leghorn full of grapes, a statement which certainly opened the door to the hypothesis that it was possible to obtain "vin de Bordeaux" *viâ* the vineyards of Tuscany.

At length, sunset being imminent, the steward announced his intention of serving dinner, which should properly have been on the table at five. He rang the warning bell, and departed for the galley in quest of the soup tureen, and precisely at that moment the *Marie Louise* made her first effort to steam out of the port of Nice. We had a harbour pilot with us, a mariner who, no doubt, had passed all his examinations, obtained all his certificates, and was in all respects a fully competent person. I am bound, however, to confess that—such is the force of prejudice—I was not favourably struck with the aspect of this Palinurus, who was quite a dandy, and looked far more like a hairdresser than a pilot.

"En avant, en avant, doucement!" he was crying when the Swiss steward, from the Canton of Berne, who had just come aft with the smoking soup tureen, hastily handed it to his assistant, and began, in a very agitated manner, to wave his table napkin as a signal to the captain on the bridge. "En avant!" The pilot had not got further than that, when the steward shrieked "Basta, arrêtez! Au nom de Dieu, *stop!*" Fortunately for the sake of the *Marie Louise*, and of our own lives, the vessel did stop. It appeared that we had been navigating right into the bows of the big Italian steamer *Muffato*, against which the poor little *Marie Louise* would probably have broken her head badly. The escape was a narrow and a fortunate one; but it was surely the first time within my experience that I had seen a collision averted by the command of a vessel being taken out of the hands of the captain and the pilot by a saloon steward.

But the end had not yet come to the misfortunes of the *Marie Louise*. We contrived to wriggle out of the way of the big *Muffato*, and the pilot was recommencing his incantations, when the chief engineer sent his compliments to the captain, at the same time categorically refusing to move any further until the vessel was properly trimmed. Was this rank mutiny, or what? But the mutinous chief engineer was not forthwith hanged up to the yardarm, any more than the adventurous saloon steward had been put in irons for daring to stop the steamer when she was running right into the *Muffato*. They manage things differently in the Mediterranean. A jury of passenger assessors, mainly composed of commercial travellers, had already pointed out to the captain that the vessel was lurching seriously to port. That estimable master mariner responded from the bridge that he could not be everywhere at once, and that it was the business of the boatswain and the stevedore to see the cargo properly bestowed; but the stevedore had gone on shore, the boatswain declared that he had had enough to do with the hands forward, getting up anchor, and meanwhile the *Marie Louise* continued to incline more and more to port, awakening in one memory at least the lines of Mr. William Cowper on the loss of the *Royal George*. Indeed, the probability of our scuttling not out of the port of Nice, but to the bottom of the harbour, seemed to be within minutely measurable distance.

Happily we had no guns to break loose and roll to leeward. No "land breeze shook the shrouds," and we were not overset; only the *Marie Louise* having been laden with inconceivable slovenliness, it was a matter of physical impossibility for her to right herself. After much shouting and bawling through speaking trumpets, a great "camion" or raft put off from the quay full of dock hands, who, amidst indescribable confusion and yelling in the Nizzard patois, and in endless varieties of the dialect of Languedoc, succeeded in redistributing the cargo, especially the empty wine casks, which, with charming carelessness, had all been placed on one side of the deck. The original stevedore I did not see again. Possibly he was tipsy, and had been replaced by another who was sober and understood his business. By about eight o'clock all was reported as having been made "snug," and the *Marie Louise* was no longer lopsided.

There are in all things compensations. The nasty little brute of a steamer had played us all kinds of mischievous tricks, but in the end she behaved extremely well, and, with the aid of the sea, which was as smooth as glass, and a bright moonlight, we had an exquisitely beautiful passage to Bastia. Old Monsieur Chose had predicted as much, as, warmly shaking hands, he had bidden me farewell at Nice. "There will be *un beau clair de lune* to-night," he said; "and you know the Provençal sailor's proverb, *La lune mange tout.*" Nobody on board had the *mal de mer*. In the watches of the night the sound of snoring from the state rooms of the passengers was quite cheerful to hear—remembering what yells and moans, what prayers and ejaculations would have been audible had there been even what sailors call "half a capful of wind" —and at sunrise it was delightful to listen to the commercial travellers loftily calling for hot coffee and nips of cognac, "pour tuer le ver"—to kill the worm—and puffing at their cigarettes quite chirpingly. Their cigarettes! Why, after a slightly rough night the mere sight of a cigar-case would have been anguish to them.

I scarcely know whether you have observed that, in the course of this pilgrimage down South, I have frequently had occasion to refer to that very characteristic type of humanity, the French commercial traveller. As a matter of fact, seafaring folk, hotel waiters, and the inevitable Figaro apart, the vast majority of my travelling companions during the last three weeks have been bagmen—not from Paris, the Southern merchants and shopkeepers would have none of what they disdainfully call "Rue St. Denisiers," but Méridionals from Nîmes and Arles, from Montpelier and Toulouse, from Fréjus and Toulon. They "do" Corsica and Sardinia four or five times a year, and a proportion of their number even extend their operations to Tuscany.

I have seen a good deal in print lately in English newspapers grievously, and to my thinking unjustly, depreciating the French *commis-voyageur*. I have read that he is "blubbery"—the exact meaning of which term, as applied to him, I fail somehow to understand—that he spits and smokes rank tobacco, that he is rude to ladies, and so forth. Amid the counts of this indictment I think that he should plead guilty to only one. The exceeding badness of his tobacco is unfortunately undeniable; and the execrable odour of the cigars with which he is supplied by a paternal and poisonous Régie can only be exceeded by the infernal stench of the paper in which the "mundungus" of his cigarette is rolled. But what else would you have? It is not his fault. It is that of La Régie Française. MM. the Receivers of the Finances, the Engineers of the Roads and Bridges, the aides-de-camp of the general commanding, smoke cigars every whit as vile as those of the *commis-voyageur*.

As, travelling in Spain, from *fonda* to *venta*, from *posada* to *meson*, from café to café, you make, unwillingly, a constantly-increasing collection of spurious money, given to you in exchange for coins of genuine mintage, so in France, if you are curious in the accumulation of foreign weeds, you may accumulate quite a "hortus siccus" of detestable cigars. I left half a drawerful at Marseilles. I flung half a bundle overboard before we reached Nice; and I am discovering, with much mortification and disappointment, that the quality of the cigars vended on the Quai Massena at Nice, by the lady who was so anxious to inform the invisible Angélique that I had returned, has grievously deteriorated. It is not the fault of that venerable Roman ruin—of that dignified old dame of the Quai Massena. It is the fault of La Régie Française. It is the fault of monopoly.

With amazing hardihood of insistence, France claims to be at the head of European civilisation; but let us just take five points by which the extent of her civilisation or otherwise may be judged. The French are a nation of smokers, yet out of Paris, from the Vosges to the Maritime Alps, it is impossible to purchase a cigar which in England the humblest patron of a "penny pickwick" would not reject with indignant contempt. Number One. France claims to be a Democratic Republic, and placards " Liberty, Equality, and Fraternity" on all her edifices; yet, in this free and democratic country, any person not being a French citizen who may by word or deed do aught to displease the Government of the day may be at once, and without any opportunity of defending himself, expelled from the territory of the Republic. Number Two. France professes to have an extreme horror of bloodshed, and is in the main so averse from the infliction of capital punishment that it is with the greatest difficulty that convictions can be obtained against the most atrocious assassin, and "extenuating circumstances" are discovered by juries in the cases of horrible miscreants who, with axes and hammers, have dashed out the brains of their infirm grandmothers in order to plunder the poor old creatures of a few hundred francs which they have been painfully hoarding for years in a long stocking; yet in this country, to whose educated classes the idea of the guillotine is so abhorrent, the guides and interpreters of public opinion systematically resort to the imbecile, the barbarous, the bloodthirsty practice of duelling. Number Three. Every lodger in a French house is subject to the insolent and degrading supervision, and very often the despotism, of a domestic called the porter, or *concierge*, who is habitually cruel and extortionate, who is often dishonest, who is always a spy of the landlord, and very frequently the spy of the police. Number Four. There is, in reality, in France no law of bail, and there is certainly no law of Habeas Corpus, and the first step taken in a prosecution for libel or "diffamation," as was recently and amusingly shown in the case of Messieurs Roustan and Challemel-Lacour versus Monsieur Henri Rochefort, is to send for the defendant to the cabinet of a *juge d'instruction,* and interrogate him privately. As it happened, Monsieur Rochefort—remembering, perhaps, the cognate case of the Chouan Georges Cadoudal, who, at his trial, told President Thuriot that he had been too long in England to be drawn into answering questions which might criminate himself—flatly refused to answer any of the *juge d'instruction's* questions. This makes Number Five, and the five points might, without much difficulty, be expanded to fifty.

Meanwhile I find the French *commis-voyageur* in the main a very good fellow. It is true that I have not had a very extended choice of associates lately—it has been, indeed, rather of the nature of Hobson's choice, of the *commis-voyageur* or nobody; still, the bagman and I have got on together capitally. "L'Illustre Gaudissart" of Balzac is not by any means an extinct type. I have met him multiplied a hundredfold any time during this journey. He is as fond of "la blague" and of "le mot pour rire" as ever. His appetite is prodigious. "There were never in the world," a gentleman from Montelimart said to me yesterday, "too many haricots for me." Most of his dishes he lubricates plentifully with oil. An American might be of opinion that the Illustrious Gaudissart was "a whale at onions;" and if he be fond of a little—or of a great deal—of garlic, you must remember that you have come South, and that the "cuisine du Midi" is not the "cuisine du Nord." All Meridional cooks are not so scrupulous in the matter of garlic as it was the pride of the exemplary Monsieur Durand of Nîmes to be. "And," remarked to me lately an excellent lady who vends fruit and vegetables in the Cours St. Louis, at Marseilles, "if we do eat a little garlic *quand le cœur nous en dit*, we sell our figs at five centimes apiece, instead of charging five francs a plate for them as your restaurant-keepers in Paris do. *Fi! les vilains gens!*"

The *Marie Louise* is full this morning of the Illustrious Gaudissart. Fortified by the calmness of the sea, a tranquil night's rest, and his coffee and "nip" of cognac, he has "spruced" himself up. He appears in a tall and shiny hat. He has even adorned his shoes with snowy white linen gaiters, with mother-of-pearl buttons. He has a walking-stick with a gold knob. In watch-chains and *breloques*—gold or plated, it is no business of mine to inquire—he was always great; but this morning he is phenomenally gleaming in the article of jewellery. He is too well bred to make any inquiries as to the particular article in which I am commercially travelling myself. Indeed, when I tell him that I am an Englishman, he is, as a rule, perfectly satisfied. "You Englishmen," he remarks, "like travelling. *Vous avez le goût de voyager, vous autres, hein?* You adore dangers and hardships and inconveniences from which the Frenchman, more delicately nurtured, shrinks." Humph! Do we? At all events the Illustrious Gaudissart was satisfied that we do.

But I am not to bid my good friends Gaudissart and Company adieu yet awhile. Commercial or non-commercial, we are all bound for the same hostelry, the Hôtel de France, in the Boulevard du Palais, "tenu par Staffe." There are other inns in this town of twenty thousand inhabitants—twenty thousand, so the natives say, although the *Guide-Joanne*, a usually trustworthy authority, states that there are less than seventeen thousand. There are the Italie, the Europe, and the Croix de Malte, all supportable, no doubt; but the France is the best. To the Hôtel de France, then; for the *Marie Louise*, with a surprisingly small amount of bungling or delay, has cast anchor in the middle of the port of Bastia, and we are in Corsica. To the Hôtel de France, "tenu par Staffe." Certainly. With all my heart. Alas! There is many a slip 'twixt the cup and the lip at Bastia, as elsewhere.

VII.

ON SHORE AT BASTIA.

BASTIA, *October* 10.

IT was apparently for the benefit of the local boatmen that the *Marie Louise* had taken up her position in the middle of the port. The harbour was not by any means crowded, and the captain could, without any difficulty, have moored his vessel close to the quay side; but there were the interests of the boatmen to be considered, and they were held to be supreme. Such a tender consideration for the material welfare of the gentlemen of the oar is, I believe, one of the peculiar features of Latin civilisation. Throughout Anglo-Saxondom you calmly and comfortably walk on board the vessel which is to take you to sea. If the vessel—as in the case of an ocean steamship—lies in the offing, you are comfortably conveyed in a tender to the monster galleon. You walk on board at Liverpool or at Southampton, and you walk on shore at New York, or Boston, or New Orleans. Out of Anglo-Saxondom things are ordered differently. You are not allowed to land directly from the steamer on the shore of Cuba. Oh, no! you must have a boat, and you must be fleeced by the boatmen. It is one of the "costumbres del pais." Precisely the same agreeable practice obtains at Vera Cruz. The steamer anchors inside the Castle of St. Juan de Ulloa, and then you fall into the hands of the inevitable boatman, who, adding insult to injury, expects you to steer the boat while he rows, and curses you in corrupt Castilian if you are clumsy at the helm. It is the same at Barcelona, the same at Cadiz; but pray mark this, *it is not the same at Gibraltar*. There you are in Anglo-Saxondom, and, if my memory serves me faithfully, you land at the sallyport direct from the steamer.

There is, perhaps, one corner of Anglo-Saxondom where the fine old tradition that those who go down to the sea in ships were normally created to be plundered and abused by boatmen yet finds acceptance. That corner may be, for aught I know, Gravesend, and I am not prepared to deny that the Portsmouth boatmen have a good many traits in common with their brethren of the Latin race. When I say that there is a strong family likeness between boatmen—I mean in the way of overcharging and using bad language—all over the world, I would except from the category the "caikjes" of Constantinople and the gondoliers of Venice. Elsewhere the boatman is little better than a foul-mouthed pirate, and Signor Tomaso Tuggi, of the port of Bastia, Corsica, is about the most piratical and the most vituperative member of the class with whom I have had lately the pleasure to come in contact.

Bastia, from the harbour, looks a much more important place than it really is. The town is displayed in amphitheatrical form round the port, and the streets make such a rapid descent to the shore as almost to produce the effect brought about by artificial perspective, as in the "built up" scenes of the ancient Roman theatre. The houses, moreover, are very tall, many of them being six and seven storeys high. Those forming the Terra Vecchia, or lower town, are more than Italian in aspect—they are mediæval; and, indeed, the majority of these structures date from the period of the Genoese occupation. They are black with age, and rich with grimy bas-reliefs, gnawed like so many bones by the hungry dogs of Time. Behind these venerable buildings rise the edifices of the Terra Nuova, or upper town, which are generally white, with green "jalousies," and affecting the villa style of architecture. Behind all is a background of steep hill, which, as I look upon it now, is as resplendent with thick-tufted vegetation as one of the Green Hills of Vermont. The hill is crowned by the donjon of the citadel—a frowning pile erected towards the close of the fifteenth century by Vicontello d'Istria.

The suburbs of Bastia afford very charming drives, the roads being bordered by olive and Barbary fig-trees, and by groves of oranges and lemons; but from the port the amphitheatre of villas, backed by the hill clad with verdure, presents the aspect of a smiling oasis in the midst of a desert, the austerity of which appals you. The appearance of the rock-bound coast is one of unrelieved savagery. You see nothing but pile after pile of jagged granite, and as these masses, which are of a monstrous tawny hue, frown down upon you, an impression, half terrifying, half grotesque, takes possession of you that you are gazing upon the menagerie turned to stone of some Van Amburg of ages long since past and gone. Stay: there are tigers in this geological wild beast show. Far away from the coast-line the tawny slopes of the rocks are thinly striped in sombre hues. Those dark stripes, undulating along the mountain sides, are, the Illustrious Gaudissart tells me, forests of pine and cypress. There are leopards, too, in this appalling Wombwell-like show, for some of the rocks are spotted with clumps of the darkly-flowering "makis."

The Illustrious Gaudissart knows his Corsica by heart; for in order to "do" it thoroughly, he is obliged to explore the interior of the island, and to penetrate by Calvi to Ajaccio. He tells me that Corsica is "un drôle de pays," but that it is not nearly so savage as the first view of the coast might lead the traveller to imagine. "Behind the fortifications of Nature"—he means the prehistoric Van Amburg's menagerie turned to stone—he tells me there is a very smiling land indeed. The arid and the desolate disappear. There are forests, it is true, of pines, and cypress, and larch; but there are also groves of almonds and chestnuts—magnificent chestnuts. At one time you might fancy yourself in Dauphiné or in Auvergne. Presto! the next moment you are in Algeria or in Sicily. Olives, oranges, lemons, and figs abound. Then comes the "makis," which may be qualified as the Corsican jungle. The French call it "le fourré." It is, in truth, an almost impenetrable underbush of dwarf oak, "alaterne," heather, laurel, thyme, myrtle, and box, mingled with rosemary, lavender, and sage bush; clematis, smilax, and bracken add to the general floral disorder. It is almost unnecessary to add, that in days gone by the "makis"—presumably derived from the Italian "macchie"—was the favourite resort of the bandits with whom the island formerly swarmed.

The Illustrious Gaudissart incidentally hinted that even in the present piping times of peace and a well-organised gen-

A CORSICAN FOREST.

darmerie the toilette of a traveller in the less frequented parts of the littoral was scarcely complete without a revolver. He hastened, however, to explain " qu'il y avait des gredins partout "—that there were scoundrels everywhere—a postulate in which I thoroughly agreed with him ; and he earnestly begged me to disbelieve all the cock-and-bull stories which I might hear about the existence among Corsican families of that vendetta about which, thanks to Monsieur Alexandre Dumas the elder, Mr. Dion Boucicault, Mr. Charles Kean, and Mr. Henry Irving, civilised Europe has heard so much. At Ajaccio, continued my informant, they will sell you stilettos with " Vendetta " and " Morte al nemico " engraved or damascened on the blades ; but these were only toys to be sold to English visitors, and manufactured, for aught he knew, in Paris or at our own Birmingham. Hereditary blood-feuds have long ceased to exist in the island. That fact, however, does not militate against the Corsican having preserved intact his essentially distrustful and vindictive character. "Il est mauvais coucheur," suspicious, unsociable, and revengeful. That is why he made such a superlatively good police agent under the Second Empire. You will hear a good deal while you are in Bastia of " la malveillance Corse."

Modern Corsican malevolence does not take the form of stabbing or shooting one's enemy, and then hiding oneself in the "makis." According to what I hear, it takes—especially among Corsicans well educated enough to know better—the guise of habitually decrying, disparaging, and scowling upon the foreigner, whether he be a Frenchman or a member of some other nationality, and of sullenly and systematically opposing, thwarting, and plotting against all or any kind of reform or enterprise introduced from the mainland, and calculated to foster the industry, develop the resources, and enhance the prosperity of the island. That the Corsicans have ceased to hate one another from generation to generation I can only vouch for on the authority of the Illustrious Gaudissart; but they are certainly unanimous in disliking the "Continentals" —a generic term which they confer upon all persons who have not been so fortunate as to draw their first breath in Corsica.

It so chanced that I learned a good deal about the town of Bastia before I became acquainted with the interior of the Hôtel de France, "tenu par Staffe." My friends the bagmen took me all over the place, and even introduced me to a highly respectable grocer, a very worthy ready-made clothes dealer, and the truly estimable proprietor of one of the dirtiest cafés I ever visited. "You must not expect anything of the nature of the taste and elegance of Marseilles here," my Meridional companions, with proper pride, were so good as to warn me. "At Bastia, with the exception of the tri-coloured flag, the red trousers of the soldiery, and the Code Napoléon, all is Italian —and Italian of the seventeenth century." I remembered, however, to have read in the pages of Monsieur Valery a much more favourable appreciation of Bastia. "This ancient capital of Corsica," wrote, in 1837, the author just named, "displays a sweetness of manners and a fine sociability for which one looks in vain in her new rival, the savage *chef-lieu* of the department, notwithstanding the grandeur of the edifices with which Ajaccio has been, at a vast expense, recently adorned." But a vast change, I was told, had taken place since 1837 in

THE FORTIFICATIONS OF BASTIA.

the relations of the two towns. Bastia is the commercial capital of Corsica. Planted right in front of the Italian mainland, it is in almost daily communication with Leghorn, which can be reached in a few hours by steamer. It is still the Place of Arms of the island, and it is here that the general commanding the garrison and his staff have their headquarters. The Supreme Court also sits at Bastia, but the Prefecture, the Treasury, and all the other administrative departments are at Ajaccio, which is the political capital and the place of periodical session for the Council-General of the department.

Communication between Ajaccio, Nice, and Marseilles is tolerably frequent, but it is with difficulty that you can reach Italy from the Corsican capital. Once a week only there is a steamer to a place called Porto Torres, in Sardinia, and thence the traveller must proceed by rail to Cagliari, where he may find a steamer bound for Leghorn. For the rest, it was a wild journey across the mountains to Ajaccio; but when I got there I should be enchanted. It was "une ville de délices." The climate was that of Paradise. It was as clean as a Swiss châlet. The public buildings were magnificent. The promenades were ravishing. The bay was more beautiful than the Bay of Naples. Finally, Ajaccio was becoming every year more fashionable as a health resort. The faculty all over the Continent were recommending its mild and balmy climate in cases of pulmonary and bronchial ailments. It had a mixed colony of Dutch, Scandinavian, and Russian invalids, to say nothing of the English, for the benefit of whom a "bonne dame Anglaise" had built a church. In fine, my friends advised me very strongly to proceed to Ajaccio with all possible despatch, making at the same time no secret of their astonishment that I should have come to Bastia at all.

How we walked about the town, to be sure! I may here state that the *Marie Louise* had arrived at a very early hour—shortly after six, if I remember aright—and that seven o'clock was just striking when the piratical boatmen had completed their work of plundering and blackguarding us. On the whole the life of a Bastian boatman must be, unlike a policeman's, a happy one. There are arrivals and departures of steamers every day. Imagine the bliss of being able to rob and abuse the travelling public from Monday morning till Saturday night!

Close to the port, on the seashore, is an open expanse of noble proportions called the Place St. Nicolas. On two sides it is bordered by tolerably handsome public buildings, but the side fronting the sea is composed of the tall, grimy, old Genoese-looking tenements of which I spoke just now. On the ground floors of these dingy houses—some of which look as though they had been transported bodily from the Old Town in Edinburgh—are a few mean shops and cafés. The Place St. Nicolas can boast neither fountains nor trees; but in the afternoon and evening it is the favourite promenade of the population, owing to the superb view of the sea which it affords. Something else, too, is visible from the place: I mean the couching masses of tawny rock—the Titanic and prehistoric Van Amburg's menagerie turned to stone.

One other feature also the expanse presents—to me a highly interesting one, and indeed I may admit that to see this feature at Bastia, and another and analogous one at

Ajaccio, were chief among the motives which impelled me to come to Corsica at all. This is a colossal statue of Napoleon I., in white marble, the work of a Florentine sculptor named Bartolini. The figure is in Roman costume, and the expression of the face good, but so austere as to resemble more closely that of an ancient Roman than of a modern Corsican, whose father must have worn powder and a pigtail—whose mother a hoop and high-heeled shoes. I have always thought that the sculptors err grievously when they attire the First Napoleon in Roman raiment. His head was purely Greek, and no artist ever understood that fact better than Canova when, in the statue now in the possession of the Duke of Wellington, he modelled the hero wholly nude. Naturally, it was not of my companions the bagmen, nor, indeed, of anybody at Bastia, that I sought for information touching the possible survival of any remnant of the Napoleonic legend at Bastia. I deferred asking any questions of that kind until I reached Ajaccio. I may just mention, however, that there is an Imperialist Newspaper at Bastia called *L'Aigle*, and that, although the Republicans have been victorious in the Parliamentary elections, the Bonapartists have a majority in the Council-General.

We visited a couple of churches. The interior of one, St. Jean Baptiste, is extremely rich in marbles of various hues, mainly from native quarries. We made acquaintance with the interior of the Hôtel de Ville, of the Palais de Justice, of the Military Hospital, of the College or Lycée, and of the theatre. There was likewise pointed out to me the public library, which contained, I was told, no less than twenty thousand volumes, the bulk of which were bequeathed to the town of Bastia by a worthy doctor named Prela, who had been physician to Pope Pius VII. I may note in this connection that at Ajaccio there is another public library of nearly thirty thousand volumes, principally the gift of Napoleon's brother, Lucien, and of his uncle, Cardinal Fesch. Remembering that the population of the island is not much more than two hundred and fifty thousand, the united libraries of Bastia and Ajaccio would give one book to every five inhabitants—a splendid literary provision. But a plenitude of books is not, unfortunately, a guarantee for the dissemination of learning. I scarcely think that, from an intellectual point of view, the denizens of the Trastevere at Rome have benefited very largely by the propinquity of the literary treasures of the Vatican, while it is certain that the slums of St. Giles's are within pistol-shot of the British Museum. It is one thing to bring a horse to the water, and another to make him drink.

It may have appeared to you passing strange that I should have been wandering about Bastia all this time without having said anything in detail concerning the Hôtel de France, "tenu par Staffe." The fact is that, although, as I have recorded, my encounter with the pirates of the port took place at seven a.m., it was half-past eleven ere I became the thoroughly wearied occupant of a bed-room at the hotel in question. Fate and the gentleman who combed his hair over his forehead were against me. When, early in the morning, the bagmen and I presented ourselves at the Hôtel de France we were received with open arms by the amiable and accomplished daughter of Monsieur Staffe. The hotel, she explained, had been, as well as its succursal, higher up the street, quite full for many days past; but there were rooms for all " ces amiables messieurs "—meaning ourselves—charming rooms, adorable rooms, if we would only wait a bit. Well, how long were we to wait? Well, Monsieur Staffe's daughter thought it might be a great half-hour; or, say, a little three-quarters of an hour; or, to make things perfectly sure—inexorably sure—suppose we said an hour. Then the charming rooms, the adorable rooms, would be ready. For the moment, "ces messieurs là-haut "—you will observe that she did not qualify them as " amiables "—were buckling the straps of their portmanteaus and paying their bills, and they were all going away by the steamer for Leghorn, which started irrevocably at ten a.m.

I could not but admire the dexterity with which the hostess executed the complicated manœuvre of welcoming the coming and speeding the parting guest. We had some *café au lait* and dry bread, and that repast, with a cigar, whiled away an hour. Then we went out for a walk, to find when, at the expiration of an hour, we returned to claim the promised shelter, that "ces messieurs" upstairs were still buckling the straps of their portmanteaus, or paying their bills, or at all events that they declined to clear out of the Hôtel de France. It was dismally aggravating; and the more so as the hitherto halcyon sky was becoming rapidly overclouded, and the hitherto cobalt-coloured sea had assumed an ugly indigo and Atlantic-looking tinge, and behind the amphitheatre of green hills there had risen a huge bank of leaden-coloured clouds, darkly menacing and throwing into ghastly relief the white villas of the Terra Vecchia. Would the Leghorn steamer never start, and would the gentleman who brushed his hair over his forehead never go away? The waiters pointed him out to me at the open window of the first-floor front room which was to be mine. He had his elbows on the sill, and displayed in an ample manner his linen cuffs, which were of great depth and ornamented with large discs of malachite. He had a beard cut "à la Henri Quatre," to match the hair which he combed over his forehead. He had an eyeglass, and smoked his cigarette in a haughtily languid manner. No *commis-voyageur* this, but one of the Gallican "upper crust" evidently. I know that I wished him at the bottom of the Mediterranean Sea. Why would he persist in not going on board the Leghorn steamer?

The Hôtel de France at Bastia is a large house, tolerably well kept. The rooms are tidy. They are destitute of chimneys; but fireplaces, they tell me, are seldom seen here. The cuisine is on the borderland between France and Italy, and, albeit susceptible of improvement, is not absolutely detestable. The drawback to the hotel is that, with the exception of a room in which to eat, and other rooms in which to sleep, it is devoid of the accommodation which travellers in European countries usually expect. There is no entrance hall, no reading-room, and no smoking-room; and when I was absolutely foot-sore with walking about Bastia—the gentleman who brushed his hair over his forehead still declining to evacuate the premises—I really do not know what I should have done, had not one of the waiters—there were three, all ferocious in aspect, but in the main civil fellows—brought me a chair, in which I sat at the hotel door, in the open street. My companions had by this time all obtained the rooms promised them, but the particular adorable apartment reserved for me was yet held by my unknown enemy. As I have said, it was half-past eleven before he took his departure, treating us all round, as he strode down the street towards the pier, with a glance of superbly patrician scorn. Was he really a patrician, I wonder, or a perfumer? Who shall say? Juvenal warned us long ago against trusting to facial appearances. The most aristocratic and the haughtiest-looking man that ever I remember to have met was a bailiff's follower.

VIII.

THE DILIGENCE COME TO LIFE AGAIN.

AJACCIO, *October* 21.

I THOUGHT that I had done with her for good and all. I allude to the diligence; and I presume that it is warrantable to assign to this happily all but obsolete vehicle the same sex imputed by immemorial courtesy to a ship, and, with equal gallantry, transferred in the earliest days of our railway economy to a locomotive. I am not quite certain about the gender of a coal-mine; but, in the French Navy at least, the powder magazine is always feminine, being christened after Sainte Barbe, the patroness of artillerymen.

I have had a good deal to do with the diligence in my time; and I reluctantly admit that just before it was ousted from the great highways of France by the introduction of railways it had attained a kind of clumsy efficiency and clumsy respectability distantly analogous to the virtual state of perfection to which English stage-coaching had attained about the period when the first sod of the London and Greenwich line was turned. The last decade has witnessed a singularly intelligent and brilliantly successful revival of four-horse vehicles, artistically driven, both in the form of private "drags" and of stage-coaches run as commercial enterprises;

but I never heard, even during the most luxurious days of the Second Empire, of any French nobleman or gentleman starting a diligence either as a private whim or as a business speculation.

The spectacle of a brand-new, bright yellow diligence at the gate of the Jockey Club, with four stalwart Picardy horses, and M. le Vicomte X—— in the gamboge buckskins, the scarlet waistcoat, the oilskin-covered hat, and the tremendously big boots of "le Postillon de Longjumeau," would have been indeed a boon to the *badauds* of the Grand Café and the Place de l'Opéra. The utmost that was done in the direction of such a revival was accomplished, I believe, by Prince Napoleon, who, when he inhabited the Palais Royal, used to delight the *flâneurs* by the periodical arrival and departure of his "berline de voyage," a most picturesque equipage of undeniably eighteenth-century character. The berline hung very high, indeed; the team four Normandy greys, their manes plaited, and their tails tied up with coloured ribbons; while the postillions, in addition to the historic Longjumeau costume, wore on their dexter arms silver badges decorated with the Prince's scutcheon, and beneath their shining hats tie-wigs, scrupulously powdered. "Vieux habits, vieux galons."

But the dear old diligence—I call her "dear" in the sense that we talk about the "dear" old schoolmaster whom we held in such lively detestation when we were under his ferule—was a widely different affair from Monseigneur's Opéra Comique "turn-out" in the courtyard of the Palais Royal. I am not old enough to remember when the French postillion was picturesque. When I first became acquainted with him on the *grande route* between Boulogne and Paris, some forty-three years ago, his red waistcoat, his gamboge buckskins, his shiny hat and parti-coloured streamers, and his preternaturally big boots had all disappeared. He was only a large shabby man, in a blouse and faded velveteen trousers, and his headgear was very often a red woollen nightcap. He no longer bestrode his team. He drove them from a very high perch in front of the *cabriolet*, or leathern-hooded *banquette*, wherein sate the *conducteur*, and two, if not three, outside travellers.

The *conducteur*, in his way, was a dandy; wore his hair and beard in the close military crop known as "à la Titus," carried his *casquette*, with its band of gold lace, on one side, in a rakish manner, and frequently sported a signet ring on his right fore-finger. It was generally understood that his political opinions were Bonapartist; and, if he had passed middle age, he had usually some stirring anecdotes to relate of his experiences with the Grande Armée, and of what King Joachim of Naples said to him—addressing him as "Mon brave Ratatouille"—on the morning of the battle of La Moskova. Apart from the martial smartness of the *conducteur*, the diligence of the past was about as dingy, dilatory, shaky, and uncomfortable an old contrivance as it was possible to imagine—in structure a monstrous conjunction of the bodies of a post-chaise, a stage-coach, and an amputated omnibus, with the hinder half of a britschka behind the driver's seat, and with the roof piled high with luggage, shielded from the weather by an enormous tarpaulin. The horses' collars were certainly covered with leather in a more or less advanced state of decay; but the rest of the harness was, as a rule, made of ropes.

This was the "dear" old diligence in which I have undergone time out of mind partial dislocation of the limbs and innumerable contusions. There was a particular kind of nausea known as the "diligence sick-headache," and which was nearly as grievous as sea-sickness; and I am not at all certain whether, about the year 1840, French medical men had not begun to recognise the existence of such a distinct muscular ailment as the "diligence leg." It was as characteristic in its way as "clergyman's sore throat" or "forkgrinder's lung;" and for days after your release from one of the "cabanons" on wheels of Messieurs Lafitte et Caillard, you felt a fearful stiffness from just above the knee to the ancle, and a vehement desire to obtain relief by kicking out at something or somebody—say the inventor of the diligence. She must have had an inventor, the appliances for inflicting torture on the passenger were so numerous and so elaborate. Albert Smith had a model of a diligence in his study in Percy Street, and was never tired of opening and shutting the doors of the *coupé*, the *intérieur*, and the *rotonde*, and of shaking his fist at the whole horrible apparatus. There should be a model of the old diligence in the Tower of London, alongside the rack, and the thumbscrews, and the scavenger's daughter.

The old diligence! I am sorry to say I saw her only the day before yesterday standing in front of the Messageries de la Corse in the main street of Bastia, and that I have since undergone nineteen hours of the acutest physical and moral suffering in the *coupé* of that appalling caravan. I had some work to do on landing at Bastia—I generally have some, in whatsoever part of the world I may be wandering—and would willingly have sojourned four or five days in the commercial capital of Corsica; but I was literally driven out of the town by the rain. The inhabitants continued to rub their hands with delight at the thought of the long-drouthy earth being at last drenched and their cisterns at length replenished, but the inmates of the Hôtel de France by no means shared in the gratification of the natives. The Illustrious Gaudissart frankly confessed that he could do no business. "Je ne fais pas les vaterproofs," he remarked, gloomily. "I do not travel in umbrellas or goloshes. Nothing else is required in this *satanée pluie*." The Upright Dutchman distinctly asseverated that he could stand it no longer.

I do not think that I have as yet mentioned this member of our company. I call him upright, because he seemed to be made all in one piece, as in days gone by it was vulgarly and erroneously supposed that the elephant's leg was made. I never met with a straighter man—not even among the officers of the Prussian Guards. The Upright Dutchman's conversation was singularly curt, but it was always brief and to the point. There is always some kind of cross-examination going on among people thrown together by the chance-medley of travelling. Politeness may prompt us to restrict within moderate limits the catechising of our companions; yet we are not disinclined to put a whole series of petty manœuvres in train in order to find out who our chance-medley friends are, and whither they are going. The Upright Dutchman met all such interrogative tactics half-way. "Retired surgeon, Dutch Navy. Traversed two oceans. Long stationed at Batavia. Going to Algeria winter. Bronchitis. Detest hotels. Going to board and lodge with Monsieur Gallonge and family, Villa Doux Sourire, near Blidah. Terrace covered with roses." I envied the Upright Dutchman.

The persistence of the downpour led to my making one discovery, interesting in itself, but scarcely important enough to compensate for the wretchedness of the rainy days of Corsica. Bastia is one of the most handsomely-paved towns in Europe; and the contrast between its magnificent side-walks and roadway and the griminess and sometimes rottenness of the superstructures is very curious. This pavement is composed of large blocks from the native quarries of Brando. It is a kind of jaspered marble, to which moisture gives a remarkable brilliancy and variety of hue. Have you ever gazed upon the wonderful façade of the Cathedral at Milan after a heavy shower of rain? If you have done so, you will have noticed that the white marble walls and pinnacles and crockets have become iridescent—now rosy, now blue, now yellow, and now sea-green. But so soon as the sun has dried the mass, the marble gleams again in monochrome almost as white as Mont Blanc. Precisely the same phenomenon is seen in the pavement of Bastia; only you scarcely care about staring all day at an expanse of paving-stones rendered rainbow-hued by a pelting and incessant rain.

There was little else to do at Bastia. As I have already hinted, the Hôtel de France offered you *alloggio* and a big bare room to take your meals in, and that was all. It was about as comfortless, and not nearly so amusing, as a Spanish *posada;* for in the *posada*, at least, is a *patio*, or courtyard, where you can watch the lading and unlading of the mules, and listen to the talk of the *arrieros*. The principal café of Bastia was one of the most dismal places of entertainment I have ever entered, and it was crowded at most hours by French soldiers reeking of *caporal* tobacco, and as rude in manner and untidy in garb as, under the rule of the Republic, the ordinary French *fantassin* has become. I specify the "ordinary" one; because, under the dispensation of universal liability to military service, and the abolition of *remplaçants*, an extraordinary private soldier has made his appearance in the ranks of the French army.

This is the "fils de famille," the "jeune homme comme il faut," the son of the wealthy merchant or manufacturer, who compromises matters between the conscription and himself by voluntarily enlisting for a year. But it is in most cases in the cavalry that these gilded youths enrol themselves. They form socially a class apart, and you can always single them out, owing to their faultlessly clean, spruce appearance and somewhat supercilious mien. They endeavour punctiliously to do their duty, but they do not fail to let it be known that they have no yearning for promotion, and that their chief ambition is to get through their twelve months' military servitude and have done with it. The ordinary conscript *tourlourous* and *pousse-cailloux*—the traditional Dumanet and Landernet—treat these young gentlemen volunteers with a sulky kind of respect. They feel that socially they have nothing in common with the "fils de famille." The sergeants and corporals call them derisively " les messieurs aux serviettes Anglaises "—the gentlemen who use English towels—and are " down upon them " mercilessly for the slightest breach of discipline.

One cannot sit in a dank, evil-smelling café all day, to have your ears tortured by the perpetual *staccato* of the dominoes on the marble tables and the rattling of the dice on the backgammon boards. The spectacle of French soldiers in greatcoats steaming with moisture, and of equally damp Corsicans in velveteen jackets and overalls and broad-brimmed felt hats, confederating in corners and muttering *patois* with their heads close together, or else playing mysterious games of skill with the bones of sheep's trotters, eventually palled upon you. It was irritating to have to pass the day in a bed-room without a chimney, and of which chamber neither the windows nor the doors would shut properly. There seemed to be much more of window and door in my sleeping apartment than wall, and where the wall did put in an appearance moisture oozed from it.

I am free, however, to admit that this bed-room at Bastia presented at least one element of diversion, in the shape of a most remarkable floor—a floor as phenomenal in its way as the rainbow-hued pavement of Bastia. This floor had been originally laid with tiles, octagonal in form and rubicund of hue ; but at some period during the sixteenth or seventeenth century—I cannot obviously be precise as to dates—the bed of plaster which should have held the tiles fast had disintegrated, and the bulk of the fictile octagons were quite loose. In the attempt to drag a heavy arm-chair—the castors to the legs had disappeared, probably about the time of Theodore Neuhoff,

King of Corsica, and afterwards of the Court for the relief of Insolvent Debtors—from the bedside to the window I displaced at least a dozen tiles; and a couple I contrived to crunch into small pieces. It was quite a change to spend a quarter of an hour now and again on one's hands and knees, replacing the loose tiles or adjusting the scattered fragments of the crunched octagons, just as though you were putting a child's puzzle map of the world together. Eventually I thought it might be as well to be a little indignant about the broken flooring; so I rang the bell, which was answered by an astonishingly old and withered woman, who might have been first cousin to Meg Merrilies, or the witch Sycorax herself. When I protested against the flooring she replied that "it had always been so," and hastily "scuttled" away, as though the subject were unworthy of being further debated; nor did I obtain any more redress when—this time furiously—I summoned the waiter, who, in his shirt-sleeves, desperately unwashed, but with great good humour, replied that the "padrone" intended to have this "maladetto tavolato" seen to "fra poco"—ere long.

There was nothing more to be done than to gaze gloomily from the window on the rain-scoured pavement and the many-coloured umbrellas, the bearers of them generally invisible in the street below. Stay—at arm's length, and no more, from the window-sill ran like the lines on a sheet of music the wires of the electric telegraph. Do you remember during the American Civil War the ingenious Confederate officer who, with a cunningly contrived instrument, used to roam about "tapping the telegraph" and intercepting the messages which the Federal generals were sending to each other? When from my window at Bastia, I saw those wires staring me in the face, how desperately did I long for the possession of some artful little instrument, in order to "tap the telegraph," and find out what was going on in the civilised world!

There was somebody dead at Zanetti's opposite. The shops at Bastia have, as a rule, no fronts. The majority of them are only so many dark and cavernous holes in the wall—like rabbit-hutches on a large scale, or those rag-festooned caves of the Triana outside Seville, where the gipsies live. A rudely-painted sign over Zanetti's hutch proclaimed what he was, or had been, a tailor. The shady recess where he—if Zanetti it was who was dead—had squatted on his board and snipped and sewn had been converted into a mortuary chapel. The front was hung with sable drapery with smirched borders and fringes, and with the initial of the name of the departed " Z." All Bastia seemed interested in the somebody lying dead at Zanetti's; and throughout the afternoon all classes of the community, men, women, and children, " dropped in," so to speak, at the mortuary chapel.

About four o'clock interest culminated in excitement. The town dog—he had welcomed us and barked at us at the port when we landed from the *Marie Louise*—trotted up and down the street, quite regardless of the pelting rain, in a state of great agitation, seemingly reminding all and sundry that they were about to bring forth the somebody who was dead at Zanetti's. Next to the tailor's habitation was a house of six storeys, the ground floor of which was tenanted by Giacometti, who asserted on his signboard that he was a hairdresser. But his " cabinet de coiffure " was only another hole in the wall, the entrance to which was completely veiled by a dingy yellow and black striped curtain. From behind this drapery came forth suddenly a figure that terrified me. It was that of a tall man shrouded from head to foot in a garberdine of some woollen fabric, a dingy sky-blue in colour, heavily barred with bands of black, relieved by bosses of tarnished silver. On the breast a black and silver cross. A hideous hood, with two holes for the eyes to see through, was drawn completely over the head and face of the man in the sky-blue gaberdine. Who was he ? I had sent for Giacometti that morning, and he had shaved me. Was it he—the figure opposite—transformed ?

There had been inside the mortuary chapel two sisters of charity all day long, for I now saw for the first time the good nuns emerge from the house of death. But it was a long time before the funeral procession could be arranged. The undertaker himself—I knew him at once by his rusty black cocked hat, his steel chain, and wand of office—seemed to be growing impatient, and looked at his watch nervously. Other figures, shrouded in sky-blue garberdines and face-concealing hoods, made their appearance on the pavement, and to them were adjoined about half a dozen little children, arrayed in the same fantastically ghastly garb. Then I began to understand that the adult figures in the blue gaberdines were members of the local Confraternity of Death; but what part the children were to play in the dismal pageant perplexed me. What were they all waiting for ? To the windows of five storeys of the house of which Giacometti occupied the ground floor there were balconies; on the other side, next to the recent Zanetti—if he, indeed, was the defunct—was another six-storeyed tenement, on the lowest floor of which was a wineshop, kept by Poggi, who, disregarding the proverb, hung out a monstrous bush, to indicate that the wine which he sold was good. Above the bush there were five tiers of balconies, and they were all full of apparently near relatives of Meg Merrilies or of the witch Sycorax herself; of slatternly girls in draggled skirts of some sleezy material of staring pink or yellow stuff, with ragged black lace veils half drawn over their heads of unkempt black hair and loosely knotted under their chins; and of little children quite innocent of shoes and stockings, and, in most instances, not boasting more than a couple of garments.

All these were spectators of the proceedings on the pavement below. A murmur of heightened interest was heard when the undertaker's assistants began to distribute tapers among those who were to join in the procession. It was very difficult, owing to the unrelenting rain, to light the candles, and it was obviously a still more difficult task to keep the candles alight, even when shielded by umbrellas. The attempts at taper-lighting were, however, watched with the liveliest curiosity. But it was five o'clock. What could they be waiting for? On the pavement, protected by umbrellas, or standing on the threshold of the mortuary chapel, were no less than four ecclesiastic persons in albs and cassocks, peeping out into the rain, and occasionally regaling themselves with a furtive although innocent pinch of snuff.

At length the town dog, coming up panting round a street corner, explained the cause of the delay. The intelligent animal was the harbinger of the superior clergy, three in number, with their thurifer and crucifer, for whom all had been waiting. So the undertaker, with the rusty black cocked hat, was able to marshal the procession at last. And they brought out the body of the somebody who had died at Zanetti's, the coffin covered with a light blue pall, and the bier borne by the blue-garberdined brethren of the Confraternity of Death. The little children walked before. As the procession crossed the street a company of French soldiers came swinging along, the buglers sounding a lively fanfare. The officer halted his men, and the *clairons* momentarily ceased their braying until the procession had gone by and disappeared down the narrow street up which the panting dog had come. Then the soldiers went on their way, the bugles sounding more shrilly than ever. Well, happy is the corpse that the rain rains on, and this one also had martial music to his obsequies.

IX.

SUNDAY AT AJACCIO.

Ajaccio, October 22.

It were in vain to dwell on the agonies undergone by the Upright Dutchman and your humble servant during our nineteen hours' close captivity in the coupé of the Diligence Come to Life Again between Bastia and Ajaccio. Æneas, you will remember, even when refreshed by a copious dinner washed down by "spuming chalices" of what some "vin-archæologists" have conjectured to have been the Carthaginian champagne, frankly admitted to Queen Dido his reluctance to recall the woes which he had undergone; and, many centuries later, the "Infandum Regina" was quoted with singular appositeness by the Winchester boy when he was interrogated by Queen Elizabeth as to the discipline of that ancient foundation. I may just hint, however, that so exiguous were the proportions and so crazy the construction of our place of torture, that it was a chronic cause of astonishment to me, during our nineteen hours' incarceration, either that the head of the Upright Dutchman did not go through the roof, or that his feet did not go through the floor of the accursed little shandrydan, for his neck seemed to be as incapable of crooking, and his knees of hingeing, as ever.

About midway I sank into a perturbed and half-strangulated slumber; and I think I dreamt that the Upright Dutchman had been metamorphosed into the sanguine Irish gentleman of the last century who, when the bottom of the sedan chair in which he was being conveyed came out, and he felt his feet touching the pavement, observed that, but for the dignity of the thing, he might as well have walked. I cannot, at the same time, refrain from paying a tribute of sincere admiration to the resolute cheerfulness displayed by my Batavian acquaintance under the most adverse viatorial circumstances. He was not to be discouraged either by the dampness of the weather or the horrible discomfort of the journey, and the only occasion of his manifesting anything approaching a feeling personally hostile to the commercial capital of Corsica was when, turning a short angle of the mountain road, and plunging into a ravine so deep and so narrow as to remind one of a *cañon* in the "Cumbus" of Mexico, we lost sight of the distant town and harbour. "Adieu, Bastia!" exclaimed the Upright Dutchman, in the most *staccato* tones of his metallic voice. "Adieu! Bastia, Basta, Bestia!" Batavia was avenged, and Voltaire's parting sneer at the country which had given him hospitality, "Adieu! Canaux, Canards, Canaille!" had found its long-deferred match.

It is but fair to record that a railway between Bastia and Ajaccio is in course of construction. As the work involves an immense amount of tunnelling through the living rock, the progress of the railway is necessarily very slow; but it is expected that within a couple of years it will be completed. The Messageries Company are even thinking of importing some traction engines from France, as a substitute for the little Tuscan horses which at present drag the diligences. The road is in tolerably good condition, but the turnings are so numerous, and the curves so sharp, that locomotion is at all times fraught with the gravest peril. Two days after my coming here the driver of the Bastia and Ajaccio diligence, in the darkness of the night, aided by the dimness of his lamps and the possibility of his having been himself asleep, missed a little wooden bridge over a mountain torrent. The three horses went over the precipice, and two of them were killed on the spot. Over their backs went the driver, to fracture his skull and die "sur place." The *conducteur* had his leg broken. Fortunately, the diligence grounded by the side of the bridge, and the passengers escaped with a plenteous allowance of bruises.

The normal danger of travelling in these badly-constructed, indifferently-horsed, and carelessly-driven machines is that they are constantly overladen, not only with luggage, but with passengers. Of the last there is a duly-settled quota; and the *conducteurs* are strictly prohibited from exceeding the capacity of their way-bills, "except in cases of absolute necessity." "Absolute necessity" contemplates some unfortunate person being found by the roadside in an absolutely footsore, exhausted, and destitute condition. Such a person the conductor is authorised, for the sake of Christian charity, to take on board his vehicle, conveying *le malheureux* to his destination, if it be in the diligence's line of route, without any kind of fee or reward; and the probability of the "absolute necessity" arising may be measured by the circumstance that the interior of Corsica—within forty hours' travelling by rail and steamer from Paris—is substantially as savage as the interior of Africa. There is no food nor lodging to be procured at the wretched little groups of stone cabins, which are by courtesy called villages. Nor board nor lodging is to be obtained at the stations where the diligence changes horses; and but for the authorised charity of the conductor the destitute wayfarer would in all probability die.

The idea of such an intervention in the *malheureux'* behalf is undeniably a very charitable one. Unfortunately, however, it practically opens the door to an extended and most impudent system of enriching the conductor at the expense of the company. This system is termed "carrottage." All kinds of persons, well able to pay their fares—priests, farmers, marketwomen—find favour in the conductor's eyes, wait for the passing of the diligence at some convenient part of the route, and, having doubtless concluded a little private arrangement equally pleasant and profitable to both parties, they are duly inscribed on the way-bill as *malheureux*, and clamber on to its overweighted sides. As the passengers in the *coupé* and the *intérieur*, already half stifled and half broken on four wheels in these wretched little cellular vans, would, in all likelihood, vehemently protest against the irruption of the sham unfortunates, these fictitious folks from Jericho are thrust into the *banquette* behind the driver, or are allowed to sprawl on the tarpaulin which covers the luggage. The result is that the vehicle is usually top-heavy; and, given a steep incline or a very sharp turn, the centre of gravity ceases to be within the base, and over the diligence goes.

I declare that I never experienced greater astonishment and delight at the gradual development to its fullest splendour of the transformation scene in a Boxing Night pantomime than I did when I found the savage desolation of our nineteen hours' journey over the mountains from Bastia transformed into the enchanting beauty of that Sunday at Ajaccio. Dark had been, indeed, the hour before the dawn, and the sun had risen in feeble struggle with the huge purple-black masses of clouds. But about ten in the morning the rain ceased, and the sun shone first through a wondrous luminous haze half of silver and half of gold, so it seemed, which, by eleven o'clock, had fully lifted. You may have seen in Cuba, or in Mexico, a sudden and violent rainstorm. The rain has come literally smashing down, as though those huge iron-shod pillars of timber that crush the silver ore at the mines of Real del Monte had become liquefied. The rain has stripped the moss and the innumerable creepers from the trees, rent away the boughs as a skilful housewife rends away the outer leaves from a lettuce, beaten the cactus and the prickly pear bushes flat, killed the birds by hundreds, and scattered wreck and desolation all around. Then the rain ceases, the sun comes out, ambiguously peeping at first through the haze, half of or, half of argent. The whole forest steams with moisture; but anon the triumphant sun consummates the transformation scene. All is brilliance of light and gorgeousness of colour. Everything is alive. The trees and shrubs seem to grow visibly. The trees are full of birds chanting merrily, as though there were not hecatombs of their tiny friends and relatives, with broken wings and legs, dead in the jungle.

So was it at Ajaccio. Not a cloud in the sky. Not a ripple on the glassy surface of the Mediterranean. The delicious odour of fruits and flowers and plants, citron and lemon, orange and myrtle, almonds and chestnuts; the singing of birds; the busy hum of human life; and last, but not least, an atmosphere warm without being sultry—elastic, balmy, and serene. This was Ajaccio at high noon when I found myself safely, but not soundly, landed from the Diligence Come to Life Again in the Messageries office, on the Cours Napoléon, resisting, with what resoluteness I was able to command, that which I considered to be a disgraceful overcharge for the conveyance of my luggage from Bastia. For the carriage of a single portmanteau of by no means unwieldy dimensions they charged me, and eventually made me pay, nine francs; the fare for a passenger in the coupé being twenty francs, and the distance traversed less than a hundred miles. For the transit of the same portmanteau between Paris and Marseilles I had likewise paid nine francs; but the distance traversed was six hundred miles.

I am sure I cannot tell how I came to part company with the Upright Dutchman. I was squabbling hotly, and he was protesting calmly, but incisively, in his usual metallically strident and laconic way, when of a sudden he was gone, and I did not see him any more. I hope that he had a good passage to Algiers, and that he is in the enjoyment of all the domestic delights of the Villa Doux Sourire, near Blidah, with the terrace all covered with roses. I dare say he thought no more about me than as a person with a bad cough and a sour temper, and who used the strongest of strong language because, during the nineteen hours' jolting through the wilds of Corsica, we had been unable to procure either bite or sup—nay, not so much as a cup of goat's milk and a piece of dry bread. I wonder whether Monsieur Fabien de' Franchi, when he travelled post-haste from the wilds of Corsica to the Forest of Fontainebleau, for the purpose of asking Monsieur de Château Renaud where his, Fabien's, brother was, brought something to eat and drink with him. If he failed to do so he must have suffered terribly from hunger and thirst *en route*.

My principal gravamen of complaint is that the people at the hotel at Bastia did not give us the slightest warning that, during the best part of a day and night, we were to be starved. In Spain you know what you have to expect when you set out on a journey in a rough part of the country. You know that you will find a few disconsolate inns, and that at the majority of them, if you ask for any solid sustenance, you will receive the courteous but hopeless reply, "No hay nada." But you can usually get bread and wine, and perhaps a little chocolate, even if the hour for the *puchero* be gone and past. In the wilds of Corsica it was a condition of "No hay nada" with a vengeance. Not only was there nothing either edible or potable to be bought for love or money, but there were neither inns nor innkeepers to announce the general nonentity of the commissariat. I have been told since that there is an inn—even two inns—at Corte. The proprietors of those establishments certainly do not make any efforts to secure the patronage of the travelling public, since neither they nor their garçons made any sign when the diligence rattled through Corte's stony main street, to change horses at a station a little way out of the town.

But I forgot all about my hunger and thirst and other miseries—I am afraid that the Upright Dutchman likewise passed out of my mind amid the new and delightful scenes among which I found myself. Certainly in the territory of the French Republic there is no lovelier spot, nor one blessed with a lovelier climate, than the birthplace of the First Emperor. The French, who dislike the Corsicans as much as the latter dislike the French—and, indeed, all "Continentals"—individually and collectively, are wont to assert that the back streets of Ajaccio are exceedingly dirty, that the lower class of the female population are terrible slovens and slatterns, and are very imperfectly attired, and that the children run about in an almost entirely nude condition. To that indictment, temporarily holding a brief for Corsica, I am afraid that I must plead guilty. The sanitation, or, rather, the want of sanitation of the back streets of Ajaccio is simply Malebolgian. As to the imperfect attire of the humbler class of females in this sunny town, I think we should be bound to consider the tolerant apophthegm of the philosopher, who remarked that it was possible to be good and happy without socks; nor should we forget the Oriental apologue of the valetudinarian Sultan, who was advised by his physician, as a remedy for all his real or fancied ailments, to change shirts with the first happy man that he could come across. But when, after long and earnest quest in many lands, such an exceptionally felicitous being was found and brought to the ailing Sultan's court, it was discovered that the happy man had no

ON THE BEACH AT AJACCIO.

shirt. I own that on week-days the display of body linen among the proletarian population of Ajaccio is not extensive, and that up to the age of ten or twelve the children of both sexes go, as a rule, barefoot. But consider the climate. The soil, too, is a soft and friable one, somewhat sandy, indeed, and rather invites impulsive youth to take off its shoes and stockings than otherwise.

But on Sunday I noticed a pleasant prevalence of hose and shoes. Coarsely-ribbed worsted, home-knitted most probably, was the most frequent fabric for the former. The shoes were not, to use a vulgarism, "up to much." Undressed calfskin, red or black bordered, and with flat soles—slippers, indeed, that would have been twin sisters to Turkish papouches had the toes only been slightly turned up—seemed to be the favourite *chaussures* worn. As for the grown-up women and girls, they affect on Sundays bodices of black serge or of velveteen, and skirts of the most *voyant* colours that the Illustrious Gaudissart can bring them from France. I saw a fair display also on their fingers and necks and in their ears of clumsily-fashioned silver ornaments—hearts and true lovers' knots, serpent and cable rings, and what not; together with those prodigious silver pins which are stuck into the back hair, and which are surmounted by effigies of butterflies, beetles, lizards, Maltese crosses, hatchets, sword-hilts, anchors, and caps of liberty. These strangely-bedizened pins always remind me of the *hâtelets* or silvered skewers, which, transfixing luscious-looking truffles, champignons, and cockscombs, are used by French *chefs* for the artistic embellishment of a "suprême de volaille" or a "chaufroid de cailles en Bellevue."

Some of the women of Ajaccio wear the ragged black veil of the Nizzardes, others tie a fazzoletto of some light-coloured stuff over the head and under the chin, after the manner of the Tuscan women, allowing the hair to "friz out" over the temples. When they go bareheaded it becomes painfully manifest that they are as shockingly ill-kempt as the Andalusian women, who time out of mind have earned the uncomplimentary sobriquet of "mal peñadas." They are very sunburnt, generally gaunt of visage and stern of mien, but now and again you come across a broad brow, a thoroughly Roman nose, high cheek-bones, firmly-chiselled lips, a superbly-rounded chin, the whole lit up by magnificent black eyes. Such a mien must have had that Corsican peasant woman who, in the last struggle of the islanders for independence, brought her young son as a recruit for Paoli. "Take care of him," she said to the patriot general. "He is the last of four brothers. You have had the other three."

Although scarcely, as a race, well favoured, the peasant and working women of Corsica walk as a rule magnificently— erect, robust, Juno-like in majesty of port. This superb carriage is due to the custom of the women repairing to the public fountains for water and bearing the jars on their heads. Nearly every muscle of the upper and lower limbs is brought into play in the at first difficult but eventually facile operation, and the result of a long apprenticeship to jar-carrying is a surprising dignity and suppleness of gait. It is true that the *contadine* of Corsica share this accomplishment with the *fellaheen* women of Egypt and with the sable Danaes of Dahomey. The French, who are for ever on the alert to discover motes in the Corsican eye, bitterly reproach the insulars for their custom of converting their women into beasts of burden. They see nothing picturesque nor poetic in the spectacle of these slim damsels and robust matrons—whose labours are often shared by mere children of ten and twelve—striding with majestic pace with the full jars nicely balanced on their parietal bones. This the ruling race term an "afflicting spectacle," and speak indignantly of "la vassalité des femmes." A recent French traveller in Corsica states that he has seen women and girls emerging from the "makis" bending under heavy fardels of brushwood for fuel, while their husbands or brothers tranquilly followed them, comfortably bestriding ponies or mules. Another explorer of the wilds of Corsica relates that one evening, passing through a village, he saw a troop of young girls carrying on their heads jars containing each from twenty to twenty-five litres—say five to six gallons —of water, while their male relatives preceded gravely, bearing flaming branches of resinous wood to light the poor thralls on their weary way. Strabo said of the ancient Corsicans that "they were not good enough to make slaves of;" but the modern Corsicans seem to be fully imbued with an idea of the capacity of their womankind for the rudest servitude.

An abundant supply of water is brought into Ajaccio by a handsome aqueduct. The house-to-house supply of the essential element leaves much to be desired; but there is plenty of water for those who choose to come and fetch it. The principal public fountain, or rather conduit, is in the Cours Napoléon, in the wall beneath the esplanade of the St. François Barracks. This watering-place is thronged from sunrise to sunset by groups of gossiping women bringing their jars to be replenished; and, to judge from their animated talk and shrill laughter, it would not seem that they suffer to any intolerable extent from the miseries of slavery. A painter, were he industrious, might fill half a sketch-book every day with studies of the varied postures of the women as they stoop to disburden themselves of the jars; as, resting the jar on one uplifted knee and holding the vessel by "the ears," they slowly fill it from the plashing jets; and as, at last, they stoop again and with amazing dexterity raise the jars to their heads and adjust the huge earthern pots full of water in their appointed place, spilling—no, not one drop. Then, with a massive squaring of the shoulders, a slight and easy undulation of the hips, and an assured tread—the right foot pointed straight forward—the poor ill-used "beasts of burden" go on their way.

I never saw any of the male Corsicans make the slightest movement in aid of these toiling yet to all appearance contented women. The male Corsicans stand apart, or prowl about, or sit on the benches superfluously abundant in this country, where the natives should be stimulated to industry, and not to idleness. There they are by the dozen, by the score, by the hundred, meagre, swarthy, and scowling, clad in shabby jackets of velveteen or some grey woollen stuff which looks like blanketing, and wearing felt wideawake hats with exaggerated brims—somewhat larger than the hat of an Italian Bersagliere, minus the feathers, and somewhat smaller than the *sombrero* of a Mexican *ranchero*. They all look like Mr. Henry Irving's country cousins in reduced circumstances.

They have, of course, no knives about them; nevertheless, you have an odd desire to exhibit Articles of the Peace against them; and if their fathers or grandfathers did not occasionally select the "makis" as a residence and follow brigandage as a profession, all that I can say is that most of the Corsicans whom I have seen might bring an action for libel against their countenances, and recover heavy damages.

But they are now, I am told, quite a harmless race, fangless wolves, reformed banditti. They are incurably idle, and they are perpetually jabbering politics—not with any patriotic or public-spirited view, but with the sole objective of obtaining some post where there will be very little to do, and where for doing that little so many francs of the money of the State will be paid them every month. They dream of becoming police agents, gendarmes, letter-carriers, post-office clerks, *gardes forestiers*, *douaniers*, and the like. Are they very much to be blamed, these men without a country—Italians by blood and language, Frenchmen only by a political accident? Are they so much to be blamed when their social superiors are incessantly plotting and intriguing to clutch the higher prizes of Government employment? Since 1870 there have been fourteen Prefects of the Département de la Corse.

X.

THE HOTEL TOO SOON.

AJACCIO, *October* 23.

I HAVE heard of a class of selfish old gentlemen who are wont to declare that the period when a West-end club is most truly enjoyable is towards the close of the dead season of the year in London, when everybody—in the "Society" sense of a few thousands of well-dressed people being everybody—is out of town. But this state of enjoyability is not, as a rule, attainable at the beginning, or even in the middle, of the dead season, for the reason that between the middle of August and the end of September the committee usually improve the opportunity of the majority of the members being in Scotland or on the Continent to have the club-house cleaned and all necessary repairs executed; and the Selfish Old Gentleman taking his tea and dry toast in a half-dismantled coffee-room, or toiling up carpetless stairs, or stumbling over paint-pots and baskets of tools, becomes to himself a burden and to others a sad and sorry spectacle. He had better betake himself to Brighton, or to some hotel near the Crystal Palace, until the painters and whitewashers, the carpenters and upholsterers have departed from Pall Mall.

It is towards the close of the recess—it is during the fortnight or so immediately preceding the coming to life again of the season—that the club is most thoroughly enjoyable. The whole splendid mansion has been swept and garnished. The new steam boiler in the kitchen, at which the smiths have been hammering these many days past, is finally fixed in its place. There is not a speck of dust on the books or on the shelves of the library. Whole stacks of magazines have come back from the binder's, spruce and shining in their brand-new jackets, and offering glad promise of comfortable winter reading. The smoky chimney in the billiard-room has been cured, and several new easy-chairs of an improved pattern have been placed in the newspaper-room. There are a new and additional umbrella-stand and a new barometer; and some stupid servants have been got rid of and replaced by new ones, who, like other new brooms, sweep clean.

Of all these the Selfish Old Gentleman, with a few of his congeners, is lord and master. He avoids his congeners as much as he can, and dislikes them as much as he should do, for in the whole catalogue of malevolence there is scarcely any kind of hatred more bitter than that which one egoist feels towards another. When the crew of the Méduse set off on the raft two men were left behind on the wrecked ship. There they lived for many days—one forward, one aft. If by chance they met on the waterlogged deck they crept by each other, each eyeing his neighbour with a wolfish glare, and grasping securely at his hip his dagger, in case the other should spring upon him with the knife concealed up his sleeve.

Fortunately for the Queen's peace, the club hours of some selfish old gentlemen are not the hours of other selfish old gentlemen, and each may in turn look round with pride on the club which he has practically to himself. The fireside is his own, for the moment. The obsequious servants are his. The hall porter, the butler, the little pages in buttons are his vassals and vavasours. The snowy damask and shining plate on the table gleam for him; for his solace is the daily bill of fare composed; for him are muffins toasted, magazines and reviews neatly cut, the newest novels sent in from the circulating library, and the latest telegrams displayed on the screen in the hall. He is monarch of all he surveys. He is the Robinson Crusoe of civilisation; but he courts the solitude, and the tameness of the waiters is far from shocking to him. On the contrary, he likes it. But this blissful state of things will endure only a few more days. The winter season will begin, and the club will have hundreds of lords and masters every day.

I feel at the present writing, at Ajaccio, very much like the Selfish Old Gentleman. I have, and have had for some days, an hotel all to myself. The real name of this hostelry is La Germania; but, for reasons which you will presently understand, I choose to call it the Hotel Too Soon. To do so may involve the commission of a solecism, since it is I that am premature, and not the house; but as the Hotel Too Soon the Germania will ever be engraved on my memory. The Germania is an edifice of considerable size, on the Cours Grandval, a spacious boulevard starting from the Place du Diamant. The avenue is planted with acacias, and in summer time I should say must be slightly, if not indeed be intolerably dusty. At the corner of the Cours and the Place du Diamant is the Military Hospital, a very large building, with a pleasant garden on the side next the sea, and which is frequently used as a sanatorium for sick soldiers from the garrisons of Algeria. There are soldiers from Tunisia—convalescents from dysentery and typhoid—at the Ajaccio hospital now.

The place—the present aspect of which is bright and smiling—has a grim interest to me, owing to a traditional story which I have read, to the effect that on the site of the hospital once stood a monastery, in the cloisters and cells of which were "interned" during the Consulate many hundreds of negro soldiers, brought hither from San Domingo after the final struggle of the negroes for independence. More mercy was shown by Napoleon to these poor slaves than he showed to their heroic chief Toussaint L'Ouverture, whom he sent to die of cold and humidity in a casemate of the fortress of Joux. The negro soldiers "interned" at Ajaccio were after a time shipped off to Malta, just wrested from the Knights of St. John; but I should like to know what became of these strangely expatriated Africans after the capture of Malta by the English. There are strange disappearances in history. What became of the bulk of the British regiments who laid down their arms at the surrender of Yorktown? Not ten per cent. of those prisoners of war ever returned, I believe, to England. They made the best, it may be, of a by' no means bad bargain, and became contented American citizens; and it is quite possible that among the patriots who were "orating" at Yorktown the other day were several lineal descendants of the British private Thomas Atkins of the year 1781.

In the Cours Grandval is the Bishop's palace, and the struggling, tumbledown-looking premises of the "Petit Séminaire," about the gateway of which you may sometimes see loitering groups of long-legged, swarthy, down-looking Corsican lads, as like Mr. Henry Irving's country cousins lounging on the Place du Marché and the Cours Napoléon as an elephant calf is like an elephant grown up. On the other side of the Cours is the Château Conti, an elegant private mansion, with a terrace and garden, thoroughly Italian in style, and then comes the Germania, the Hotel Too Soon. It is a large, roomy edifice, with lofty and airy apartments, and is throughout scrupulously neat and clean. In the *salle à manger* I should say from eighty to a hundred guests might dine. The drawing-room on the ground floor is a superb saloon, luxuriously furnished, with a pianoforte and a large bookcase containing a small but carefully-selected library of French, German, and English literature. The reading-room is supplied with the latest— well, not the very latest—issues of *Galignani*, some German-Swiss papers, and the *Petit Marseillais*; but on the 25th of this instant October a copious "abonnement" to the chief journals of England and the cities of the Continent is to begin.

On the 25th, you will be good enough to understand. The *salle à manger* is not being used for the purpose of a *table d'hôte* just now; it is being dusted and decorated, and the chairs are being marshalled with mathematical precision up and down the sides of the interminable table. That which may be termed the Elkington paraphernalia is being unpacked; cruet-stands and mustard-pots are scattered about on buffets; the branches of candelabra begin to show themselves through reft veils of canvas matting, and there are distant visions of plated épergnes and cake-baskets. By the 25th all will be ranged in proper order, and sable-clad, white-cravated waiters, hailing mainly from the Canton of Zurich, will glide about and serve the viands to the milords Anglais and the miladis, the charming English "meesses," the Russian princes and princesses, the high, well-born Teutons, the "first families" of the United States of America, the distinguished guests from Scandinavia and the Low Countries, who are coming to pass the winter in the delicious climate of Ajaccio and the pleasant and refined society of the Germania. Always on the 25th. I have told you before that there is a commodious Anglican Church at Ajaccio, built by an English lady, who for some years since has taken a kindly interest in the little place. "Monsieur le Ministre Anglican" has not yet arrived. The reverend gentleman is expected at the very latest by the 25th. With justifiable pride they show me letters endorsed "pour attendre l'arrivée," and addressed to the estimable ecclesiastic who is due on the 25th. It is by that date that the sable-clad waiters from the Canton of Zurich are due at Ajaccio.

At present the waiting department is undertaken by a solitary stout Swiss female, who speaks many tongues, and who tells me that for four years she was a chambermaid at the Midland Grand Hotel, St. Pancras, London. Daily she serves luncheon and dinner of a *cuisine* which may be qualified as of a "simple but fortifying order." There is a cook, she informs me, in the house; but he is not *the* cook—the real *chef* will arrive on the 25th. In my mind's eye I see him leisurely scanning, over a cigarette and a glass of vermouth, the pages of Jules Gouffé and Urbain Dubois in quest of fresh culinary combinations to tempt the palates of the English milords and the Muscovite boyards, the barons from the Vaterland and the cattle kings from Nebraska. By the 25th what "salmis" and "sautés" may he not have devised; what "jeune poularde en entrée de broche" may he not have excogitated from his busy brain! For the nonce one submits resignedly to the "simple but fortifying" *menu* in which the not always tractable "biftek" and the sometimes unconquerable mutton cutlet—unconquerable, I mean, from the point of view of gristle—are normally too conspicuous. But the fish is very fine; and the dessert—the figs and grapes especially—superb.

Nor should the native Corsican wines be despised. That called "Pompeiano" is excellent, although a little too sweet for some palates; but the ordinary red wine of the country is a sound and pleasant vintage, not unlike the Chianti of Tuscany, and is certainly to be preferred to the "vins coupés," the equivocal Médocs and ambiguous St. Estephes, which are being sold at present all over the civilised world. It is certainly not the fault of the innkeepers, either at home or abroad, if the phylloxera has ruined the French vineyards, and if an enormous proportion of the wines sold as Bordeaux in England and the Continent are manufactured articles in which the basis is either wine or dried grapes—"dell' uva passa"—from Italy and Spain; but the Italians are beginning, not without some reason, to complain that, while many millions of francs' worth of their wines are being annually exported from Genoa and Leghorn to be manipulated into spurious Bordeaux at Cette, at Bercy, or at Bordeaux itself, the Italian vintages honestly sold as such are at a discount in the way of *prestige* as compared with so-called French wines, which in many instances have nothing French about them beyond their bottles and their labels.

What a wondrous change will come over the Germania after the 25th! At present it is the Hotel Too Soon; and I am the only guest in it. The solitary Swiss chambermaid is unremitting in her attention. She answers the electric bell almost as soon as I press the little button. Indeed, I fancy that she hears me rise from my chair to sound the alarm, for she is generally knitting stockings at a little table just outside my door. There is a strong young man from Marseilles—a young man with a brown countenance, merry black eyes, a jovial smile, and a tremendous head of bushy black hair—who officiates as porter, boots, coachman, and groom to the establishment. Saddle-horses, with real English side-saddles for ladies, are obtainable at the Germania, and after the 25th there will be frequent equestrian excursions of the most picturesque nature to the environs of Ajaccio. There is a nice little basket-phaeton, too, with a clever pony, attached to the hotel; and when I am well enough to move about, the strong young man, donning a cap with a gold-laced band and a blue coat with plated buttons, and looking quite gallant and dashing in that garb, drives me along a capital road round the beautiful shores of the bay.

I like the drive towards the lighthouse and the Sanguinary Islands best. A strange name for a group of islets—"Les Iles Sanguinaires." Was some grim vendetta accomplished there in days gone by? On your way to these uncomfortably-named islands you pass a pretty infirmary called the Hôpital Eugénie, and named indeed after the illustrious and unhappy lady who was its founder, and to whom that House in St. Charles Street belongs. On the green hills gently declining to the shore are the smiling villas of the nobility and gentry of Ajaccio. The slopes are all thick and gorgeous with sub-tropical vegetation; while the inner side of the carriage road itself is dotted with pretty little edifices, now resembling Greek temples, now like Tuscan villas, now like Venetian casini. They are embosomed in lovely plants, and the façades of some are bright with flowers. I think of the Villa Doux Sourire, near Blidah, to which the Upright Dutchman was bound. But when you approach one of these gay and smiling little structures closely, you find that the roof is surmounted by a cross, that the walls are blind of windows, and that the solitary door is closely sealed. The gay and smiling structures are, in truth, so many mortuary chapels, in which repose the ashes of the Corsican nobility and gentry defunct. An entombment pleasant to think of—at the base of the verdant hill, among the cacti and the bamboos, the Barbary figs and prickly pears, the innumerable flowers of radiant hues, the birds carolling, and the blue, tideless Mediterranean laving the steps of the sepulchre. Nothing of the dank earthiness of the churchyard; no pert or canting or stupid epitaphs; nothing of the undertaking statuary of the Euston-road type—only a cross over the tomb by the shore of the sea.

But for the inscrutable decree of Fate, the man who was born in the house in St. Charles Street yonder might have had his bones laid there in peace with those of his forefathers. He was not the eldest son. But for Fate they might have made a priest of him, as his uncle Luciano, his uncle Fesch were. Or a monk? He would have made, I take it, in time, a very vigorous bishop of Ajaccio, or a terribly earnest abbot of a convent of Dominican friars. Or suppose that—the times being troublous—he had taken to the "makis" and turned bandit. Assuredly he would have risen to be chief of a band of brigands. It would have been better, perhaps, all things considered, if he had been shot by the gendarmerie in some skirmish in the "makis," or, after a quiet provincial life as priest, or monk, or advocate, found tranquil sepulture here among the flowers and shrubs on the road to the Isles Sanguinaires, than that he should have been appointed to cross over, lean, hungry, rapacious, with nothing but his sword and his superhuman will to help him to plunder crowns and sceptres, and set the world in a blaze.

At the extremity of the Cours Grandval, and within a few minutes' walk of the Germania, is a garden called the Casone, planted with magnificent olive-trees. In the Casone is the famous grotto in which, according to the legend, Napoleon, as a child, used to spend long hours in solitary musing. The always-sceptical French traveller Valéry has not failed to point out that, before the Revolution, the Casone was a villa belonging to the Jesuits; that when the Order was suppressed in Corsica the grotto and garden became the property of the State, and, as a "bien national," were purchased by the Bonaparte family. Napoleon was then more than twenty years of age, and, according to Valéry, he could not as a child have enacted the part of a juvenile Zimmermann in a grotto which did not belong to his papa. There is nothing, however, to prove that the youthful Bonapartes had not access to the Jesuits' garden; and it is even within the domain of possibility that, for a short time, just before he was sent to the military school of Brienne, the young Napoleon may have been a pupil of the Jesuits, and may have picked up from them the very small modicum of Latin and the respectable amount of mathematics which he took with him to France. Be it as it may, there is the grotto of the Casone, formed by two granite rocks inclining inwards, until their summits nearly touch, and crowned by an enormous block of stone, almost Druidical or cromlech-looking in its antique savagery of aspect.

I am sorry to say that on the walls of the grotto thousands of pilgrims have hacked or hewed or carved their long-since-forgotten names. This is, no doubt, a highly reprehensible practice; and, if the Metropolitan Board of Works held sway in Ajaccio, these objectionable *graffiti* would be made a Star Chamber matter, or at least a local police-court one. In reality, this propensity to scratch and scrawl your name on famous places is the most natural thing in the world. It is a trick common to all humanity. In the school-room at Westminster or Harrow, in the chapel at Hougoumont, in the bed-chamber of the house at Stratford-on-Avon, on the balcony of the loggia of the Doge's Palace at Venice, on the Pyramids of Egypt, " they all do it "—from Walter Scott to John Smith, from Byron to Brown, from Victor Hugo to Joseph Prudhomme. When Queen Isabel Segunda of Spain visited the Pantheon or Royal vault in the Escorial she scratched her name with a pair of scissors on the marble ledge of one of the empty shelves. I never owned a diamond ring myself, but did I possess such a bauble I will not guarantee—although I am come to more than years of discretion—that were I left to myself in a room of the Ship Hotel, Greenwich, I should not find myself scratching my name on the window-pane. The act would be idiotic, but it would be natural.

When I am not well enough to avail myself of the services as charioteer of the strong young man from Marseilles, I wander in the picturesque garden of the Hotel Too Soon. Almost everything seems to grow here, and you begin to think that Mr. William Morris's Earthly Paradise must have been at Ajaccio. When I am not well enough to move about at all—for eleven very ugly days have been my lot since I came from Bastia—I sit in my room pondering over the metamorphosis which will be undergone by the Hotel Too Soon when the much-proclaimed 25th has come and gone. In imagination, I hear the pianoforte in the drawing-room harmoniously resonant with complicated concertos of Schubert and Chopin and Mendelssohn, executed by the nimble hands of the accomplished female guests of the Hotel Too Soon. I hear the laughter of the children in the corridor—romping British children, untamable American urchins. But, always to my imagining, the children's merriment turns to shriller tones. It is in Corsican *patois* that they are prattling.

No longer is this the Germania, but the House in St. Charles Street, and the drawing-room piano has become a little old harpsichord on which Madame Letizia is playing to her young ones—to Giuseppe, and Luciano, and Luigi—to Alisa, and Paolina, and Carolina. Young Napoleone is not there.

He is away in the grotto of the Casone. Then I turn to the window and look wistfully at the mountains by the hour at a time. Over the heights, bathed in hues of crimson and purple, of azure and gold, hovers the ever-shifting panorama of the clouds. There are some that are dragonish; there are vapours like bears and lions; but to my imagining they all resolve themselves into one Figure. Now he stands enthroned in Notre Dame, in the Imperial robes, powdered with golden bees, the golden laurel on his brow, the sceptre in his right hand, the orb in his left; now reaching to the cloud-billows, and dominating them, is Napoleone il Grande, on his war-horse, his mantle flying loose in the wintry blast, as you see him in David's picture, crossing the snow-clad Alps.

XI.

THE HOUSE IN ST. CHARLES STREET, AJACCIO.

AJACCIO, *October* 26.

THERE is very little indeed at Bastia, with the exception of the Florentine Bartolini's marble statue, to remind you of Napoleon the Great; and the municipality have not even had the grace to call the area in which the Roman-clad effigy stands by the name of its illustrious original. They might at least have remembered that there is, or was, a Saint Napoleon in the calendar; but the dusty expanse where stands the Napoleonic monument is dubbed the Place St. Nicolas. At a kind of everything-shop on the Boulevard du Palais I found, among ready-made clothing, preserved meat from Australia and preserved tomatoes from Wilmington, Delaware, U.S.A., macintoshes from England and chocolat Menier from Paris, a coarsely-executed lithographic print of the "Adieux de Fontainebleau;" but this solitary vestige of the Bonapartist legend looked sadly crestfallen and woe-begone among German oleographs of fat Teutonic children getting into mischief, and fatter tavern-wenches handing beer flagons to pipe-smoking old peasants; which productions, together with photographs of Monsieur Gambetta, Citizen Rochefort, Citoyenne Louise Michel, and Mr. Charles Stewart Parnell,

M.P., "Leader Irlandais," make up the staple of the works of art at present on view in the shop-windows in France and its dependencies. At Ajaccio, on the contrary, you shall scarcely walk ten paces without being reminded of the wonderful family of which Carlo Buonaparte, Advocate of the Royal Court, was the immediate progenitor.

The town of Ajaccio is most beautifully built in amphitheatrical form, on the flanks of a steep range of hills forming the base and two sides of a bay which vies with those of Naples and Dublin for loveliness. That part of the town which surrounds the harbour is built on a tongue of land at the extremity of which is an old fort, erected in the middle of the sixteenth century by the commander of the French expedition sent to help the Corsican Sampiero against the Genoese. The first public place which you reach on landing—of course, in a boat, but the boatmen are not such buccaneers as their brethren at Bastia—is the Piazza del Mercato, or Place du Marché, where stands the Hôtel de Ville, an edifice of considerable size and comeliness. There are one or two more administrative buildings here; but the shops, well-stocked book and stationery warehouses excepted, are the merest hovels devoted to the sale of secondhand clothes, old rags and bones, pots and pans, and ship chandlery, to say nothing of an inordinate number of low *buvettes* and dram-shops, usually thronged from morning to night with sailors and French soldiers. The native Corsicans are temperate, and do not seem to trouble the liquor-shops much. They prefer to hang about in knots at the street-corners, weaving goodness knows what occult *congiurazioni* in their muttered patois.

In the centre of the square gleams graceful and beautiful an ornamental fountain, surmounted by a white marble statue of Napoleon I. as First Consul. The monument is remarkable for the extreme richness and minute finish of the details. French critics object not only to the excessive delicacy of the chiselling, but to the quiet simplicity of the attitude of the figure. It wants *fougue,* it wants *verve,* they say ; and they contend that the Napoleon here portrayed is not the First Consul fresh from the triumphs of Marengo—the Great Captain who has made all Europe tremble—but rather the precariously restored Emperor of the Hundred Days, the Cæsar on a new trial, the ruler who has made concessions and promises to make more—the Napoleon of the " Acte Additionnel." These critics forget that the sculptor of the statue, Monsieur Laboureur—the fountain is the work of Monsieur Maglioli, architect of the town of Ajaccio—has simply been true to history. The First Consul was in 1804 a somewhat cadaverous, careworn, meagre, puny man. The expression was rather pensive than stern, and his features, while they had lost the boyish beauty of the sub-lieutenant in the regiment of La Fère, had not acquired the massive breadth and roundness of the Imperial mask in 1816. Monsieur Laboureur's statue seems to me as faithful to the record of the Hour and the Man as Isabey's full-length picture of the First Consul taken on the eve of his grasping—to his destruction—the Imperial dignity.

You are acquainted with that picture. It is known among the students of the legend as the " Adieu, Malmaison." He is standing, alone, but all the world watching him, in the garden of the country-house where he has enjoyed the few brief snatches of repose and tranquillity which, in his troublous life, he has known or shall know. Adieu, Malmaison! His baggage is packed, his household are astir to change quarters, and Josephine is busied with the safe removal of her beloved singing birds and the packing of her innumerable gowns and bonnets. Adieu, Malmaison! The travelling carriages are at the gate. The postmaster of Rueil is busy with the relays; you almost hear the horses stamp and snort. The First Consul is waited for. The Senate wait for him in the antechambers of the Tuileries. They are eager to hail him Imperator, and to lick the dust from off his boots. He is going to win Austerlitz and Jena; to clutch the sword of the Great Frederick in the vault at Potsdam; to dictate peace on the raft on the Niemen; to repudiate the wife who loved him so fondly, and marry the Kaiser's fat, foolish, blue-eyed daughter; to hear the hundred and one guns fired on that night in 1811, and to hold in his arms the baby King of Rome; to see the Moskova won in bloody fight, and to behold the Kremlin blaze; to run away from his army, leaving thousands of brave men to die on the Beresina's icy bosom. He is going away—to Leipzic, to Montmirail, to Fontainebleau, to Elba, to Waterloo, to Longwood. Adieu, Malmaison!

That is Isabey's, and that, in a most sympathetic degree, is Monsieur Laboureur's First Consul. The municipality of Ajaccio have wisely surrounded the monument—at the base of which are four lions of Corsican granite, spouting water—with a delightfully pretty *giardinetto*, a parterre of serried tropical flowers and plants, among which the orange, the lemon, and the bamboo are conspicuous. I say that wisdom, as well as taste, has dictated the planning of this garden and of the light but strong iron railing which protects it, because otherwise there would be no knowing, in these days, when the Napoleonic legend is apparently at such a hopeless discount, what mischievous injury might be done to the statue. Over and over again, lately, when turning over a handful of silver, have I noticed that on coins bearing the effigy of Napoleon III. a deep line has been jagged right across the neck of the profile — this stupid and barbarous indignity being probably the product of the leisure of some patriot with a clasp-knife in his possession; and I did actually at Ajaccio see one of a knot of blackguard Corsican boys calmly jobbing away at the inscription on the pedestal of another of the Napoleonic monuments, which is not protected by a railing, but which, in the interests of historic decency, ought to be so protected forthwith. I offered to conduct, by the ear, this perverted disciple of Old Mortality; but he ran away swiftly, howling, with his bare-legged companions, who, gaunt and fierce and panting, looked like a pack of young wolves. Stay. The simile will not hold good. When the Corsican blackguards had reached what they deemed to be a safe distance they threw *ciottolini* at me. Now wolves do not throw stones.

The second monument of which I speak is situated on the Place du Diamant or Place Bonaparte, which you reach by following from the Place du Marché the rue of that name and the Rue Napoléon. The Place du Diamant is the largest and handsomest in Ajaccio. Its base is washed by the Mediterranean, and it commands a magnificent view of the gulf. In the centre is the memorial of Napoleon the Great and his four brothers, Joseph, King of Spain; Louis, King of Holland; Jérome, King of Westphalia; and Lucien, Prince of Canino. The monument was composed—yes, "composed" is the word—from the designs of M. Viollet le Duc, a most accomplished authority on architecture and art decoration, but who, I venture to think, has failed lamentably as an adventurer in monumental sculpture. The equestrian statue of the Emperor, in bronze and in Roman costume, is not without a certain dignity and some little grace. But the Brothers Bonaparte, who in postures of uneasy rigidity stand at the four corners of the pedestal, like so many pawns on a chessboard, struck me as being, their big proportions notwithstanding, singularly insignificant personages. If the sculptor had only provided them with periwigs they would have been ludicrously suggestive of the "Quatre-z-officiers" who followed the funeral car of M. de Malbrouck:

> L'un portait son beau sabre,
>   Mironton, mironton, mirontaine !
> L'un portait son beau sabre,
>   Et l'autre son bouclier ;
> L'un portait sa cuirasse,
>   Mironton, mironton, mirontaine !
> L'un portait sa cuirasse,
>   Et l'autre ne portait rien.

The Three Kings—not of Brentford, but of Spain, Holland, and Westphalia respectively—are hugging their regal sceptres; but poor Lucien has not got so much as an umbrella. They are accoutred in togas and sandals, after the antique fashion of the wardrobe of the Théâtre Français, and, on the whole, if you know your legend by heart, you feel that you would much rather not have seen this monumental group, of which the *ensemble* is not unlike a *surtout de table*. Joseph might hold a platter of preserved ginger, and Jérome might carry macaroons. The almonds and raisins might be assigned to Louis, and Lucien would make a fit supporter of the sponge-cakes; while the Imperial centrepiece might be surmounted by a handsome pineapple and two luscious bunches of grapes. This pretentious performance was inaugurated on the 15th of May, 1865, by Prince Napoléon Jérome Buonaparte. The omens on the occasion were curiously inauspicious. Prince Napoleon made, on unveiling the monument, a speech which gave high displeasure to the Emperor Napoleon III., who was then making a triumphal progress through Algeria, and who administered a terrible epistolary scolding to his cousin. It does not matter much now. " Adieu, paniers ! vendanges sont faites." It was my lot to follow the triumphant ruler through Algeria, even to the borders of Kabylia; and I saw the great Bedouin Emirs and Sheiks come into the Imperial camp to have the Cross of the Legion of Honour pinned to their snowy burnouses by Imperial hands. It would not seem that French dominion in Cæsarian Mauritania has been much strengthened by that triumphal progress in 1865. The Imperial hands are cold in the vault at Chislehurst; and here am I at Ajaccio spying the blackguard Corsican boy with his clasp-knife as he jobs into the inscription on the pedestal of the Imperial statue.

This big *surtout de table* on the Place du Diamant leaves, somehow, an unpleasant taste in your mouth. The Second Empire is a little too close to you. The "Family Monument" smells of the Bourse and the "Cabinet Noir"—of official *communiqués* and official candidates; while the Brothers Buonaparte bear an uncomfortable likeness to Four Shams whose real names are Meanness, Servility, Corruption, and Humbug, supporting Impudent Usurpation. It is a relief to debouch from the Place du Diamant into the Cours Napoléon, the principal thoroughfare in Ajaccio, a broad and noble thoroughfare, planted throughout its length with elms and acacias. At the angle of the Rue du Marché and the Cours is the Hôtel de France, on the ground floor of which is the really handsome Café du Roi Jérome. There is another spacious and well-appointed café on the Cours opposite the Prefecture, which, although built in the villa style of architecture, might, without any exaggeration, be called a palace, so extensive are its dimensions and so imposing is its aspect. It is surrounded by a splendidly-planted garden—a Kew in miniature, but with the glass roofs of the hot-houses removed. This is the official residence which, as I have already incidentally remarked, has had fourteen occupants since the year 1870. A little above the Prefecture is the Théâtre St. Gabriel, where, in the winter season—that is, from the middle of October until the end of March—comic operas and vaudevilles of the stereotyped Bouffes and Palais Royal pattern are given. Occasionally the programme is varied by the performance of Italian operas. Beyond the theatre is the Hôtel Sebastiani, in the rear of which is a beauteously picturesque park, stretching far up the mountain side. At the extremity of the Cours Napoléon farthest from the Place du Diamant is a statue of the youthful General Charles Abbatucci, who was killed in 1796, at the defence of Huninguen.

Sebastiani! Abbatucci! these names take me back to the past and help me to forget the impertinent brazen protuberances on the sea-shore. They take me back to the old days of the legend, and make me live among the shadows. I need no more statues nor monuments of him now. I see him, in my mind's eye, all over Ajaccio. I meet him on the Cours Grandval, on the Boulevard Lantivy, on the Boulevard du Roi Jérome, in the Rue du Cardinal Fesch. Now I meet him as a mere child, sallow, delicate, and with great wistful grey eyes, his long dark-brown locks curling like the young tendrils of the vine about his temples, and falling over the broad frill of his shirt collar. I wonder whether he ever scampered about the dusty and then unpaved streets of Ajaccio barefooted. I am quite aware that there has been traditionally preserved a scrap of a ballad sung by his school companions, in which he is ridiculed as "a mezza calzetta," and accused of having in that ungartered condition paid court to one Giacominetta, and the inattention he displayed with regard to his stockings rather favours the inference that at an earlier stage of his nonage he had dispensed with stockings altogether. Madame Letizia had a very numerous family, and it may have been sometimes a matter of some difficulty to provide hose and shoes for all the little feet—the feet which were afterwards to climb the steps of thrones. But from the possibly barefooted little Napoleon my thoughts wandered backward in his strange life history. It was in August of the year 1769. It was the Feast of the Assumption of the Virgin, and, sprawling and feebly wailing on a piece of antique tapestry woven with some dimly-pictured story of the Iliad, there arose before me the vision of a naked new-born babe. I would delay no longer, I thought. I must see the house where he was born.

Like a greedy child who has put aside on the corner of his plate the sweetest and most toothsome morsel of his portion of pudding, and keeps until the last, but opening trenches with his spoon around it, and, although trembling with desire, deferring and still deferring the final storming of the sugary citadel, so for days I had lingered and loitered round a certain house in St. Charles Street, Ajaccio, still repeating to myself that it should be for to-morrow, positively for to-morrow, and still postponing the doing of that which in reality I had come solely to Ajaccio to do. The Rue St. Charles is one of the narrowest in the town. If the municipality were to adopt a system of Italian instead of French street nomenclature, the thoroughfare erst inhabited by Carlo Buonaparte and his family could scarcely be qualified as more than a *vicolo*. It is certainly not broader than the narrowest part of Hanway Street. Opposite the house, which is a great square block of plain masonry, I know not how many storeys high, on the other side of the *vicolo*, is a tiny quadrangular expanse, called the Place Letizia. It is one mass of flowers and shrubs, which make the air heavy with their delicious fragrance.

On a slab of grey marble over the central door of the house

is an inscription in French, reciting that here, on August 15, 1769, was born Napoleon Buonaparte. The door was closed, but there was no need to knock. A charming old lady, with hair like white floss silk, neatly braided and prying from beneath her black Corsican coif, emerged from a little door in the wall of the Place Letizia, and bade me wait " un momentino," and she would fetch the keys. Ere long she came back, opened the heavily-timbered door, and preceded me up a very short flight of stairs to rooms formerly occupied by the advocate of the Royal Court. I took no notes, but unless I err she conducted me through nine different apartments. One was the ball-room ; the old mirrors, with their faded gilt frames and sconces, and the once bravely-flowered but now dim and ghostlike paper on the walls yet remaining.

It was formerly the practice of politicians and publicists who called Napoleon the "Corsican Ogre" and the "Jacobin Usurper," to assert that Carlo Buonaparte was a poverty-stricken and pettifogging attorney at Ajaccio, and that it was only through the disgraceful fact of Madame Buonaparte having been the mistress of the Count de Marbœuf, the French Governor of Corsica, that by this latter's influence the young Napoleon obtained admission as a foundationer to the military school at Brienne. I have read the statement, made with charming naïveté, that "he was the son of a base-born pauper, and was brought up at a charity school." The majority of these lies were invented by Bourbonist pamphleteers, refugees in London of the type of Peltier, whom Erskine defended when Napoleon prosecuted him in the English courts for libel.

But if pettifogging was the business of Carlo Buonaparte, it must have been a very profitable business in the Ajaccio of the time, seeing that he accupied a large mansion, which had even the luxury of a ball-room attached to it. In reality, in addition to his profession as a lawyer, Carlo Buonaparte was a considerable landed proprietor and vine-grower. Touching his social position in the Ajaccio community, it is sufficient to remark that in a recently published tract entitled "La Vérité sur l'Origine de nos Bonaparte," M. Caraffa, the curator of the public library of Bastia, has proved from indisputable documentary authority that in the year 1759 thè Buonaparte family made good their claim to rank as nobles, and that in 1771 the Superior Council of the island, on the petition of Luciano and Carlo Buonaparte, confirmed this claim, and declared the father and brother of Napoleon to be " nobles of a nobility proved extending over two hundred years."

The old lady took me into a room half darkened by the flowers and plants shrouding the window outside. In the midst of the room was the framework of a bed—the traverse, the head and foot boards, all now painted in a stone grey monochrome, but in times gone by gay, no doubt, with colour and gilding, for the curves and beading of the head and foot-board gave evidence of the bed having been what was known as " un lit Pompadour." " He was born there," the charming old lady with the white floss silk hair said simply. Did many strangers visit the house? I asked. Well, all the English and all the Americans. Many Italians. All the Russians. She could not remember one Spanish visitor. Any Germans? —Very few. Any French ?—The old lady shook her head. "Corsica is in France, and in the Republic," she remarked.

I saw nothing else in the room where he was born save on the chimney-piece a little marble bust of the Prince Imperial. In another room is a little old harpsichord, and in another the wreck of a sedan chair, once resplendent with carving and gilding and crimson plush lining. In this sedan chair Madame Letizia was carried to and from high mass on the day on which Napoleon was born. The ashes of the noble lady moulder peacefully hard by, in the mausoleum of the Chapelle Fesch. There also sleep the Cardinal himself and Charles Buonaparte, Prince of Canino. The inscription on the tomb of Madame Letizia styles her "Mater Regum"— the Mother of Kings.

XII.

A WINTER CITY.

AJACCIO, *October* 27.

WHEN I left Paris on this journey due South, I took with me something else besides my luggage, a goodly assortment of Murray's handbooks, and some circular notes. This something else was a slight cold. I went down with it to Marseilles, a long and uncomfortable journey of some six hundred miles. There was no accident, and I was not smashed *en route*, as some pessimist friends in Paris suggested that I should surely be; but the windows of the compartment in which I sate would not close properly—the rolling stock of the Paris, Lyons, and Mediterranean Railway is in a positively disgraceful state of disrepair—and by the time we reached Marseilles my cold had developed into catarrh.

During two days it was tropically hot in the City of the Cannebière; but on the third day the mistral blew great guns. That abominable mistral. It is the fora of the Adriatic and the norte of the Gulf of Mexico. The only thing that can be said in favour of this throat-cutting blast is that it departs as suddenly as it comes. On the fourth day it was tropically hot at Marseilles again, and, like the mariners "from Bristol

City," in Mr. Thackeray's ballad, "I took a wessel and I went to sea." That is to say, I took passage for Bastia, in Corsica, touching at Nice by the way.

The trip was a beautifully fine one; but, as I have already mentioned, a few hours after I had landed it began to rain. You remember Southey's lines describing how "the waters come down at Lodore." I never learned those lines by heart, and am far from any accessible edition of the late Laureate's poems; but I think that he said something about the cascade at Lodore descending in a dashing, splashing, crashing, smashing, roaring, pouring, rushing, gushing, teeming, screaming, streaming, gleaming, tumbling, rumbling, jumbling manner. At all events, that is how the rain came down at Bastia. And it rained three whole days and nights, to the great joy of the inhabitants. No rain had fallen for three months. The beds of the mountain torrents were dry, and the cisterns of Bastia were nearly empty. Cataclysm! how it rained!

Bronchitis and spasmodic asthma came down upon me like two armed men in the night at Bastia, at the Hôtel de France "tenu par Staffe," and gripped me by the throat. So soon as it was morning, and the shops were open, I sent to an apothecary to have a prescription, without which I never travel, made up. It was given to me nearly twenty years ago by a celebrated English surgeon, and has done me good, I may say scores of times. In the course of an hour the *pharmacien*—he was a Frenchman, mind, not a Corsican, and described himself on his *enseigne* as a *lauréat*, and *médaillé*, and all the rest of it—sent word to say that he could make nothing of the prescription. It was Chinese to him. Those were his literal words.

In despair, I made inquiries for a doctor. They brought me one—a Corsican. This *medico* could make nothing of the prescription. Of course he understood the Latin in which it was framed, but the handwriting was, according to his contention, illegible. I may remark that I have had it made up with scrupulous exactitude of formula in Paris, in Frankfort, in Berlin, in Venice, in Rome, in Geneva, in Richmond, in Baltimore, in New Orleans, and in St. Petersburg. The Corsican *medico* gave me a "potion" composed of thirty *grammes* of syrup of belladonna and some vile stuff which he called "sirop pectoral," and which made me a great deal worse than I had been before. Then I tried some rough-and-ready palliatives of the "old woman" order: mustard plasters, linseed tea, the inhalation of the fumes of lighted brown paper saturated with saltpetre, by means of which I contrived to half suffocate the inmates of the Hôtel de France "tenu par Staffe," but failed to experience any personal relief from the experiment, and so forth. An Italian barber, to whom I confided my woes, obligingly offered to bleed me; but I have a horror of phlebotomy, and declined his friendly proposal.

At length, the dreadful feeling of congestion increasing every half-hour—if you wish to know what that feeling is, try to realise the idea that you are Mark Twain's Celebrated Jumping Frog, and that somebody has "prized" your mouth open, and forced you to swallow a soup-ladleful of number seven shot—I arrived at the conclusion that the sooner I got out of Bastia the Barbarous the better it would be. It was five in the evening, and the diligence was just starting for Ajaccio. Fortunately, there was a place vacant in the *coupé* ; and, as fortunately, I discovered in the remotest recesses of my travelling bag a tin box of Keating's Cough Lozenges. I had laid in a stock of half-a-dozen boxes at Roberts's, the English chemist, in the Rue de la Paix, before leaving Paris ; but I had overlooked this particular box, and thought that my supply of Keatings was exhausted. That beneficent box ! Mithridates, they say, fed on poisons until they became antidotes. I fed on Keatings nearly throughout a nineteen hours' miserable bumping and jolting along the mountain roads from one end of the island of Corsica to the other. I will not say how many lozenges I swallowed, lest you should think that I was taking advantage of the travelling adage, " A beau mentir qui vient de loin."

It was in a most pitiable condition that I arrived at Ajaccio, and in a condition as pitiable did I remain for eight or nine days longer. When I found myself approaching convalescence, I was for taking the first steamer to Marseilles, and returning home at once ; but the skilful and humane physician into whose hands I had been so fortunate as to fall, said "No." He told me that I had still enough bronchitis and asthma about me to last me three weeks longer ; that a sudden change of climate would probably bring about a relapse, and that if I had a relapse I should possibly die. "Go to Italy," he concluded, "as quickly as you can, and get well. You will get well." He tended me all these days as tenderly as though I had been a child, and so stoutly refused to accept any kind of fee or honorarium, that I was compelled, with the friendly connivance of the landlord of the hotel, to resort to a (I hope not unworthy) subterfuge, in order to let the learned Professor H——, of Zurich, know that I was not ungrateful for the kindness which he had shown to an entire stranger.

You are not, if you please, to consider these paragraphs as the mere gossiping experiences of an egotistical valetudinarian. Invalids, I grant, are always to a certain extent selfish. "The sick man's horizon," wrote Honoré de Balzac, "is at the foot of his bed." What I have said concerning my troubles in Corsica has been penned with a deliberate and practical purpose, not devoid, I hope, of utility.

In the first place, I would call the attention of the medical profession both at home and abroad, to the vital necessity of framing some universally accepted mode of expression in writing prescriptions. I bought at Euston Station, some months ago, for the sum of one shilling, a paper-knife, on the obverse and reverse blades of which were neatly printed the English and the decimal system of weights, measures, and distances; an exhaustive table of foreign moneys and their respective value in English money; a comprehensive international Postal Guide, and a variety of other highly useful information. Are we never to have an International Pharmacopœia? Just before I left home there was held in London a Pharmaceutical Congress, and I remember writing a leading article strongly advocating the adoption of some generally recognised medical formula. A first step in the direction would be the abolition of our own absurd system of hieroglyphics to denote the weights and measures of drugs. I copy one of the prescriptions of my skilful professor at Ajaccio.

Sulph : Aurat	0,05 grammes
Pulv : Opii	0,05 ,,
Syrop 15. Aq	1,80 ,,
quatre fois par jour une cuill :	

Would this prescription, I wonder, be "Chinese" to the English chemist and druggist to whom it was sent to be compounded?

Whether Latin should be the language universally employed is, of course, a moot point; still, I venture to think it highly expedient that if Latin is to continue to be the general form of pharmaceutical expression all abbreviations should be avoided. You are ready to pay the physician for the time which he bestows on you; why should he truncate the healing words which he writes on paper for you? Again, in all cases I think that Arabic numerals should be substituted for the mysterious hieroglyphics, and the weight or measure of the drug plainly stated in words.

Finally, should not the physician be bound to write the directions for use in the vernacular tongue of the person for whom the prescription is intended? The chronic invalid pores over his prescriptions as Mr. Soapy Spunge used to pore over Mogg's Ten Thousand Cab Fares, until he knows them—the prescriptions, not the fares—by heart. I may be told that the chemist will take care to translate the doctor's directions into a language "understanded of the vulgar:" that is, by yourself. Well; I remember once sending an English doctor's prescription to be made up by an apothecary at Constantinople. The sage of the Grande Rue de Pera was good enough to translate into choice Italian the Latin behests of my English M.R.C.S., and on the label of the bottle of physic which he sent me I was bidden to take the medicine twice every hour. Fortunately, I remembered that the directions were to take the stuff, which was very powerful, twice every day. But suppose I had lent the prescription to a suffering friend, and he had implicitly followed the directions given by the sage of the Grande Rue de Pera? A nice time I should have had with my suffering friend's widow.

Then there comes the scarcely less important matter of writing prescriptions legibly. The one which I sent to the *pharmacien* at Bastia was really—although the Corsican *medico* declared it to be "illisible"—indited in a very neat and flowing hand. But the prescriptions of some doctors are the very vilest of scrawls. An illegible "fist," abbreviations, and hieroglyphics more mysterious than the Rosetta inscription, all belong to the mummy and stuffed lizard period of medicine, to the days when "Miriam cured wounds and Pharaoh was sold for balsam"—I know not whether I am quoting Sir Thomas Browne correctly—when the healing art was looked upon as a kind of thaumaturgic one, full of weird "hocus-pocus," and the leech occupied an ambiguous middle station between an alchemist and a wizard. In any case, as things go at present, it would be a blessed thing if every medical man "composed" his prescriptions through the intermediary of a Remington Type Writer.

Yet all personal suffering notwithstanding, I do not, for two reasons, regret my journey to Corsica. In the first place, I have seen the house, the room, the bed in which Napoleon the Great was born. I saw him buried in the Invalides, in 1840; and could I only hope to see the house at Longwood, I should be satisfied. I should have learned, to the end, the Legend—to me a marvellously fascinating one—which I have been studying my whole thinking life long.

In the next place, I am positively delighted at having been privileged to make the acquaintance of, perhaps, the most enchanting "winter city" that I have ever visited. I know the majority of the "winter cities"—the Cities of Refuge for the unfortunates who suffer from pulmonary or from bronchitic affections pretty well. But do not talk to me, if you please, about Nice, Cannes, or Montpelier; about Antibes, or Frejus, or the Golfe Juan; about Mentone, San Remo, or Bordighera; about Madeira, or about St. Augustin in Florida, U.S.A. Cease to laud the balmy climate of Seville and Malaga; withhold your praises from the oranges and bananas of Havana; moderate your transports touching Algiers, and be even reticent as to the curative virtues of Ventnor and St. Leonards. From my fidelity to Brighton I will never swerve. It is to me the place *par excellence* to get well and to keep well in; but, after Brighton, give me Ajaccio. I look upon this charming little town of fifteen thousand inhabitants as the Queen of the Mediterranean.

It is as warm here in October as it should be warm in Devonshire in July. The sun has shone continuously during my stay, and even when I was at my worst the doctor insisted that the window should be partially opened. The air is the most fragrant that I have ever breathed. After sunset comes a deliciously soft and cool breeze—like the "frio" of the Valley of Mexico. The Bay of Ajaccio is as beautiful as the Bay of Naples. The drives and promenades are numerous and picturesque. The markets teem with fruit and vegetables of every conceivable kind. You may have—read this, ye Americans!—your corn cobs, your "succotash," and your "egg plant" for breakfast. You revel in tomatoes. It is a land of figs and grapes, and luscious pears, and sweet lemons. "La Germania" is a delightfully clean, airy, and comfortable hotel; and, for the benefit of the steadily increasing English colony, as I have already informed my readers, an exemplary English lady has built a church.

I dare say that what I have said about this delightful little watering-place will not be by any means a new thing to some of my readers. There may be those who found out Ajaccio long ago, and I can only hope that such persons will concur in my favourable estimate of the place. But it is on behalf of those who have not visited Ajaccio that I write. In scenery and climate it is just such another Earthly Paradise as Monte Carlo, only, unlike the lovely plateau on which the "Principino" of Monaco has suffered the proprietor of a common gaming-house to spread a detestable *tapis vert*, the Paradise has not an Inferno for a next door neighbour.

In the course of my wanderings in many lands, I have picked up a good deal of what we conventionally call " bric-

A PRICKLY PEAR TREE.

P. 168.

à-brac," and what the Americans sometimes irreverently term "truck." Even from Russia, when I went thither, after the assassination of the Tsar Alexander II., I contrived to bring home some " truck " of an interesting kind : some old china, both of Dresden and Muscovite manufacture ; a little very old silver ; a model *samovar;* some " Apostle " teaspoons ; some peasant women's needlework ; a bit of bronze, and so forth. But now that my Corsican trip is coming to an end, I look ruefully at my wallet and find that in the Island I have secured scarcely anything at all. During my few days of convalescence at Ajaccio, I have searched diligently through main streets and back streets for " curios ; " but my search has been almost wholly barren of result.

I am not aware whether the philosopher Seneca was a collector of " curios," but he certainly seems to have been lacking in appreciation of the resources of Corsica. He was exiled there A.D. 45, and remained in banishment eight long years. " Can aught be more arid and denuded than this rock ? " wrote Seneca to the freed man Polybius, Minister of Claudius. "Is there a place where man could undergo greater misery ? The earth here has neither fruits for use nor trees for shelter, and it can scarcely nourish the wretches who cultivate it." It is plain that there was no clean and tidy precursor of the Hôtel Germania at Ajaccio in Seneca's time. So far as I am concerned, I am and always shall be in love with Ajaccio and the Germania. I only grumble at the paucity of local "curios." All that I have been able to buy is a "vendetta " dagger, with " Morte al nemico " inscribed on the blade ; a toy model of the same in coral, silver, and mother-of-pearl, for a lady's *châtelaine,* and a couple of curiously incised gourds for holding water, with silver chains and stoppers. I am not prepared to maintain that the real dagger and the toy stiletto are not "articles de Paris," and manufactured at Belleville or Montmartre; but I know that the gourds are veritably Corsican, because I saw the man incising them.

But that which grieved and irritated me most of all was that in Ajaccio I could not obtain a single memento of the Great Napoleon. I did not hunger after sham relics; spurious eagles, counterfeit military buttons, fraudulent gun-locks, "bogus" bayonets; such as they will sell you by the hundredweight on the field of Waterloo. I only wanted a bust, a medal, a photograph, a print, to hang up at home as a reminiscence of my visit to Corsica. You bring away analogous trifles from Stratford-on-Avon, and they are a continual delight to you in after years. In Ajaccio I could find nothing; not even a photograph of the house in the Rue St. Charles, or of the bed-chamber in which the Conqueror and Captive of the Earth was born. Evidently I could not bring away his equestrian statue, surrounded with the effigies of his four brothers, from the Place Diamant. There was nothing; and it was most exasperating.

In the course of my researches I espied in the window of a stationer's shop a profile medallion in alabaster surrounded by an ebony frame. In my shortsightedness I deemed for an instant that this was a portrait of Napoleon. No; I was informed by the clown-looking Corsican shopkeeper to whom I addressed myself: it was a portrait of Torquato Tasso. But I am purblind. Had the stationer no portrait of Napoleon? There was none. Why? I asked, quite out of patience. "For the reason," replied, with a scowl and in the Tuscan tongue, the clown-looking Corsican stationer, "that if we sold busts of Napoleon we should be obliged to import them from Paris, and to charge a considerable sum for them. In the meantimet he wicked Italian continentals who are always going about with plaster of Paris would take moulds of our busts and sell copies up and down the country at five-and-twenty sous apiece." The idea of the "cattivi Italiani" from the mainland prowling about Corsica with their pockets full of plaster of Paris was, at least, droll.

XIII.

GENOA, THE SUPERB.—THE CITY OF THE LEANING TOWER.

PISA, *November* 4.

THE chief cities of Italy are, with the exception of Venice, normally noisy; and even in la Bella Venezia I am informed there is at present much more clamour than existed in the old days of the domination of the Tedeschi, when the loudest sounds to be heard were the strains of the Austrian military bands discoursing sweet music on St. Mark's Place. Now that Venice has become one of the brightest jewels in the crown of United Italy, they tell me that the newsboys make a terrible noise on the Piazza and on the Rialto, yelling their publications; and I even learn, with a sinking of the heart, that the distracting "tic-tac" of steam-launches is audible on the Grand Canal. From the crowning nuisance of tramways, the Queen of the Adriatic is, I should say, secure.

I have come to Pisa from Genoa, which, Naples alone left out, I hold to be the noisiest city in the whole Italian Peninsula. For some occult reason of his own, Dante, in the "Inferno," took occasion to anathematise the Genoese, to denounce them as men of heterogeneous races and conflicting customs, full of fraud and spite, and to inquire why they were not swept from the face of the earth. I only wonder that the immortal Alighieri did not taunt the Genoese with the desperate din which, I have not the slightest doubt, they were making five hundred years ago, just as they were making it the day before yesterday. Surely that atrabilious critic, whoever he may have been, who invented the proverb reciting that on the Ligurian shore was a city cursed with "a sea without fish, hills without trees, men without probity, and women without modesty"—all purely libellous and calumnious accusations, for Genoa is renowned for its mullets and sardines, the population are laborious and honest, and the women are the gracefullest in North Italy— might have aggravated the venom of his sneer by declaring a Genoese night to be one without sleep, owing to the infernal disturbance made by belated brawlers in the streets.

The architectural attractions of Genova la Superba have lately been enhanced by the construction of an inordinately protracted arcade or passage roofed with glass, a Ligurian rival of the magnificent Galleria Vittorio Emanuele at Milan, which, standing as it does in the very heart of the city, and leading directly to the Piazza del Duomo, is as useful as it is ornamental. The Genoese arcade, which is called the Galleria Mazzini, leads from the post office to nowhere in particular; and the post-office itself is just as easily reached by the Via Roma, a new street running exactly parallel to the Galleria Mazzini, from which it is accessible by a series of archways. The Galleria Mazzini contains two or three café-restaurants, and the back door of the Grand Hôtel Isotta opens into it. Otherwise the preposterous passage has proved commercially as dead a failure as that dismal Rue de la République at Marseilles. The shop windows are mean and gloomy, and appear to be chiefly repositories for the sale of cheap photographs, squeaking dolls, wretchedly bad cigars, translations into Italian of "Nana," "Le Ventre de Paris," and "L'Assommoir"—the last-named, as "Lo Scannatojo," the cut-throat place, has gone through I know not how many editions—together with wax-matches, with scenes and portraits from "Nana" on the lids of the boxes, and cheap dream-books—the last devoutly believed in by the common people as an infallible guide for speculations in that hebdomadally recurring lottery which literally pauperises the mass of the Italian people, the thrifty and laborious as well as the idle and improvident. Those ladies and gentlemen in England who are so fond of lecturing us upon the blessings of thrift would do well to visit, first France, and then Italy, and study on the spot a few of the disadvantages attendant on rigid and habitual parsimony. They would find that in France excessive thrift has too frequently the terrible concomitant of the brutal—nay, murderous—covetousness of your neighbour's money; while in Italy the industrious classes toil painfully and economise unremittingly in order to gamble away their savings in the lottery.

There are also one or two "Bersagli" at twopence a shot in the Galleria Mazzini, and a hybrid establishment which seemed, in the origin, to have been a wax-work show on a small scale. That enterprise having collapsed, the proprietor appears to have turned his energies partially towards the sale of German oleographs, and partially in the direction of a boot-blacking and clothes-brushing saloon; while in his back shop there is a faint suspicion of shaving and hairdressing. Altogether, in view of the comfort and luxury of the Milan Galleries, the aspect of the arcade named after the late patriarch of Young Italy is somewhat depressing. It is an example of vaulting—or rather vaulted —ambition which has overleaped itself, and fallen on the other side.

The upper classes in Genoese society steadily refuse to patronise the Galleria Mazzini as a promenade, and, as no well-dressed ladies are ever seen in it—save a few chance guests from the hotel—its prospects as a resort for shopping purposes are the reverse of bright. The best shops are in the Via Roma and in the Via Carlo Felice, and the favourite mart for filigree jewellery, coral, velvet, and lace is still that dear old Dædalus of narrow lanes round about the port, between the Fontane Amorose and the Exchange. There are complaints, moreover, of deficient ventilation in the Galleria. Personally, I found its atmosphere that which is vulgarly termed "stuffy." It suited me exactly, for in the open there was a terrible north-east wind blowing—a compound of the Mediterranean mistral and the Adriatic "bora," and not unlike that awful blast from the Guardarrama at Madrid, which is proverbially said to be at the same time so keen and so subtle that it will kill a man without blowing out a candle.

I rejoiced in the stuffiness of the Gallery. My bed-room window at the Hôtel Isotta opened into it; and I fancied that I had been recommended by the faculty to live under glass as the best European substitute for the Mammoth Cave of Kentucky. Some speculative philanthropists built a number of houses, you may remember, in the Mammoth Cave several years ago as residences for consumptive and bronchitic patients. The undertaking, I am afraid, was scarcely a successful one. The *poitrinaires* suffered the agonies of *ennui* until they began to hate each other bitterly, as you are apt to do when you are desperately bored by dining at the same table d'hôte day after day for three weeks opposite the same old lady with the ear-trumpet, the same wolfish little boy who always over-eats himself, and is constantly being detected by the waiter in the act of furtively pocketing the almonds and raisins and macaroons at dessert, and the same old French gentleman in the black velvet skull-cap, who always goes to sleep between the fish and the roast—and at length the consumptive and bronchitic patients fled from the Mammoth Cave in despair. Better a hyperborean attic in the unglazed lantern of a lighthouse than a tempered atmosphere where you are being slowly bored to death.

Whenever it rains in Genoa—and it rained pretty steadily during the greater part of my stay there—the Galleria Mazzini is crowded by the unwashed Ligurians of both sexes. The air—or so much of it as penetrates into the arcade—reeks with the odour of bad Cavours and the even worse paper in which the tobacco used for cigarettes is rolled. A distractingly tumultuous jabbering rises, towards sunset, into a *grida*, or shout, and, should the rain continue, this *grida* culminates in a hideous howling, which endures until long after midnight. Then you cease to be astonished that Dante should have denounced the Genovesi as "Uomini diversi, d'ogni costume, e pieni d'ogni magagna."

I came away from this turbulent city by perhaps the noisiest railway that I have ever travelled by. It skirts the seashore; and why it is so turbulent is for the reason that, for at least a third of the way—at least so it seemed to me— the track is an underground one, and the train rattles and roars and screeches through the bowels of the land. How many tunnels there are, hewn through the living rock, between Genoa and Pisa, I do not know. Some people told me that there were eighty, others ninety, while others went as far as a hundred; but I do know that the sound which you most commonly hear on this stentorian railway is "Wra-a-a-a-ah!" and that no sooner do you catch sight of a fragment of blue sky, a strip of blue sea, a sunlit rock, a white villa, and a clump of olive-trees, and congratulate yourself on being out of a tunnel, than you are in another. Egyptian darkness encompasses you, and the roar of "Wr-a-a-a-ah!" is more horrible than ever. It was, indeed, a relief for which much thanks were due after about nine hours' plunging in and out of the tunnels to emerge into the roomy and brilliantly lighted terminus at Pisa, and to wake up next morning at a very clean and comfortable hostelry called the Hôtel Vittoria, on the Lung' Arno, right over against the post-office, which is on the other side of the old bridge called the Ponte di Mezzo.

The Arno, swollen by many days' almost incessant downpour, made turbid by the accretion of mountain torrents, and holding in solution a vast amount of loam turned to mud, was certainly not lovely to look upon; but the day was beautifully fine. The well-paved streets were quite dry; the sun shone very brightly; and the atmosphere was nearly as warm as at Ajaccio. I was told, indeed, that it was very seldom cold at Pisa, and that a tolerably large number of English people, pulmonary and bronchitic sufferers, came every season to pass the winter there. The rest of the travelling world who are neither invalids nor archæologists, just "pop into Pisa," if I may be allowed the use of an inelegant but expressive colloquialism, scamper to the Quattro Monumenti, peep at the Leaning Tower, and "pop back" again. Whither? Well, into the "Ewigkeit," I suppose.

I remained four days at Pisa, and during that period I made the knife-and-fork acquaintance of two Swedish gentlemen, a dozen Germans, a Polish count, a Spanish grandee and family, and at least twenty Americans of both sexes; but we were never more than six at the table d'hôte. People who made a fitful appearance at breakfast went away before dinner. Next morning you asked after the agreeable lady and gentleman with whom you had supped the night before; but they were gone. There used, in former days, to be an excellent *pension* at Havana in the Island of Cuba, kept, if I remember aright, by a Madame Almé. You used to meet the most charming people there, but, missing them from the table, and asking after them, you would be told with melancholy piquancy that the charming people had died that morning of consumption or of the Yellow Fever, and that they were to be buried at sunset, in the Potter's Field. The rapid succession of charming people at the inn at Pisa, however, went away, I hope, to enjoy good health and to live long years.

At the same time I cannot help thinking that it is slightly unjust to treat Pisa in so cavalier a manner. The following piece of advice from *Murray*, although doubtless well meant, strikes me as being positively cruel to Pisa. "If the traveller," I read, "only wishes to see the Cathedral, Leaning Tower, &c., he can leave his luggage at the station and follow the new street running to the new bridge, Ponte Solferino, and thence straight to the Cathedral if walking. No guide necessary. Distance about one mile. Cab fare one franc." I believe that there are thousands of tourists who in the course of every year follow this perfectly practical but cold-blooded and unsympathetic advice.

For my part I would willingly have sojourned at least a month in this venerable, comely, tranquil city; but if the municipality of Pisa are anxious to induce strangers to abide within their gates for a longer period than is merely required for a scamper to and from the Four Monuments, I should strongly advise them to apply to the Italian Parliament for a special local statute empowering them to put down the workers in alabaster. I grant that the nature of the law of which I presume to suggest the enactment would be exceptional, and that its operation would be despotic; but in the interests of the hotel, lodging-house, and restaurant keepers, and of the barbers, hackney cab-drivers, and washerwomen of Pisa, I would have such a law swiftly passed and mercilessly enforced. Down with the sculptors in alabaster!

I think that I have read in ancient history that if among the silver image-workers of Ephesus there happened to arrive a strange craftsman who excelled in a particular degree in the working of silver, the vigilance committee of the guild were accustomed to erect before the shop-door of the new-comer a gallows, to which was attached a written intimation requesting the alien silversmith to go and excel elsewhere. This was the antique method of "rattening;" but it is no such barbarous exercise of trades-unionism that I would advocate. I would suppress the alabaster image-workers of Pisa altogether. Their productions become an intolerable nuisance. They put ratsbane in your porridge and halters in your pew. They poison your existence. Even riding at night in the hotel omnibus from the railway station to the Lung' Arno I became uneasily conscious of passing a number of little shops of the usual rabbit-hutch formation, in which were displayed alabaster models of various sizes of the Leaning Tower, the Duomo, the Baptistery, and the Campo Santo; but it was the next morning, and in the salle-à-manger of the hotel, that the plague came down upon you with more than Egyptian unrelentingness.

On a side table, which should properly have been garnished with cold galantine, aromatic Gorgonzola, "zesty" Stracchino, ruddy tomatoes, and luscious grapes, alabaster trophies of the Four Monuments grinned upon you in the ghastliest manner. The Baptistery, about the size of and looking remarkably like a wedding-cake in a pastrycook's shop-window, price fifty francs; the Baptistery, the size of and with the aspect of a Melton Mowbray pork-pie, whitewashed, with a potato cut in half for the cupola, price fifteen francs; the Baptistery, the size of a threepenny Savoy cake, price five francs; the Baptistery, the size of the smallest of jelly moulds, three francs; the Baptistery, the size of Columbus' egg after it had been made to stand upright, one franc fifty centimes. The Duomo, spectrally gleaming with hundreds of little arches and columns, and reminding you of that traditional little plaster-of-Paris structure in the Lowther Arcade—the chalky-faced cabin in the interior of which you placed a lighted candle so as to show off the stained-glass windows, and which successively, from the enterprising salesman's point of view, did duty as Rosslyn Chapel, Garibaldi's hermitage at Caprera, William Tell's cottage, and the birth-place of Jenny Lind. As to the Leaning Tower, it made its simulated appearance in the guise of a post-office letter pillar sadly out of the perpendicular, of a chimney-pot after a heavy gale, of a lamp-post after an Irish riot, and of a drain-pipe gone wrong; but always whitewashed, always sepulchral in the whitest alabaster.

The exasperation produced by the contemplation of these gewgaws was aggravated by the circumstance of their being intermingled with photographs of the sculpture and frescoes in the Campo Santo, and of Galileo's lamp, and Nicolo Pisano's pulpit in the Duomo. Nor was this all. There was more alabaster—alabaster models of pigeons and puppy dogs, alabaster cups and dishes, alabaster profiles of Galileo and Lorenzo de' Medici, and, more dreadful than all, the Bagnatrice—the Bathing Girl, the statue which created so great a sensation in the Paris Exposition of 1878. All the world knows that example of the plastic art to be an exquisitely beauteous one, but I object to a thousand and one more or less corrupted, perverted, and vulgarised reproductions of the figure of a bold young woman in an abbreviated "combination" of some knitted fabric, idiotically simpering as she poises her finger-tips high above her silly head, and prepares to take a "sensation header" into an imaginary bath. The Bagnatrice, as tall as an umbrella, price one hundred francs; the Bagnatrice, the height of an office ruler, price thirty francs; the Bagnatrice, the altitude of a stick of sealing-wax, price ten francs; the Bagnatrice, the length of your little finger, price one franc twenty-five centimes. This art exhibition—there was, besides, a large cupboardful of Quattro Monumenti, puppy dogs, and bathing girls—completely sufficed to spoil my breakfast, and I despatched the meal in sulky apprehension, dreading every moment the appearance of the Torre Pendente in barley sugar or of the Bagnatrice in alto-relievo on a pat of butter.

Outside, under the blue sky, in the lovely balmy air, with the sun shining on the sullen turbid Arno as though to coax it into smoothing its brow, I felt decidedly better. I had a purpose in view. I wished to discover the Four Monuments for and by myself, without the aid of the guide-book, without the help of the hotel cicerone, without even the assistance of a cab-driver. I should come upon the Quattro Monumenti, I thought, unawares. You know how, at Nismes, you are transported, as if by magic, into the presence of the beauteous Maison Carrée, still fresh, sparkling, as though in ineffaceable youth, and smiling half saucily, half compassionately upon poor old Time, who, in all these centuries, has been able to do the enchanting edifice so little harm. You know how in Granada some mysterious finger seems to be pointing out to you the long straight avenue, and to guide you through the towering Moorish archway, and to lead you, how you scarcely know, into the Court of the Lions. You know how, purposely losing your way in the labyrinth of little lanes and alleys encompassing the Mercuria of Venice, you are sure, after crossing innumerable bridges and catching innumerable glimpses of gondolas, to find yourself either on the steps of the Rialto or the Piazzo San Marco. You know how in Rome, wandering away at random from the Corso, you turn a corner and find yourself suddenly confronted by the Pantheon of Agrippa, gigantic, black, inexpugnable, awful. You have but to lose your way, and you are sure to find these fanes.

But I lost my way at Pisa, on purpose, at least a dozen times, and I could not find the Quattro Monumenti. I knew that I was on the right side of the Arno, that the city was of no very vast extent, and that I could not be more than a quarter of an hour's walk from the Monuments; but where were they? In vain did my eyes sweep the sky line of the distant buildings, but no Leaning Tower, no Duomo, no Baptistery in sight appeared. I had, somewhat contumeliously, rejected the proffered aid of a very civil charioteer, who was plying for hire at the hotel door. He was quite a patriarchal-looking cabman, with a long white beard, gentle eyes, and a pleasant smile. His victoria was drawn by a plump Tuscan horse, very well groomed, with a tuft of feathers in his headstall, and a row of bells on his collar jingling softly. I was sorry ere long that I had rejected the proposal of the patriarchal cabdriver. He was such a very pleasant-looking, civil-spoken old gentleman.

Conscience doth make cowards of us all, and as in dogged disappointment, verging on despair, I wearily plodded along in vain quest of the Quattro Monumenti, I could not help imagining that I could hear behind me the jingling, jingling, jingling of the bells; until at last I began to think that my name was Matthias, and my native land Alsace; that my daughter was married to a brigadier of gendarmerie, and that, through greed of gold, I had murdered a Polish Jew. At length, fairly worn out, I hailed a passing victoria, and bade the *vetturino* drive me to the Duomo. It was idle fancy, no doubt, but still it struck me that I had seen that vetturino before; that he was a patriarchal old man, with gentle eyes and a pleasant smile—a very pleasant smile. In less than three minutes he set me down in the very midst of the Four Monuments.

XIV.

AUSTERE BOLOGNA.

BOLOGNA, *November* 13.

To a person in indifferent health and afflicted besides with occasional attacks of that unheroic form of hypochondria known as "the blues," I should be reluctant to suggest as a place of temporary sojourn the city of Bologna in the middle of November. Ferrara is certainly the reverse of a lively place; and, so strong is the force of imagination, you cannot help fancying when you are in the antique "Forum Alieni" that strange chemical savours hover about the dishes offered you at the table d'hôte; you eye askance the lowering portal of the huge Castello, "moated and flanked with towers in the heart of the subjugated town, like a tyrant intrenched among slaves;" and quicken your pace lest Rustighello, with a halter in his pocket, should be waiting round the corner to pounce upon you, and drag you into the presence of Don Alfonso d'Este, there to answer for the high crime and misdemeanour of having scrawled on the ducal gate some *graffiti*, implying aspersions on the fair fame of his Highness's august spouse. Still, although Ferrara be silent and mournful and grim, although the grass grows in her streets and in the interstices of the stones of her decaying palaces, and the druggists' shops are to your thinking a great deal too numerous, and you have an uncomfortable feeling at the pit of your stomach and a burning sensation in your throat when you see the black-eyebrowed assistant at the *farmacia* of the Fratelli Avellenagente pestling something in a huge mortar, while at the Stabilimento Panziarotto, the apothecary's opposite, a lean and shrivelled man, that Romeo might have known, is pouring a suspicious-looking liquid from one phial into another, to which a label as big as a barrister's bands is attached—although, on the whole, when the railway takes you away from Ferrara you feel that you are "well out of" the city of Lucrezia Borgia, I will back Bologna in November, and on a Sunday—and a cold Sunday, be it remembered—as a home of dismal sensations and unmitigated gloom.

I was unfortunate this time in my experience of the ancient Felsina. It was fifteen years since I had been there; and on the last occasion of my visiting Bologna I had as travelling companion a very diminutive but fire-eating officer in Garibaldi's legion of "camicie rosse," fresh from campaigning in the Trentino. The appearance of my friend in a red-flannel shirt, much weather-stained, and with a very big sabre at his hip, made a noise in Bologna. We were received with great ceremony at the Hôtel Brun. Deputations waited on the gallant Garibaldino, poetry was recited by the Bolognese youth in his praise: the "wine of honour" was offered to us; and the Prefetto or the Sindaco—I forget which—perhaps both—asked us to dinner. "Sic transit." I came in, alone, very late at night to the capital of the old Etruscan kings and bestowed myself in the hotel omnibus with that feeling of being generally miserable which sometimes comes over you when you remember that you are in a city of more than a hundred thousand inhabitants, and that you do not know one single soul there.

No such feeling of dejection need oppress you when you arrive as a total stranger in an American city. The hotel clerk shakes hands with you to begin with—and if he does not, I should strongly advise you to shake hands with him, although you may never have seen him in your life before—and that is something. Then, when you are two hours older, you will probably be "interviewed" by the reporters of at least two local newspapers—possibly by half a dozen; and when you have been twenty-four hours in town it is quite "on the cards" that you will be made an honorary member of one or more clubs, and that you will receive a letter written on four sides of foolscap and purporting to come from a gentleman whose grand uncle, so he contends, was at school with you at Rotherhithe, London, England, forty years ago; who is, as he puts it, Young, Impulsive, and Impassioned, and who is anxious to know whether, in the event of his crossing the Atlantic to the Old Country you can secure him remunerative enjoyment as an epic poet, or as clerk in a dry goods store. I wonder whether the Americans, who are continually wandering up and down Europe, ever feel wretched when they find themselves in large cities where they have never been before, and where they know absolutely nobody.

Yes, the Fates were against me at Bologna. Of course I went to the Hôtel Brun, the excellent hostelry and Pension Suisse, so long established in the vast premises of the Palazzo

Malvasia. As I knew it in days gone by, the Albergo Brun was an exceptionally clean, comfortable, and civilly conducted house, famed for its capital cuisine, and especially for its fragrant coffee. The house, some friends in Rome had told me, was as good and indeed better than ever; but, alas! when the omnibus deposited me in the vast courtyard of the ci-devant Palazzo Malvasia, a serene German waiter informed me, to my extreme discomfiture, that the hotel was full, almost to overflowing. The Indian mail, he added, had just come in; and the best apartments were occupied by English generals and colonels with their consorts, who had come from the far East viâ Brindisi, and, not liking to travel on a Sunday, had broken their journey home, at Bologna. Exemplary travellers!

The serene waiter had a choice of only two rooms to offer me. One was in a dark corridor, on a remote staircase at an uncertain altitude—an irregular polygon in form, with one window and no fireplace. Its sides looked uncomfortably collapsible; and, remembering Mr. Wilkie Collins's tale of "A Terribly Strange Bed," I declined to occupy the polygonal sleeping accommodation. The remaining alternative was on the ground floor, opening, indeed, into the court-yard. It was a vast old chamber, with a ceiling supported by heavy beams, and one huge window looking on a side street, but placed so high up in the wall that you had to ascend a flight of three steep steps before you found your chin on a level with the sill. This alarming casement was protected by double rows of iron bars, crossing each other at right angles. There was, as in the polygonal packing-case at the uncertain altitude, no fireplace in this all-too-roomy apartment, in the midst of which the white-covered pallet bed looked remarkably like a sepulchre for one; but, in the way of compensation, there was plenty of ventilation. Rarely have I heard the wind whistle so shrilly as it did throughout that night in the courtyard, and through undiscoverable chinks and crannies into my room. But I made the best of circumstances, and ordered four *bougies* as a first step towards making things cheerful. The serene waiter stared. What, he was perhaps thinking, could a traveller want with four candles at half an hour after midnight! But I had my two brace of *bougies* nevertheless, and kept them burning royally, all night: simply to dispel the illusion which was fast gaining ground in my mind that this dungeon-like den at Bologna was the condemned hold in Newgate, and that my name was Captain Macheath, but that I was deserted both by Polly and Lucy, without hope of a reprieve, and fated on the morrow to travel in the cart up the Heavy Hill, to take my last sup from St. Giles's bowl, and make my will, at Tyburn.

I was up betimes on the morrow, hoping to see something of the picturesque life and movement which you rarely fail to find on Sunday morning in the dullest of Italian towns, even in the bleakest and most sunless late autumnal weather. But the great, populous, wealthy, and intelligent city of Bologna seemed, with one exception, Dead. The exception was in these doubtless useful and convenient but artistically abominable tramway cars, which ceased not the pursuit of their jingling way throughout the principal streets. Wonderfully few foot passengers were visible. There were no chattering groups at the caffé or the wine-house doors, and no quidnuncs gossiping in the apothecaries' shops. There were no beggars even on the steps of the many churches or on the Mercato di Mezzo. Nearly all the shops were shut; and in the few which remained open only that which appeared to be the paltriest description of merchandise was on sale.

Could this be Bologna "La Grassa," the city of joviality and good cheer? Where were the bunches of succulent yellow grapes—the "uva paradisa;" where the renowned "cervellato," the Bolognese equivalent for plum-pudding, which only comes into season at the beginning of November; and where, above all, was the incomparable "mortadella," the unconquered Bologna sausage? The rare people of the ruder sex that you came across were swathed to the eyes in cloaks, of which the cut and mode of carriage so exactly resembled Roman togas dyed in sombre hues, that you felt angry with the men for wearing laced-up boots and wide-awake hats. At least, to have been consistent, they should have donned sandals and gone bare-headed. Antiquarian research has not enabled me to discover whether the ancient Felsinians were in the habit of scowling at strangers whom they passed on chilly Sunday mornings in November: but I fancied that I had not been so malevolently regarded since I abode among the frowning country cousins of Mr. Henry Irving in the island of Corsica.

Never mind, I thought, I had not been the first to give the Bolognese—whom I did not know from Adam—a bad character. Tassoni called them "un popol del demonio," whom "no bridle would curb." "Vathek" Beckford, too, I remembered spoke contemptuously of Bologna as "a city of puppy dogs and sausages." The sausages, however, as I have said, were invisible, and I looked in vain for the dear friend of my youth, the four-footed creature which, perhaps, next to the white Pomeranian, is the sweetest of all dogs, the black Bolognese poodle. Have they all been bought up by the officers of her Majesty's Household Brigade? On the other hand, I noticed among the few members of the softer sex whom I encountered in my rambles a far from pleasing prevalence of pug noses. Should the Preobajinski Russian Guard regiment be at any future period in want of a supply of *vivandières*, the commanding officer of that distinguished corps could not do better than send a recruiting party among the damsels of Bologna.

The only satisfactory impression produced in my dejected mind on this exceptionally cheerless morning was that Bologna might be considered in one sense an eminently Shakespearian place. It is essentially a City of Arcades; and it is precisely in thoroughfares under cover that the action of those Shakespearian dramas the locality of which is laid in Italy should most appropriately occur. "Scene, a Street." Remembering the intolerable heat of an Italian summer and the torrential character of the rainy season on this side the Apennines, this stage direction, so frequent in the Shakespearian repertory, might seem false to the "genius loci" did you not bear in mind the fact that the piazzas in Italian towns are nearly always surrounded by coolly-shady arcades—the very places for chatting, and leasing, and love-making, and conspiring, and, occasionally, for smiting your foeman under the fifth rib. There is, it is true, in Venice only one principal series of colonnades, that surrounding the Piazza San Marco, and so turning at a right angle into the Piazzetta; but then St. Mark's Place is the universal Venetian rendezvous; and, again, the cabins of the gondolas, may, one and all, be considered as so many isolated arcades upon the bosom of the sea. Among North Italian towns, Padua, Verona, Ferrara, Rovigo, and Vicenza are all much arcaded; but in Bologna, so it strikes the stranger, nine-tenths of the houses are built on arches, and you may walk for miles under shelter.

The pleasure to be derived from this mode of peregrination very soon palled on me, however. It became, after a time, distressingly monotonous to trudge through gloomy covered side-walks, in which scarcely any shops were open, and to meet nobody but men in togas who scowled on you and pug-nosed women with large feet. There is certainly no excess on the side of gracefulness among the female population of Bologna. I mean the women of the humbler classes. The Bolognese ladies were not "on hand." It was too early for them—this reflection occurred to me shortly before noon—or perhaps they were at mass. At length, in sheer despair at the shut-up shops and the sparseness of humanity, the absence of poodle dogs and the perpetually jingling tramway car bells, I did a deed which, under ordinary circumstances, my soul abhors. I went sight-seeing. I hailed a hackney carriage, and informed the driver that I should require his services for a period of one hour, or, possibly, of one hour and a half. This hackney driver was, perhaps, the most genial, and, at the same time, the most impudent, character that I had met with during my journeyings. When I mentioned an hour and a half as the maximum term of our engagement, he smiled with an air of gentle derision and made answer that I meant three hours and a half. In stern accents I repeated my former observation and bade him drive to the Duomo. His back being towards me I could not tell whether he smiled again, but from the wriggling of his shoulders I inferred that he was still in a merry mood; and, as he urged his horse to speed, I heard him say cheerfully, "We shall see, we shall see."

We did see; and among the sights one at least most unexpected by me. We followed the Via Ugo Bassi, a long street leading from the Hôtel Brun to the heart of the ancient city, and which has been re-named after one of the Italian patriots of 1848. Of course the great central entrance, the Piazza Maggiore, has also been re-christened. It is now the Piazza Vittorio Emanuele. It should be intensely and magnificently mediæval, and through its commanding vistas of mediæval splendour should be dimly visible the phantom of its yet more antique aspect as the indubitable forum of a Roman city; but its scenic and historic aspect has been utterly and irremediably spoilt by the intolerable tramway lines which here converge, and by the hideous cars of which the Piazza Vittorio Emanuele is the central starting point. I am perfectly well aware that it is useless to protest against tramway cars in the populous cities of this once beauteous land. I am as well aware that, in the course of a year or so, gondolas on the Grand Canal at Venice will be superseded by penny steamers. Every age has its requirements, and those requirements must be satisfied. The beautiful and useless must bow the head before the barbarous and useful. If the Torre Pendente, at Pisa, were to go by the board some fine morning, the Italians would never think of building it up again as a Leaning Tower. In greater probability, they would utilise the site for the erection of a soap or a macaroni manufactory, with a tall brick shaft faultlessly adhering to the perpendicular line.

This Piazza Maggiore, at Bologna, was no doubt, in the days of old, a superbly handsome area. John Evelyn, who knew something about architecture, considered it to be, with the exception of St. Mark's, the most superb piazza in Italy. The Fontana Pubblica, surmounted by a statue which is one of the finest works of the famous sculptor Giovanni di Bologna, and which cost seventy thousand golden crowns, has scarcely, as a fountain, its equal even in Rome. Then, in front of you, looms immense the Cathedral of San Petronio, a sublime specimen of the Italian pointed architecture of the fourteenth century. The effect of the wondrous bas reliefs in the three canopied doorways of the façade is altogether ruined by the propinquity of those accursed and highly-convenient tramway cars. The colossal pile called the Palazzo del Governo, once the residence of the Papal Legates and of the Senators of Bologna, is now partially occupied by the bureaux of the municipality and by the Royal Post-office. The Palazzo del Podestà, which was begun nearly seven hundred years ago, and is yet unfinished, affords accommodation for the offices of receivers of taxes and the administration of the "Regia" of salt and tobacco. Opposite is the Portico de' Banchi, occupying one entire side of the Piazza, and, as the Loggie del Pavaglione, continued along the entire length of the Church of San Petronio, forming an unbroken arcade a thousand feet long. This masterpiece of the illustrious architect Vignola has its frontage defaced by all kinds of mean shop signs and quack placards.

How is all this to be helped? I conceive that it cannot be helped. Italy has become a country for the Italians, who, it would seem, are entitled to do what they like with their own, and are certainly not bound to place their monuments under glass cases, to be stared at by the *forestieri* at so much a head. The fact is, I suppose, that from that which was once the home of Romance everything which is Romantic is swiftly departing. It may grieve many to hear that Italy is growing uglier every day; but it may gratify others to learn that a country which was once the untidiest in Europe is daily becoming cleaner and more industrious, and, consequently, more prosperous. Hideous as Bologna, as Pisa, as Milan, as Imperial Rome herself has been made by tramway cars, it is impossible to deny that the people who flock to ride in these unpicturesque vehicles are cleaner and better dressed, and look better fed, than the Italians whom I remember twenty and fifteen and even ten years ago.

XV.

A DAY OF THE DEAD.

BOLOGNA, *November* 15.

YES, I went sight-seeing that bitter November Sunday at Bologna; and I confess that on the whole I enjoyed the prolonged round of pictorial and archæological shows no more than, I fancy, I should have enjoyed Trimalcion's banquet. How oppressively wearisome that symposium must have appeared to a guest who halted on this side of being an inordinate glutton, and who was doomed to behold and to inhale the fumes, even if he escaped partaking, of the multitudinous array of hors d'œuvres, removes, entrées, roasts, and entremets which stretched in an intolerable line of gormandising between the bringing in of the egg and the coming on of the apple! An analogous feeling of jaded satiety may even nowadays be experienced by the person who is bidden to dine with the Worshipful Company of Knife Grinders at their sumptuous hall in Whetstone Park-lane. It is the grandest of imaginable feasts, prepared by a *chef* as cunning as Trypherus of old; only it seems as though it would never come to an end. Sometimes you begin to indulge in a faint hope that you are "through," that the cloth will speedily be drawn, and the loving cup make its appearance; but you have reckoned without your host, and the protracted repast breaks out again in a fresh place—now with a truffle roasted whole, and now with some ruffs and reeves: now with a Spanish ham served with *garbanzos*, and now with a "warden pie," the recipe for which has been in the possession of the Court of the Worshipful Company of Knife Grinders for the last four hundred and fifty years. What would have become of you had you tasted of all the dainties which obsequious waiters had been pressing on you during the last two hours, or had you listened to the blandishments of the bald-headed butler with his bland whispers about '47 port and Sunnyside Madeira, about Schloss Johannisberg, and Imperial Tokay? Of course you have been duly impressed with the general grandeur of the festival, the richness of the viands, the rarity of the vintages, the fragrance of the flowers, the glittering sheen of the Worshipful Company's plate, and the sonorous voices of the gentlemen from the Temple Choir, who sang "Non Nobis Domine" before the dessert and the speechmaking began; but, in fine, when the convivial pageant has come to an end, and the Worshipful Company's beadle has presented you, as a parting gift, with a highly-ornamental casket full of chocolate creams and candied greengages, are you much better off than if you had dined heartily on boiled leg of mutton with turnips and caper sauce?

I questioned myself, in somewhat similar spirit, at the end of two hours' sight-seeing at Bologna. Had I profited aught by staring at all these things? Had I brought away anything tangible—even the equivalent of the beadle's box of sweetmeats—from this overwhelming banquet of art and antiquity? I am afraid that I had not. From church to church, from palace to palace, from tower to tower, from gallery to gallery, had I wandered, the cunning hack-driver always inveigling me with fresh promises of something very wonderful to be seen round the corner. Bologna is all corners and dark arches, with masterpieces at the extremities thereof, and back staircases, and other mysteries. Your head gets full of a "galimatias" of saints, of pictures of martyrs broiled and martyrs roasted, and martyrs skinned alive, of shavenpated monks, and fat-faced cherubs and angels playing on the violoncello. The Bolognese school of painting is doubtless very grand, but it is slightly too robust for me. You become terrified at last at Simoni di Crocifissi's vast anatomical knowledge and the violent osteology and myology of Pellegrino Tibaldi, who is suggestive of a kind of nightmare of Michael Angelo. The meekly devotional Francia soothes you for a while; but after a little you are thrown into dire perturbation again by the tremendous turbulence of the Caracci—Ludovico and his cousins Agostino and Annibale, the Three Bounding Brothers of a Babylonish art—acrobats of the easel, gymnasts in form and colour, taking the most surprising leaps, and generally alarming and perplexing you till a little rest and peace are found in the contemplation of the calmly grand and serene work of Domenichino and of Guido Reni.

But, if you could live a year at Bologna, and quaff your wine as Béranger counsels you to quaff it, "à petits coups," you would not find the cup overcharged: nor would the liquor mount to your brain. It is having to see so much in so short a time that disturbs and half maddens you; for it makes havoc, for the nonce, of your memory; and when memory is absent perfect sanity for the moment cannot be said to exist. I was heartily glad and grateful when the driver deposited me at the gateway of the Accademia delle Belle Arti, which is installed in the premises of a suppressed Jesuit monastery, and when, on ascending the staircase leading to the Pinacoteca, or picture gallery, the civil guardian told me that the hour was twenty minutes to three, and that at three precisely the gallery closed "irrevocably." I felt relieved. It was pictorially dinner-time, and I determined to dine on one dish. Not for me the prodigious productions of the Caracci. Not for me even the Guidos, the Domenichinos, and the Guercinos. The picture on which I had resolved to feast should be, I knew from my catalogue, in the sixth room; but, when I sought it, I found, to my dismay, that the pictures in the collection were in course of re-arrangement, and that the masterpieces in particular were, for the time being, in a topsy-turvy condition as regarded enumeration.

I sought the aid of the civil guardian, and he kindly set me in the right path. I found my dinner—I mean my picture—in a side room, on an easel. It was the world-famous Rafaelle—the Santa Cecilia in ecstasy on hearing the heavenly music of the Angelic Choir, and surrounded by St. Paul, St. John the Evangelist, St. Augustine, and St. Mary Magdalene. It was enough for twenty minutes' enjoyment. It would have been enough for a day, for a week, for a month. The picture, like most of the masterpieces stolen by the First Napoleon, and removed to the Louvre, has been under the paw of the French restorer, and has even, I believe, been transferred from panel to canvas; but neither the drawing nor the expression has lost in the process of restoration. One should be thankful for the beneficence of photography, which enables you to purchase for a few francs either a copy of the picture itself or a fac-simile of the exquisite line engraving taken from it. Forty years ago the engraving would be found only in the portfolio of the wealthy amateur, and all that the common people in England knew about Rafaelle's St. Cecilia would have been from a rude woodcut in the "Penny Magazine."

There was to be no more sightseeing, I told the hackdriver, when I emerged from the Accademia. As it was, I had overstayed by a full hour the maximum which I had fixed. No more sightseeing! The artful charioteer got up a spasm of simulated surprise. It was unheard of. It was disastrous. It was deplorable—nay, monstrous. Surely the Excellency could not leave Bologna without seeing its most ancient and most interesting ecclesiastical edifice—San Stefano of the Seven Churches. There were there seven wonders of the world under one roof. Sulkily I allowed the cunning charioteer to hold me with his glittering eye; and he drove me through the streets—now more silent and deserted than ever—to San Stefano. In the Seven Churches I counted just twenty women, mostly of the humbler classes, at different altars, praying. The churches, I was told, were served by no less than thirty secular priests, but not a single cleric was visible.

On the other hand, a peculiarly mouldy old lady, with a *fazzoletto* of the hue of a pickled cabbage twisted round her head, introduced me to a verger in a rustly black gown, who, in his turn, presented me to a most affable old gentleman in a black velveteen waistcoat, profusely decorated with mother-o'-pearl buttons, and he, in good time, made me known to a plump little sacristan, with a headdress remarkably like one of the iron extinguishers which, secured to the railings of a few old-fashioned mansions near Grosvenor Square, yet recall the days when there were running footmen and link-boys in the land. These acquaintances all meant as a final cause the administration of a *buonamano* or *backshish* ; but ah ! on so modest a scale. The sacristan with the extinguisher cap made me at least twenty bows for the couple of lire which I slipped into his hand; and the old lady with the pickle-cabbage *coiffure* looked as pleased as Punch for a donation of fifty centesimi, or fourpence three-farthings sterling. They all had their several parts of the wonderful old building to show, and were as gently and persuasively voluble as it is the gift of Italian *ciceroni* to be. The French guide is only tolerable when he is an old soldier ; and the French sacristan is either pompously taciturn or disagreeably garrulous, when he half deafens you with his impertinences.

As for San Stefano of the Seven Churches, it is certainly, next to the Mesquita, at Cordova, about the most amazing olla-podrida of ancient and moyenage architecture that I have ever beheld. That which was originally and undoubtedly an ancient Roman basilica has been, in successive ages, cut up into a wilderness of sectional "risks," as Captain Shaw would call them, and amidst all these corridors and cloisters and crypts, these naves and aisles and transepts, these apses and chancels and side chapels, the Seven Churches have, I suppose, a several and distinct existence. There might have been seventy for aught that I could tell. Had I given a day to the exploration of each church I might have been a little more enlightened. As it was I could not but take note of the to me edifying fact that, in this extraordinary jumbling of architectonic forms, the Bolognese had once more gratified that which appears their traditional propensity for seeing everything through an arch, darkly. The intersection of archways is something wonderful to behold.

For the rest, all is confusion, as the Campo Santo at Pisa, between classicalism and mediævalism. The ashes of highborn dames of the Cinque Cento period moulder in antique Roman sarcophagi. The Church of the Santo Sepolcro, supposed to be a Lombard Baptistery of the twelfth century, has its roof supported by marble columns, reputed to have come from an ancient Temple of Isis. One of the churches, founded by San Faustiniano in the fourth century, has a quantity of Roman materials built into its walls. In a room called the Atrium of Pilate, the sacristan told me some wondrous tales; but they would read more fitly in the pages of Alban Butler than in these. The heterogeneous aspect of this labyrinth of brick walls and stone arches is aggravated by a multiplicity of pictures, some of them gems of art, others the merest daubs; by half-effaced frescoes of saints and martyrs peeping through whitewash; by rough mosaics in coloured brickwork and exquisitely-enamelled reliquaries; by sumptuously-carved panels and benches, and by tawdry tinselled figures and wreaths of artificial flowers.

Of treasures in the way of plate and jewels I saw nothing. Napoleon and his hungry and ragged heroes were here at the close of the last century; and recalling that circumstance I remembered the indignant and slightly turgid language of Edmund Burke, "The Pontiff has seen his free, fertile, and happy city and state of Bologna, the cradle of regenerated law, the seat of sciences and of arts, the chosen spot of plenty and delight, converted into a Jacobin ferocious republic dependent on the homicides of France." It is undeniable that Napoleon the Great had an illimitable capacity for stealing plate and pictures. The traces of the crowbar, the centrebit, and the "jemmy" of this most burglarious of Cæsars are yet visible all over Italy and Spain.

But I emerged from San Stefano, dazed and dizzy, and authoritatively informed the artful hackney man that my career of sight-seeing had come to an end. On the contrary, he confidently replied. There remained to be seen a spectacle which did I omit to witness it would be in my memory a perpetual reproach and remorse to me. It was impossible that I could return to my esteemed country and honoured family without seeing this sight, which, moreover, was only on view once a year. This happened to be the Day of the Dead in Bologna; and he must positively have the honour of driving me out to the Campo Santo. It was a *festa*, a high day and holiday, and the entire population of Bologna would be there. I had seen so very few human beings during the exceptionally miserable morning and afternoon that I could not say the cunning man nay. So he had his will of me; and "Via!" for the Campo Santo.

The public cemetery of Bologna is situated at about a mile and a half from the Porta Isaia, on the west side of the city. As we drove out to it along a narrow but well-kept road, through a fat hemp and flax-growing country—they grow hemp enough about Bologna to hang half the rogues in Christendom—there came over me an odd impression to the effect that this was no Italian November Sunday, but the last Wednesday in an English May, and that I was going under the certainly shabby circumstances of a "one-horse shay," but still going, to the Derby. I have known many Derbies that were cold and comfortless. Other roads converged into the main highway, and they were all densely crowded with vehicles and with pedestrians. There were a few broughams and barouches; but the great majority of the carriages were open victorias or "one-horse shays," designed to carry at the utmost three passengers, but very frequently containing six or eight, or, inclusive of small children, ten or twelve.

You have seen in a reality, or in a picture, a Neapolitan *calescino*. It is a kind of high perched curricle between two very big wheels. A ragged man, not unlike a Connemara bog-trotter, drives; and the cargo of humanity heaped up on the *calescino* comprises a very corpulent priest with a shovel hat and a huge crimson umbrella tucked under his arm, a couple of gentlemen so picturesque in appearance as to look suspiciously like the brothers of Fra Diavolo or the cousins of Pascal Bruno, a deformed cripple without arms and legs, who, it is to be supposed, pays a proportionately diminished quota of the fare, a stout matron, a white-headed patriarch of eighty, two strapping damsels of eighteen, and an indefinite number of brats and babies. Two or three free and independent lazzaroni hang on behind this chariot, which is drawn by one wretched little horse with a bunch of feathers in his head-stall.

This is the way in which a *calescino* used to travel from Naples to Torre del Greco; and, in degree, this was the way in which the Bolognese victorias were journeying to the Campo Santo. Nobody that I could see was in mourning; and the men all seemed to be smoking, and the women and children laughing. As we neared the cemetery the road became more and more like the road to Epsom, or to a fair. There were sellers of fruit and flowers, of baked apples and roasted chestnuts, the season for which last edibles has just begun, and of which the Bolognese are amazingly fond. The demand for very greasy-looking pies, tartlets, and cakes was seemingly unappeasable, and the consumption of lollipops phenomenal. Rudely-printed ballads of the popular or "Catnach" order were being vended at a few centesimi a yard; and there was a brisk business done in dream-books and Oracles of Fate, with a view to lucky combinations of numbers to be backed in next week's lottery. There was nothing to suggest that this was the solemn anniversary on which the people were accustomed to visit the graves of their kindred and their friends—nothing beyond a few stentorian lunged fellows with tiers upon tiers of wreaths of yellow immortelles on their arms, noisily bawling out their wares.

It was now close upon four o'clock; and this strange carnival,

I was told, had been going on since early morning. As we neared the great gate of the cemetery the crowd had assumed the dimensions of a dense mass of humanity, slowly surging onward, to all appearance imperturbably good-humoured, and very easily kept in order by certainly not more than a dozen agents "di pubblica sicurezza," or "capelloni"—"tall-hat" wearers, as, from their exaggerated "stove-pipe" head-gear, they are more popularly called. These municipal functionaries wear also a long double-breasted surtout of stout black cloth with metallic buttons, reaching nearly to their heels, and they carry long bamboo canes with metal knobs. I was gravely informed that, in organisation as well as in uniform, the worthy fellows exactly resembled our British policeman; but the Italian authorities seem to have selected an English police-constable of the last generation for their model, and to be totally unaware that the force have long since had their "chimney-pot" hats replaced by shapely helmets.

The buildings of the Campo Santo of Bologna belonged in olden time to a foundation of Carthusian monks, and their disestablished monastery is still familiarly known as the Certosa. The monks were turned out of their dwelling in 1797; and 1801 the place was consecrated as a public cemetery: one of the first acts of that *régime* which Mr. Burke styled furious and Jacobinical and homicidal being utterly to prohibit intramural interments. In our own highly conservative country intramural interments were not forbidden until the year 1850. In making excavations for the catacombs of the new Campo Santo, extensive remains were found of the ancient Etruscan cemetery of Felsina. Most of the tombs, the skeletons, and the relics in glass, bronze, and the precious metals found here have been 'removed to the new Museo Civico; but a few of the Etruscan tombs have been purposely left at the Certosa, with the intention of constituting a link between the present and the past. The link is further strengthened by several Roman tombs, bas-reliefs, and mural inscriptions of the Imperial period, and by some highly interesting Renaissance monuments left in the forecourt of the old monastery. Among these are the marble effigies of illustrious members of the Malvezzi, the Romanzi, and the Zambeccari families, wonderfully elaborate specimens of decorative statuary.

The transition from these vestiges of the Prehistoric, the Roman, and the Mediæval eras to mortuary mementoes of the present century and our own actual time is indeed strange. The cloisters of the Carthusians have been prolonged on every side by vast halls, the roofs supported by marble columns, and here again the Bolognese have been able to gratify their insatiable passion for arcades. These halls are all catacombs, the dead lying on shelves one above the other, and the mouths of the sepulchres securely walled up by marble tablets containing some noble and pathetic and a great many stilted and nonsensical inscriptions. Many of the niches are family tombs, still awaiting occupants, and their fronts bear simply the owner's name and the reminder, "Sibi et Suis."

On this Day of the Dead, before hundreds of the tombs, lighted lamps and tapers were burning; while the marble pavement was thickly strewn with crosses, wreaths, and bouquets of brilliant flowers, placed there to mark the resting-place of those interred beneath. The care taken by the enormous crowd to avoid treading on these floral tributes was very admirable and beautiful to see. Otherwise the multitude seemed to be rather in a jocular than in a mournful temper; and appeared to look on this Day of the Dead as a merry festival, and not as a season for grief and lamentation. Possibly the people of old Bononia, and older still Felsina, were accustomed to keep their Days of the Dead in a similarly mirthful mood.

As for the statuary tombs lining the centres of the arcades, and in places grouped together under a cupola so as to form a kind of Pantheon, they are so numerous, and mainly in such very poor modern Italian and sham classical taste, as to remind one of nothing half so much as of a tombstone-sculptor's yard in the Euston Road. Some of these effigies are so vapid and so meretricious that you almost expect—on turning a corner—to come upon a replica of the "Veiled Slave" or of the inevitable "Bather" who haunted you so at Pisa. The majority of these effigies had wreaths of flowers or of immortelles hung round them, or floral crosses piled around their bases. In numerous instances a curious survival of an ancient Roman funerary custom was visible in the shape of tablets bearing the life-sized photographic portraits, garishly framed, of the deceased.

In front of one statuesque monument I lingered for a good many minutes. On a pedestal of the purest Carrara marble was graven in low relief a female head adorned with those clustering ringlets which were fashionable about forty years ago. The inscription beneath recited that this was the tomb of the Marchioness Pepoli, and that her sons, anticipating her wish, had reared above her grave the marble image of her father whom she loved so well. Then I remembered whose daughter the Marchioness Pepoli was; and, looking up, I beheld, heroic of stature, audaciously handsome of mien, luxuriant in ringlet and whisker and moustache, the statue of the warrior of " the snow-white plume, Whose realm refused him e'en a tomb." He stands in full hussar uniform, with richly embroidered dolman, with sabretasche and sabre trailing as his side, with spurs on his heels, and in his right hand a little lithe riding-whip. Waving that whip, he was wont to lead his squadrons to battle; but the sculptor, in subtle cunning of suggestiveness, had made the hand that held the whip to point downwards to where, at the feet, were an eagle and a Royal crown. And then I remembered that in the days when this man sate upon a throne he used to keep in one of the saloons of his palace at Capo di Monte, on a cushion of crimson velvet under a glass shade, a common postillion's whip; and that he was wont to point out this instrument to his friends, and to say laughingly, "Je suis venu de là "—I sprang from that. He had been, indeed, a common postillion at an inn near Avignon; and was not ashamed of his origin when Joachim Murat had become Grand Duke of Berg and King of Naples.

Now and again I looked out of the great barred windows at the ends of the arcades on to the great expanse of greensward surrounded by the cloisters. In these areas the poor folk are buried. The turf was dotted by multitudes of humble little wooden crosses : but round many of them were wreaths, and some had little tapers twinkling before them, where poorly-clad women and children were kneeling on the grass. There were a good many sore hearts there, perhaps, beating not altogether in unison with those of the mob of merrymakers in the grand arcades of the prattling Campo Santo.

XVI.

VENICE PRESERVED?

VENICE, *November* 20.

I HAVE appended a note of interrogation to the title of this chapter, because in the first place one cannot be certain about anything; and in the next, because there may be considerable differences of opinion among recent visitors to Venice respecting the precise state of preservation, or the contrary, in which the Queen of the Adriatic happens to be at present. For example, I was told at the very comfortable hotel which used to be Barbesi's, on the Grand Canal, over against the Church of Santa Maria della Salute, that, for many years past, Venice had not been so brilliantly prosperous as had been the case during the tourist season which had recently come to a close. The same gratifying tale was related to me when I went to call on a friend at the historic Danieli's, on the Riva de' Schiavoni, and my ears were saluted by similar pleasant tidings conveyed to me by sundry intelligent tradesmen keeping shops for the sale of photographs, beads, and Murano glass nick-nacks on St. Mark's Place. They were doing nothing now, they candidly admitted—could they show me any more selenographs, any more pelerines of seed-pearls, any more picture frames apparently formed of vitrified lollypops? Certainly the season just terminated had been a wonderful, a deliriously exciting, a superlatively excellent one. Never, perhaps, might Venice behold such a season again; and this last remark was uttered with something like a sigh.

The fact is that a Geographical Congress had been meeting at Venice, and the session of the *savants* had attracted a crowd of visitors, with plenty of money in their pockets, not only from outlying Italy, but from all parts of Europe. For a short time the hotels had been full to repletion; some of the shops on the Piazza San Marco had made wonderful sales, and Florian's, the Specchi, and the other world-famed cafés had had plenty of customers. So the landlords and the waiters, the shopkeepers and the *valets de place*, had all had reason to rejoice greatly; but, as I heard their gladsome accounts of the halcyon time—not unmingled with melancholy at the remembrance that the time had come to an end—I could not help reflecting that the people who had made money out of the deliriously exciting, the superlatively excellent season of the Geographical Congress must be reckoned by scores, or at the most by hundreds, and that the population of Venice is close upon a hundred and thirty thousand, made up of a people who, as a rule, belong to the non-productive classes.

There are to me two delightful ways of entering Venice. The first is to approach it by the railway from Mestre, late at night; the second is to come upon it by the steamer from Trieste at early morning. In the last case, if the morning be fine, the view which you obtain of the city is almost supernaturally enchanting. The cobalt blue of the sky should match exactly with the cobalt blue of the Adriatic Sea; so that Venice itself should have the appearance of being suspended in mid-air—a glorious mirage gilded by the rays of the young sun. When I say that, beholding Venice thus from the steamer's deck, it seems as though you could cover the whole prospect—the Ducal Palace, the Riva de' Schiavoni, the Giardini Pubblici, the Piazzetta, the Campanile, the Royal Palace, the Salute, the Dogana, and San Giorgio Maggiore—" with a pocket-handkerchief," there is in my mind less the remembrance of a well-known sporting expression applying to the competitors at a horse-race lying very closely together as they run, than the more recent memory of having recently seen, fluttering from a linendraper's doorpost in the Merceria a number of cotton pocket-handkerchiefs, price fifty centesimi, or fourpence-halfpenny each, on which were printed in a lively pink pigment bird's-eye views of Venice. This is a city in which the picturesque and the prosaic are most whimsically intermingled. Few things had you ever beheld so exquisitely lovely as that rose-coloured vision of a city tipped with golden sunshine and embosomed in the blue sky and the blue sea; yet here was another pink Venice, undeniably gay in its colouring and tolerably accurate in its perspective, possibly printed at Manchester, and decidedly cheap at fourpence halfpenny.

To behold, however, the real Venice from an incoming steamer's deck implies a visit to Trieste, which is at the best of times a far from agreeable city, and when the "Bora" is blowing is an outrageously disagreeable one. On the whole I was glad that I came in at night, and very late, by rail from the mainland. The Venice train left Bologna, or rather should have left that affluent and austere city, at five in the afternoon, and, according to the *orario*, we should have reached our destination by ten o'clock; but punctuality is not one of the virtues that the modern Italians have acquired. Time, we have all been told, is meant for slaves, and it may be that, now the Italians have become altogether a free people, they disdain the servile obligation to keep time on their railways. So it was midnight ere we crossed the causeway from Mestre, and were safely landed at the Venice terminus.

I had made, also, a mistake in my train, and instead of taking the express, found myself, to my dismay, in an "omnibus" train, which meant that it blundered on with painful slowness, stopped at every station, and was continually crowded with fresh parties travelling short distances. One group of "short-timers," who joined us, I think, at Padua, and left us at Ponte di Brenta, I shall not readily forget. They were five in number: a handsome dark lady of matronly age; a handsome and younger matronly lady; two very pretty girls with many-caped ulsters, Gainsborough hats, kilted skirts, Balmoral hosiery, and all the paraphernalia of the modern Italian belle, who, but for her gloriously flashing black eyes, might be mistaken for one of Mr. Du Maurier's Notting Hill houris or Haverstock Hill Helens, and a corpulent little girl of six, who, having in view her general viciousness and "cantankerousness," might have been sixty and Mother —— well, Mother Shipton to boot. I have rarely met with such a fiendish little girl; not even in the United States, where fiend-children abound, and where, travelling per Pullman, your slumbers are disturbed by terrific dreams that you have murdered the Sleeping-Car Baby. To those dreams, however, pleasanter visions may succeed. You may dream of being tried for killing the Sleeping-Car Baby, and of a jury of fellow-sufferers unanimously and enthusiastically bringing in a verdict of justifiable homicide.

The grown-up members of the group that joined us at Padua were, I apprehend, the mamma, the grandmamma, and the aunts or cousins of the little fat child, whose name I gathered was Paolina. They all made much of her, and loaded her with caresses and sweetmeats—the last produced from a large number of bags and reticules of various shapes and sizes. The Italians are, when travelling, a wonderfully marsupial race; and I fancy that one reason for the multiplicity of pouches and wallets with which they cram railway compartments, and which are continually tumbling about the carriage—sometimes on your head—is the extortionately high tariff of charges exacted by the railway companies for the conveyance of luggage. On some of the lines also they have a bad habit of breaking open your trunks and portmanteaus *en route*, and stealing whatever valuables may be among the contents. Madame de Metternich lost quite recently, in this manner, a large quantity of precious jewellery, and the thieves, it was discovered, were in the employ of the railway company.

Paolina was the mistress, tyrant, and oppressor of her parent, her grandparent, and her remaining female relatives.

She repulsed their caresses as well as she could with her pudgy little hands; nor was she backward, in the same intent, in using her mites of feet. She ate as much sweet-stuff as ever she inconveniently could, and then she howled because she could not eat any more. There had been some *festa* in the neighbourhood which Paolina and her grown-up kindred had attended, and the ladies were full of the praises of St. Somebody and the local clergy. They had brought, as well as the sweetstuff, a superabundance of cheap toys from the *festa*, all on account of Paolina; and she destroyed at least a lira and a half's worth of playthings during her short journey. I see her now, a sullen, sticky, wrathful child, clutching a paper-bagful of the Italian substitute for brandy-balls in one hand and a headless doll in the other. That doll's head she had wrenched off ere we steamed out of Padua Station. On no feminine knee would she remain quietly, and on no male toes did she refrain from treading. I tried my best to conciliate her; but she repelled my advances scornfully. I asked her to give me a brandy-ball; but she sulkily declined to do so. Now, ninety-nine children out of a hundred, to the very tiniest, will give you of the "goodies" of which they are eating. The little hand that has scarcely cunning in it, yet, to hold the toffy or the hardbake securely will stretch it forth to the stranger who asks a dole.

Paolina didn't see it. She was one of the extremely few children that I have met with in the course of a roving life at whom I should have liked dearly to "make faces." I was heartily glad when the little wretch and her belongings went away at Ponte di Brenta; and more glad when I noted that the liveried footman of the family—they were evidently people of some consequence—who opened the door of the compartment, and touching his hat, announced that the carriage was waiting, was about the ugliest servitor, liberally marked with the small-pox, and with a huge pair of blacking-brush whiskers, that I had seen for many years. I was glad; for I fancied that, when Paolina had an exceptionally acute attack of viciousness, the ugly footman might be utilised as Bogey, and frighten her a little. I did not fail to observe that her mamma and her grandmamma frequently spoke of her as an "Angeletta." Well, she may have been normally a little angel, only I had been so unfortunate as to make her acquaintance on one of her non-angelic evenings. Anger transforms us all; and does not the Roman poet tell us that a radically bad temper was the cause of all the woes of Thyestes?

They all went away into the dark night—the nice people and the people who were not nice; the noisy people and the quiet ones; the gentleman with a cough, who insisted on having both windows up; the gentleman with a temper—it was mild and meek in comparison with Paolina's, though—who violently pulled both windows down. It was good at length to find yourself alone in the carriage, the lamp in the roof throwing dimly fantastic shadows around. Dolo, Mestre; and then, two miles further, and you know that you have entered upon the Lagoons and that the train is putting out to sea. The darkest of nights, but quite calm and still. Not more than once in two minutes can you discern a light faintly flickering in the casement of some island cottage. Now you are fairly out on the water; and full ten minutes pass, with total darkness without. Not a breath of wind is stirring. Presently you discern the horizon bounded by a long line of pale light sending a paler reflex to the sky. Instant by instant the glow grows broader and more brilliant. The train touches land at the island of Santa Lucia. A minute's more semi-darkness as you rattle through what may be called the slums of the station—by engine-sheds, luggage trains, store-houses, signalmen's huts, and the like—and then you are in Venice, and one of the noisiest and most inconveniently crowded railway termini in Italy.

It is quite a purgatorial passage, that jostling of your way through the mob of touting hotel porters and gesticulating *facchini* to the quay of the canal. When you have secured your gondola you have to wait an unconscionable time before your luggage is brought down to the water-side, and to pay an unconscionable number of small fees before your gondolier finally makes play with his oar, and wafts you—yes, "wafts" is the word—to the heart of that Bella Venezia which you have known so well, and which you love so dearly. Again, you have the inestimable boon of a full half-hour's peace and darkness before you reach your hostelry on the Grand Canal, hard by the Palazzo Reale. It is on the Grand Canal, and so is the railway terminus; but a full hour would be consumed were your gondolier to follow the course of the Canalazzo, of which the form is that of an inverted S, throughout is length. So "the hansom cabman of the sea" makes unexpected turns, and takes cunningly short cuts, and conducts you up all manner of strange streets or canals. Sometimes you begin to grow slightly dubious as to whether he may not be rowing you back to the Lagoons again, or even, by a back way, to the Lido, there to sell you and your belongings to potential pirates from Barbary; but the gondolier knows his way thoroughly well, as his fathers before him have known it for ages; and while you are wondering in what kind of watery Seven Dials labyrinth he is disporting, he brings you on to the Grand Canal again, but only for a spell; for there are more cunning short cuts to be made, and more windings of the Canalazzo to avoid.

Few things are there more pleasant to one accustomed to the ways of the City on the Sea than this gondola voyage alone, and late in the night. You have, to begin with, a feeling of perfect ease and security. You know that the gondolier has been rowing ever since he was a boy, and that probably the oar has been a bread-winner in his family for the last five hundred years. Why not a thousand? You are certain, humanly speaking, that there is not going to be a collision between your gondola and another. You are as certain that the gondolier has in reality not the slightest intention of selling you and your portmanteau to the potential and mythical Barbary pirates, or of robbing you of your watch and chain and flinging you into the Grand Canal. That kind of thing is not done in Venice. The gondoliers are a traditionally honest, civil, and gentle race; and, on the whole, apart from a great deal of begging and a little pilfering among the lowest class of the population, Venice is about as innocent a city for its size as can be found in Europe. Finally, in your narrow little caboose of the gondola after midnight, you feel quite cheerful and quite at ease, because you know that at the bourne whither you are bound you will find brilliantly-lighted rooms, tasteful comfort, civil attendance, and good cheer. Venice is a city where it is never too late to get some supper; and I was cheerfully reminded of that reassuring fact when I sate down at one a.m. to an excellent potage, and was aware that a chicken was being broiled and potatoes sautéd; but had even an hotel supper failed me I could have gone to Florian's. Has not that renowned caffé been open night and day ever since the time of Marino Faliero? We used to say so in days gone by.

Was it for the reason that we had only the most meagre allowance of sunshine, and that the temperature was cold and raw, during my five days' stay in Venice, that I was induced to think the city altered, and for the worse? We are all creatures of circumstance, and it is obvious that colour has a great deal to do with our appreciation of various countries, and especially of cities. For example, the architectural splendour of St. Petersburg has been very much overrated. Izaak's Cathedral is colossal but lumbering in form, and for all its hugeness relatively squat; the remaining public buildings are mainly of the barrack order; and at the utmost Petropolis can only be considered structurally as Berlin's big brother. In summer-time, however, St. Petersburg is a city of most beauteous colour. The hue of the Neva is pure ultramarine; the islands on the river are delicious spots of verdure; the marble façades of the palaces glisten like basalt in the sun; the caftans, sashes, and headdresses of the people are variegated in tint; and, above all, the gilded domes, cupolas, and spires with which the city abounds, flashing diamond-bright at noon, but in the sunset, glowing with crimson and orange, purple, and even apple-green tints, give an Oriental and fantastic aspect to the whole place, ravishing to the view.

Constantinople is about the dirtiest hole in uncivilised Europe; its finest public building is St. Sophia, which was erected, not by the Turks, but by the Christian Emperor Justinian; yet Stamboul and Pera, from the Golden Horn and the Bosphorus, with their abundant wealth of colour, and under the influence of bright sunshine, look supremely lovely. It is only when you land that you discover that you would have done much better to have remained on shipboard and returned to Malta or to Marseilles with the least possible delay.

The chief cities of the United States are liberally provided with imposing public edifices, which it has taken many millions of dollars to build; yet in the whole of the Great Republic the eye that seeks for colour can only be gratified by two patches of rural scenery—on the banks of the Hudson River between New York and Albany, and in the hills of Vermont, which in autumn are so many delightful replicas of our Clifton and our Wharfedale, and by two cities, New Orleans and San Francisco. The Pacific slope has a prismatic charm of its own; while sub-tropical vegetation, orange and bananas, cypress and myrtle, in all their affluence of gay and sombre tones, make beautiful the capital of Louisiana, which architecturally is not handsome, and topographically is built in a half-moon-shaped trench below the level of the muddy Mississippi, with an immense swamp in its rear.

P

Now Venice is, architecturally, a marvel of marvels. Every façade is a study; every soffit and spandril, glowing with mosaic, is a thing to be rapturous over. But—it does not matter whether I am a Philistine or not—I merely wish for the nonce to change minds with the ordinary British travelling Philistine who has never read the "Seven Lamps of Architecture," and who scarcely knows the difference between Byzantine and Florentine mosaic, or between Florentine and Roman. Venice, to be thoroughly enjoyable, wants plenty of sunshine, because sunshine means largely distributed masses of light and shade; and in local colour Venice is sadly deficient. I mean that there is scarcely any vegetation, that there are few white houses, and that the costumes of the people are no longer picturesque. One great element of picturesqueness has been taken away from the city by the disappearance of the "Tedeschi." The white uniforms and gold embroidery of the Austrian officers gave charming variety of hue to the dark masses for ever struggling, like the souls in the Halls of Eblis in Beckford's "Vathek," through the tortuous alleys of the Merceria; but Italian independence is of slightly too much value to be surrendered in order that pictorial Venice might get back a certain number of Austrian staff-officers, Croat grenadiers, and Hungarian hussars to enliven with their gay costumes the sadly-clad masses of the population.

It has been indeed my lot to see out-door Venice as dazzlingly radiant in colour as though a Titian, a Paul Veronese, a Giorgione, or a Tintoretto had had the ordinance of her pageants. I was here when, after the war of 1866, and the cession of the Dominio Veneto to France—which, through the interme-

ST. MARK'S PLACE, VENICE.

P. 223.

diary of Bazaine, handed it over to Italy—Victor Emmanuel entered Venice at the head of the Italian troops. On the day of the Royal entry the old sumptuary observance by virtue of which the Venetian gondolas look like so many floating hearses was suspended, and the Canalazzo was covered by barques and shallops and barges of mediæval form, glowing with gilding and gay colours, and with the rowers dressed in splendidly *bizarre* liveries. In these gorgeous galleys the ladies of the Venetian nobility, who for years had worn nothing but funereal sables, sat in low-necked ball-dresses, with flowers on their heads, and with piles of flowery wreaths all round them to be flung into the Royal barge as the "Rè Eletto" came along, to the clangour of trumpets, the roar of artillery, and the shouts of a hundred thousand people. On that day, from every window of every grey old palace on the Grand Canal hung pieces of rare tapestry, Eastern carpets, or festoons of bright-coloured silks and satins, or cloth of gold and silver. On that day the front of St. Mark's, the arcades of the Procuratin, and the colonnade of the Piazzetta were hidden by flags, and the Italian banner streamed from the three masts of cedar whence erst floated the gonfalons of Candia, Cyprus, and the Morea—but sights such as these are not to be seen twice in a lifetime.

I am dealing now with the Venice of to-day—the Venice in which small and ragged boys are bawling cheap and nasty newspapers all over St. Mark's Place; the Venice in which the flower-girls have lost their good looks and graceful manners, and are now so many haggard importunate elderly slatterns, with voices as hoarse as those of London night cabmen: the Venice of which the Grand Canal is now profaned, not only by puffing, gasping, and clattering steam launches, but by twopenny steamers, of which the largely-patronised traffic literally takes the bread out of the mouth of the wretched gondoliers. This Venice, I am bound to own—being for the present time a Philistine—appears, without sunshine, very similar to what, in the days of old, Vauxhall Gardens by daylight used to look like. The aspect of the Waterloo Ground, the Italian Walk, and the great orchestra, with its shell-shaped sounding-board, was, on a cold and muggy afternoon in November, anything but exhilarating to the sight. It was, on the contrary, depressing, almost to the lachrymose stage—and so was Venice, under conditions of Philistian metempsychosis, to me.

XVII.

THE TWO ROMES.—THE OLD.

ROME, *November* 26.

THE last time that I visited Rome was more than eleven years ago—a serious slice out of the life of a man; yet it does not seem to me to be much longer than the day before yesterday since I was here. Nothing in the Via Bocca di Leone or at the cosy and comfortable Hôtel d'Angleterre appears in the least changed. There is the same well-supplied, chatty, and cheerful table d'hôte, at which one hears, perhaps, now that Strauss is dead, the best talk—artistic, archæological, ecclesiological, political, and mundane—to be listened to over any public dinner table in Europe; there is the same marble tablet on the first-floor landing, with the inscription handing down to posterity the imperishable record of a visit paid to Don Pedro the Fifth, King of Portugal, by his Holiness Pope Pius the Ninth, and reciting likewise the feelings of joyful gratitude and inextinguishable loyalty which filled the bosom of the landlord, Monsieur Antonio Gendre, after the visit of the Supreme Pontiff to the illustrious sojourner at the Albergo d'Inghilterra. Dead the Supreme Pontiff; dead Don Pedro the Fifth, King of Portugal; dead worthy Antonio Gendre, most courteous of Frenchmen, of the "ancien régime;" but the brave old hotel keeps its ground, and, amidst a crowd of new competitors, finds a plenitude of patrons.

No; there is nothing changed in the Via Bocca di Leone. There is the fountain by the wall, shadowed by the graceful pepper tree—the waters plashing musically into the great marble basin, rich with antique bas-reliefs, the gift of some bygone Prince of the plutocratic Torlonia family. And there, over against the fountain, is the Torlonia Palace itself, as big as several cavalry barracks piled on top of each other, with a bank, an insurance office, and the offices of a local Board of Works thrown in as make-weights, and rejoicing in the custodianship of one of the stateliest "Suisses" to be found in this city of palaces and hall-porters. The "proud young porter" immortalised in the ballad of "Lord Bateman" carried himself not more superbly than does the Torlonia "Suisse;" and the beadle of the old British Museum might have envied his Roman *confrère* his stupendous cocked hat and his gilt-knobbed bamboo cane, high, in degree, as "the mast of some great ammiral." The eleven years have passed lightly over that cocked hat, although they may have slightly flecked with grey the bushy black whiskers beneath. I fancy, too, that our own porter at the Angleterre has grown slightly stouter, and that he makes more frequent use of a double eye-glass than he was wont to do eleven years syne. It is the common lot.

For the rest, little, if anything, is altered at mine inn. The ladies after dinner persist in their old and charming practice of invading the gentlemen's smoking-room, instead of patronising the elegant *salon* reserved for their own use. Let us hope that their sweet presence soothes, as music is said to do, the savage breasts of the slaves of nicotine. Between the *fumoir* and the *salle-à-manger* yet remains all day long the patient Roman citizen who sells jewellery. He continues to display fresh trays full of cameo and mosaic brooches, bracelets, *porte-bonheurs*, studs, sleeve-buttons, lockets, chains and ouches, until I begin to look upon him as a kind of beneficent pastrycook, busily withdrawing baking-sheet after baking-sheet laden with tarts, puffs, cakes, and bath-buns, all piping hot from the oven, in view of an entire Collegiate School for Young Gentlemen and the Upper-crust High School for Girls, on a half-holiday, in the back shop clamouring for goodies.

Without it is the same Via Condotti — the English chemist's shop; the dainty *boutiques* full of glowing Roman jewellery, Roman scarves, Roman photographs, Roman mosaics, doubtful Roman antiquities, and, happily, indubitable English pickles, preserves, potted anchovies, Worcestershire Sauce, and Old Brown Windsor Soap. It is the same Piazza di Spagna : only I miss the picturesquely-costumed artists' models plying for hire on the steps of the Trinità di Monte. It is the same Via Frattina, handsome, gay, bustling, sparking, and with quite as much English as foreign conversation audible on the side-walk. It is the same—no ; it is *not* the same Corso. A dozen years have wrought stupendous changes in the capital of United Italy ; and I am in New Rome.

You see that when I came hither in the late autumn of

1870 the Eternal City had only been the capital of United Italy during a space of about four-and-twenty hours. I was just a day after the fair which had consisted in the Italian army marching through the Porta Pia, knocking down a few stone walls, and overcoming a few gallant Papal Zouaves on their march to the Quirinal. There had been no time for Papal Rome to change its ordinary guise. The supply even of Italian flags for window decoration had run short, and the *imbandierazione* of the city was but partial. The comparative paucity of triumphal arches and waving banners was compensated by the enthusiasm of a patriotic populace, and especially of the juvenile section thereof, who ceased not to yell Garibaldi's Hymn and to make the night hideous with howls of "Viva l'Armata Italiana" and "Rè Eletto en Campidoglio!" But, when I began to walk about emancipated Rome, it was as though the Pope-King yet reigned, but that several excursion trains, full of Italian officers and soldiers, had just arrived to have a look at the Forum and the Coliseum, the Pantheon of Agrippa, and the Baths of Caracalla.

Every day, however, that I remained Rome continued to change. Every train seemed to be laden, not only with piles of Milanese, Genoese, and Florentine newspapers, hitherto inaccessible to Romans of Liberal opinions—who, when they declined to read the orthodox *Osservatore*, had been fain to content themselves with an occultly-seditious little print, entitled *Roma dei Romani*, which made its appearance at irregular intervals, and which was ostensibly edited in an underground kitchen, and printed up a chimney—but also with enterprising gentlemen of advanced political views, who, so soon as ever they had deposited their carpet-bag at an hotel, proceeded to organise, to edit, and to publish brand-new newspapers for themselves. Every morning witnessed the dawn of some fresh organ of public opinion. The *Capitoline Wolf*, the *Broken Chains*, *Free Rome*, the *People's Forum*, the *Italian Banner*, the *Groans of Tyranny*, the *Shout of Freedom*, the *Porta del Popolo*—I know not how many journals, with titles such as those I have fancied, sprang up every morning fully armed, like Minerva from the head of Jove. Innumerable little Roman boys, who hitherto had wasted their energies in paddling barefooted in the mud of the Tiber, by the steps of the Ripetta, or had earned a precarious livelihood as downright beggars, were in the twinkling of an eye transformed into peripatetic newsvendors, and ere the first week of enfranchisement had expired Rome had ceased to be a Silent City. It will never be a Silent City again, I suppose, until universal cataclysm comes, and everybody is tumbled over the Tarpeian Rock, and the long-expected New Zealander arrives, having finished his sketch of St. Paul's, to photograph, by means of the electric light, the last remains of the Ministry of Finance, the Hôtel Costanzi, and the other imposing structures which at present form a portion of New Rome.

After the impromptu newspaper proprietors and the improvised army of newsvendors came the Deluge. Hitherto unheard-of hairdressers hung up their signboards at street corners, quite unexpectedly. A strange man from Turin suddenly proclaimed, in printed placards on the walls, that he had twenty thousand pairs of ladies' and gentlemen's boots to dispose of for ready money at surprisingly low prices. In the very midst of the Corso, between two ancestral palaces, a ready-made clothes warehouse started up as suddenly as though it had been the Palace of Aladdin; and from under the very lees of venerable monasteries and austere theological seminaries new cafés and new restaurants made an unblushing appearance; while—scandal upon scandal!—coquettishly-attired young females of alluring mien, and bearing trim little baskets full of flowers on their left arms, tripped saucily from café to café, accosting gentlemen to whom they had never been introduced, and, in the coolest manner imaginable, sticking posies into the stranger's button-hole, and expecting *centesimi* in return.

It was also worthy of melancholy remark in these first few days of transformation that as the new things appeared the old, pleasant landmarks of Roman life disappeared. That very clean and urbane Franciscan monk outside the portal of the Albergo d'Inghilterra, and to whom it was quite a pleasure to give an alms before you set out for a morning walk, was not to be discouraged by the altered state of political circumstances, and begged on as blithely as ever. It was good to be kind to him, remembering how churlishly his predecessor was treated long years ago in the inn-yard at Calais by the Reverend Laurence Sterne. But there was every day an appreciable falling off of the monks and friars, barefooted or shod, shaven-crowned or bushy-headed, cowled or shovel-hatted—friars in brown, friars in grey, friars in white, friars in black, who were wont to throng the streets. The long-

ARRIVAL OF THE CARDINALS AT THE QUIRINAL.

bearded beggars with tin badges on their breasts, licensed, under the Papal rule, "per domandare in Roma," unaccountably disappeared. The great leathern screen which veils the portal of St. Peter's still gave egress to that basilica of basilicas; but the Bronze Gate of the Vatican was shut close, and no sign of a Papal gendarme or a Swiss Guard in his striped doublet and hose of red and yellow and black appeared. As for the Papal Zouaves and the warriors of the Antibes Legion, you might as well have looked for the Prætorians of the Empire, or the barbaric body-guard of Theodoric the Goth, as for even a remnant of the last defenders of the Temporal Power. Then, on the Pincian Hill, a crowd of compact new broughams and barouches, highly varnished and expensively horsed, the property of astute speculators, who, hungrier than the Goths, the Visigoths, and the Huns of old, had made an irruption on Rome with their heads and their portfolios full of schemes, and with pockets of illimitable capacity. Concurrently the stately old gilded and painted coaches of the cardinals, with the placid old gentlemen in scarlet and point lace inside, utterly vanished, and of the Papal hierarchy you saw, in the open, not so much as a purple-stockinged monsignore.

There was an end, then, for us heretics of the grand sights and spectacles with which Rome so abounded in the days of the "Papa Rè." No more processions of the Bambino on the steps of the Ara Cœli; no more sermons from itinerant friars by the Stations in the arena of the Coliseum; no more grand "functions" in St. Peter's, the carrying round of the Pontifice Massimo on the Sedia Gestatoria, the waving of the giant fans of peacocks' plumes; the glittering throng of prelates and priests, the Guardia Nobile, radiant in scarlet and gold, the air thick and heavy with the mingled odour of incense and waxen tapers. I had seen for the last time the good old Pio Nono, in his long white flannel "soutane" and shovel hat of crimson velvet, alighting from his carriage on the Pincian, smilingly trotting along with his chamberlains in his wake, and blessing the kneeling crowd on either side. Good-bye, Pontifical Rome! So I went away to see the Red Flag waving over Lyons, and made the best of my way through distracted and bleeding France to England, at that time far more interested in the fortunes of the Franco-German war than in the transformation of Old into New Rome.

THE POPE IN THE SEDIA AT ST. PETER'S.

P. 232.

XVIII.

THE TWO ROMES.—THE NEW.

ROME, *November* 28.

THE Rome of United Italy has added to her population, since the memorable year Seventy, something closely approaching one hundred thousand inhabitants. The Italians assert that the capital now contains three hundred thousand souls ; but more cautious statists are of opinion that the aggregate of humanity within the walls should be placed some ten or even twenty thousand lower. In any case, the vast increase of the population since the old Papal times must be apparent to the most superficial observer. The Corso is thronged with people from morning till night, and movement is always difficult owing to the incurable narrowness of the foot-pavement. I say incurable, since, if the *marciapiede* were widened, the already restricted roadway would become more exiguous, whilst the thoroughfare itself could not be made structurally broader without pulling down some of the historic palaces, a contingency certainly not to be dreamt of in this generation at least. It is one thing to dispossess monks and nuns, and turn monasteries into post-offices and cavalry barracks, but it is quite another and a far less practicable thing to contemplate the demolition of the grim old fortress-palaces of the Roman nobility — huge piles, the frowning stones of which may have been plundered from the Coliseum or from the Baths of Caracalla, which have stood in their time several stout sieges and assaults, and which look, now, externally like so many Newgates, but are full within of priceless art treasures.

The normal narrowness of the *trottoir* in the Corso, and the vast increase in the number of Romans who frequent it, render circulation at most times somewhat difficult, very uncomfortable, and slightly dangerous; for the wheeled traffic of Rome has increased in proportion with that of the pedestrians, and when you are forced to step into the gutter owing to the footway being blocked by groups of the "gentile e colta cittadinanza della capitale," as a local organ terms the crowd in the Corso, you run a very tolerable risk of being run over by some passing omnibus, or at least having your toes crushed by the wheels of a passing victoria. Yes; there are omnibuses on the Corso of Rome. I do not speak of the hotel omnibuses. Those commodious caravans—every important hotel-keeper in London ought to start an omnibus for the convenience of his guests and for the dealing of a death-blow to the four-wheeled cab nuisance—existed in the old days; but the omnibuses which, to my amazement, I notice in New Rome are of the approved London and Paris pattern plying duly for hire, and belonging to a company called the Impresa Romana.

More than this, the broader thoroughfares of Rome are now blessed, or cursed—there are two opinions on the matter —with tramway cars. They are all built on the pattern which I took note of at Nice. Mere platforms or "floats" on wheels, open at the sides, furnished with parallel rows of seats of the *char-à-bancs* kind, and canopied by a linen awning from the sun or the rain. These tramway cars are now abundant in every considerable town in Italy, and the alacrity with which the Italians have taken to that which is ostensibly a purely modern and American invention would be astonishing were it not remembered first that there is nothing new under the sun, and next that humanity is, as a rule, addicted to returning to its first loves. If you will turn to any copious dictionary of Roman antiquities—say the exhaustive work by Anthony Rich—you will find the tramway car in its *char-à-bancs* aspect neatly figured, I think—but am not quite certain—as a "carpentum;" but there sure enough is the caravan, with the passengers sitting back to back. While, touching the tramway itself, who that has wandered in Pompeii has not seen the deep ruts worn by the chariot wheels in the stony roadways of the Dead City? What were those ruts but sunken trams?

The crowd in the Corso is not, I regret to say, made up of opulent foreigners anxious to purchase Roman jewellery or Roman antiquities—the first as beautiful, the last as doubtful as ever. The main thoroughfare of "Roma Redenta" is plagued by a multitudinous and ignoble army of "loafers." There are the haggard and unwholesome-looking youths, by hundreds, who ought to be serving behind shop counters, or better still, whistling at the plough, or toiling at the loom, but who now embellish the kerbstone, jabbering about the policy of the "Destra," and the "Sinistra," denouncing the alliance with Austria, demanding the withdrawal of the Papal guarantees, or bragging about Castel Fidardo and Aspromonte and Mentana, which were fought before many of them were born. They suck their halfpenny Cavours, and recite, in parrot-like fashion, the "screaming" leading articles which they have read in a host of halfpenny newspapers, which are issued "hot and hot" from sunrise to sunset.

Then there is the older class of "loafers," sallow, wrinkled, grizzled, woe-begone men, with rusty hats and shabby cloaks, worn as the togas of the ancient Romans were worn—that is to say, with one end of the garment flung over the shoulder and falling in picturesque folds over the back. Who are these elderly men, I wonder? They are evidently discontented with something or somebody, for, as they "collogue" together, you may see them clench their fists menacingly, or throw their fingers upwards in disdainful disparagement; while painfully edging by them you may hear them, with no bated breath, utter such uncomplimentary expressions as "falsehood," "calumny," "intrigue," "corruption," "spoliation of the revenue," "ruin of the country," and so forth. They have a curious family likeness, these old gentlemen, to the ex-"empleados" or cashiered Government clerks over whom the earlier editions of the "Handbook of Spain" used to make so merry. I have not the slightest desire to be funny at the expense of these dilapidated obstructors of the kerbstone in the Corso. They may be old Pontifical *impiegati*, waifs and strays of the Pontifical police, superannuated and unpensioned attachés of the office of the Cardinal Secretary of State, or discharged subordinates of the Pontifical

Dogana. I compassionate these venerable Mariuses amidst the ruins of Carthage. Still, I cannot help wishing that the poor old fellows in the cloaks would not block up the foot pavement in the Corso, while they gird at existing institutions.

Rome, since her redemption from Theocratical rule, has seen an astounding multiplicity of new caffès, *liquoristi*, and *birrerie*, or downright Vienna and Chiavenna beer saloons, spring up. The Romans are, as a body, doubtless, as sober as ever they were. Still, there seems to be a good deal of hot punch—not "ponche à la Romaine," but the actual rum punch now all but obsolete in England—sold by retail from an early hour in the forenoon. I should not counsel the old gentlemen to drink punch before dinner, or, for the matter of that, after dinner, yet surely they might remember that among the pleasantest of Italian customs, is the privilege of sitting all day long in a caffè, at an expense which certainly need not exceed twopence-halfpenny, inclusive of the *buona mano* to the waiter. With some few exceptions—the splendid Caffè di Roma, in the Corso, for example—the Roman coffee-houses are as dark and dismal as their congeners in other Italian cities. They are the very places to which all those who are discontented should preferentially resort as to a Cave of Adullam. Why cannot they foregather in shady caffè corners, these Roman Adullamites, and denounce the wickedness of a corrupt Administration at their leisure over tepid chicory and beet-root sugar?

No; the Italian, and especially the Roman, likes to ventilate his grievances in the open air. As it was with the Old so it is with the New. He likes to hang about the butchers' and fruiterers' stalls on the Forum. Failing the Forum, the modern Roman hangs about the Corso. It is precisely the same with that extremely Roman-like people the modern Spaniards. To say that a person is "en foro" instead of "en su casa" is yet common in the South of Spain.

That Caffè di Roma, of which I spoke just now, is an eminently characteristic feature of New Rome. In my time —the old one—when you wished to vary the monotony of the hotel *table d'hôte*, you lunched or dined at Spillmann's or at Nazzari's. These establishments, I apprehend, yet maintain their well-earned reputation; but if, being at Rome, you wish to do as the Romans do, you lunch at Morteo's and dine at the Caffè di Roma. I have never, during many years of discourse on culinary topics, disguised my opinion that the modern Italian *cuisine* is, next to the Spanish, the most detestable in Europe. It has, indeed, hopelessly degenerated since the days when part of Cardinal Campeggio's mission to the Court of Henry VIII. was, at the express command of the Supreme Pontiff, to ascertain whether English cookery presented any dish worthy of being included in the already splendid *répertoire* of the kitchen of the Vatican. The reply of Cardinal Campeggio was to the effect that there was in English cookery " assolutamente nienti "—absolutely nothing worthy of transplantation beyond the Alps.

And now, lo! how all is changed! From Calais to Constantinople the English beefsteak and potatoes reign disagreeably supreme. I say disagreeably, because there are persons who abhor beefsteak and potatoes. You will have little else offered you for breakfast—as an alternative to badly-fried fish and ill-made omelettes, from one end of modern Italy to the other. The beefsteak and potatoes have even crossed the sea to the mainland of Greece; and the first item which you see in the bill of fare in a restaurant at Athens is " mpiphtaik me' geomela." You begin to wonder what on earth " mpiphtaik "—sometimes it is spelt " mpiphteki "—can mean, when you remember that the modern Greeks have no letter " b " in their language, and that they call Lord Byron " Ho Lordos Mpiron." Then you awake to the consciousness that the mystic entry in the Romaic *menu* refers to beefsteak with " earth-apples "—otherwise potatoes.

This virtual abandonment of cunningly-prepared dishes in favour of a flap of broiled bullock's flesh, either half burnt or half raw, and on the Continent wholly destitute of fat, is, to me, worthy of the most serious attention not only of the culinary expert but of the student of civilisation generally. To me the universal supremacy of the " bifteck " represents not so much the prevalence of Anglo-Saxon ideas—for an underdone steak is in reality quite as Abyssinian or as Kaffir-like, that is to say, as savage as it is English—as it does the feverish haste, flurry, and excitement of modern life, and the almost wolf-like desire to devour the largest amount of solid succulents in the shortest possible time. But even the heartiest of English people eschew, as a rule, beef or rump steak, or, as the prudish among the Americans call it, " tender loin " steak, at the early morning repast. We reserve steak for late luncheon or for dinner. The Americans habitually eat beefsteak at eight or nine o'clock in the morning, and

French and Italian hotel and restaurant keepers are naturally led to imagine that English appetites are of the Transatlantic calibre.

As for the most monstrous delusion prevalent, not among the Italians, but among the French, that every Englishman likes to have his meat "bien saignant"—in a blue-raw condition of under-cooking—I can only account for it by the supposition that once upon a time—possibly in the fantastic epoch of "milords excentriques"—some fashionable Paris restaurant was patronised by an ogre, accidentally of British extraction, who lived on half-raw beef-steaks, plum-pudding, "porter-beer," and "colossal grogs," prior to returning to his native land, there to oppress the wretched natives of Ireland and Hindustan, to sell his wife "dans le Smithfield," with a rope round her neck, for a shilling and "un tob de gin," and finally to die of "le spleen." There is not the slightest use in arguing with a French waiter on the subject. If you decline to partake of the eternal steak, and order mutton cutlets instead, he replies with a grin, "Parfaitement. Bien saignantes, n'est-ce-pas?"

You can obtain a very fair dinner at the Caffè di Roma, if you know how to order it; and Giovanni, tallest and most obliging of waiters, will help you to acquire that knowledge. You have only to explain to him that English people are in the habit of eating something else besides beefsteaks, roast beef, and mutton chops; and that as regards fish their views extend further than sprats, gudgeons, and "slip" soles, fried in oil, without any sauce. Tell Giovanni to serve you such Italian dishes as are eatable, especially those of the "paste" kind—macaroni, "stuffato," "ravioli," "polpetti," "lasagne," "spaghetti," and so forth; cutlets of "gallinaccio," or turkey, served with "funghi" or mushrooms, a really dainty dish; and especially "uccellini," or small birds of the quail order, served on a bed of boiled polenta. Stay, you may indulge, also, in the tasty "risotto," or rice boiled and dressed with butter and grated parmesan, and rendered wholesome by a slight infusion of saffron.

Into the mysteries of Italian cookery—the sweet creams and pastry generally of which are very good—I would not advise you further to enter. Years ago I own that I liked the wild boar with "agro-dolce"—sweet-sour sauce, which is a standing dish at some Roman dinner tables; but tastes change, albeit we may be unconscious of the change, with age. One talks about the delicacy of roast pig, because Charles Lamb's "Essay on Roast Pig" reads as delightfully as ever; but who eats baby-porkers now, out of the rural districts? Does anybody eat tripe nowadays? I remember, when stewed in milk and smothered in onions—Portugal onions, mind—it was a delicacy that even epicures of the Silver Fork School did not despise. The modern Romans eat tripe, and a good many other dreadful things, fried in batter. If you are offered a "frittura," avoid it; fly from "frattaglie," of which most Romans are immoderately fond.

You will get good wine at the Roma; and if you be wise you will temporarily forget the existence of so-called Médocs and St. Julliens, and adhere to the wine of the country, which is cheap, unadulterated, well-flavoured, and, when moderately diluted with water, not "heady." Try Chianti; at least it tastes of the grape. The so-called Bordeaux tastes of anything but the grape. If you be a party of four, Giovanni brings you the wine in a *fiascone* which resembles the Brobdingnagian brother of the Florence oil flask, with its elegant form and rush-covered bulb, with which we are familiar in England. The *fiascone* holds, they tell me, four good litres or quart bottles. It is placed on the table in a kind of iron rack, on which when empty it sways slowly backwards and forwards, mournfully. Guests with tender consciences may feel a guilty feeling creeping over them as they watch this mute reminder that they have drunk a gallon of Chianti between them; but stouter spirits may pluck up heart, and reciting the well-known lines from "Bacco in Toscana"—the author of which famous poem was a confirmed water-drinker—order t'other *fiascone*.

Outside Florence they say there are *osterie* where the hugest of *fiasconi* are to be seen. The landlord weighs the "diva bottiglia" when it is placed on the table; it is weighed again when the Tuscan topers have finished their bout, and the quantity consumed can thus be accurately gauged and duly charged for. "A pint is a pound, all the world round," it would appear, especially in Tuscany. But surely when the "sederunt" is at an end they should weigh the wine-bibbers as well as the bottle. Retribution would thus overtake him who had not "drunk fair."

I knew this Caffè di Roma long years ago, in the days of the Papal Zouaves and the Antibes Legion, of the officers of both which distinguished corps the Roma was the habitual afternoon resort. It was patronised by only a few native gentlemen, who sate apart and scowled at the "Mercenarii stranieri," as the Zouaves and the Antibes soldiers are pithily styled in the Roman commentary on the monument erected in the Campo Verano at Rome to the memory of the brave defenders of the Papacy who fell at Mentana. The original inscription is a Latin one, composed under the Pontifical rule, and reciting the virtues of the warriors, strangers as well as natives, who fought victoriously for the Holy See and the Eternal City against "a copious horde of parricides." If the French had been in the place of the Romans they would, most assuredly, when they gained the upper hand, have hacked this inscription from the marble of the Mentana monument. But the Italians, notwithstanding their occasional vehemence, are a remarkably shrewd and long-headed people, with a subtle sense of humour combined with dignity of expression. Beneath the Latin inscription now runs a postscript, in Italian, to the effect that the monument erected by "the Theocratical Government" in memory of foreign mercenaries, " Roma Redenta "—Enfranchised Rome —has left to posterity as a record of calamitous times.

They were brave and devoted fellows, nevertheless, the Paladins of the Temporal Power. I can see them now, with their sabres clattering, flocking into the Roma about five in the afternoon on vermouth and absinthe intent, and shaking hands with each other, as though they were all new acquaintances, with quite a desperate cordiality. The fact was that, out of their own immediate circle and the precincts of the Vatican, the poor gallant gentlemen experienced some difficulty in getting anybody to shake hands with them. The bulk of the Romans loathed the " Mercenarii stranieri " even more bitterly than they had hated the French garrison. But the Roma at which they foregathered and sipped their vermouth and their absinthe was not the Roma where you take counsel with Giovanni as to dinner, and where you sit around the *fiascone* of Chianti, gently swaying in its iron cradle. The Caffè of the New Rome. is frequented by ministers, deputies, journalists, and advocates of renown, bankers and stockbrokers, and "moneyed men" of all nations. Last evening the whole staff of the Japanese Legation were dining at the next table. Ladies in goodly number may be seen at the new Caffè di Roma, not at the old. The Caffè bore the same name, but it was on the other side of the Corso, nearly opposite the present handsome and luxurious establishment.

As for Morteo's, it is a capital restaurant, slightly more Italian and less expensive than the Roma, and where you will find excellent oysters at two francs a dozen, and a succulent lunch, in ordering which you will be on the safest side if you call for the "piatto del giorno" —the dish of the day. On the morning when I lunched at Morteo's the "dish of the day" was a wonderful preparation of roast veal with a marrow-bone in the middle, on the top of a mountain of "spaghetti" with saffron and grated cheese, and a fine sauce, made of I know not what; but it was toothsome. Try Morteo's. It has one entrance, I think, in the Corso, opposite the Chigi Palace; but there is a back entrance to the restaurant, to which I was conducted, through a labyrinth of narrow streets, by an English friend, who knows

ancient and modern Rome as familiarly as he knows Pall
Mall. Life is a curious play, full of odd "situations." As
my English friend walks me about and drives me about New
Rome, and enumerates all the transformations which have
taken place—as he kindly rubs up my decaying memory of
bygone Roman things, and sets me right about the Domenichino in this church and the mosaics in that basilica—as he
does all this with genial prolixity, and with a knowing air,
we recall, with a smile, that fifteen years ago 'twas I who
awaited his arrival for the first time in Rome, and that we
spent Christmas together, and that I had the honour of
being his cicerone through the city, which he knows now
"like a book," but which to me is so new and so strange.

XIX.

THE TWO ROMES—THE NEW—(*continued*).

ROME, *November* 30.

ADMITTING the practical impossibility of widening the Corso and confessing the inadequacy, as the main thoroughfare of the capital of Italy, of a narrow street which bears a curious resemblance to Hanway Yard amalgamated with Birchin Lane, Cornhill, and indefinitely prolonged, the masters of new Rome decreed the construction of the Via Nazionale, a thoroughfare which, when fully completed, will equal in magnificence the Ringstrasse at Vienna, or any of the surprisingly handsome boulevards in the Quartier Leopold of New Brussels. To remember such boulevards, full of lofty mansions, of which the ground floors are occupied by splendid shops, makes one indignantly ashamed of one's own country and its metropolis —London. We have been tinkering at Victoria Street, Westminster, for more than thirty years, and the unfinished street still exhibits gaps of land not yet built over; while one side of it has for a considerable portion of its length a fringe of slums as vile as any in St. Giles's.

That is our good old national custom. Ladies of fashion who indulge in the recreation of shopping in Regent Street the Superb, may not be aware that one side of our Via—not

Nazionale, but "Nashonale"—has behind it a very noisome little labyrinth of slums indeed. They have been left there for more than sixty years, when old Great Swallow Street was architecturally licked into the comely shape of Regent Street; and it has been nobody's business to take the slums away. Carnaby Street and its congeners will continue to flourish, I have little doubt, long after I am dead.

With equally exemplary adherence to the good old system of allowing the slums to look after themselves, we are driving a very grand new boulevard indeed all the way from New Oxford Street through Theobald's Road and into Clerkenwell; and this boulevard is to end, we are told, in the wilds of Hoxton. A considerable portion of this new "via" runs through the most noisome of slums, which will be left cheerfully undisturbed; and on the ground which has become available for building purposes I fail to remark—with the exception of the Holborn Town Hall—any buildings more remarkable than several towering gin-shops.

When the Parisians built their Boulevard Haussmann, their Avenue de l'Opéra, and their Rue du Quatre Septembre, it was insisted upon by the authorities that the style of architecture adopted should be not only handsome but uniform. We have only one street in London where the expediency of such structural uniformity has been borne in mind. The façades of the houses built by Nash from Langham Place to Waterloo Place are only repetitions of one architectural scheme, and, although the fronts are of stucco, the general result is certainly harmonious, and would be handsome but for the fact that Nash, banished by the duresse of warlike times from the contemplation of the architectural Renaissance which Napoleon had promoted in his grand Parisian monuments, was unable to realise the idea that private as well as public buildings may be conveniently erected of an imposing height, and thus built his façades so low as to dwarf his columns, truncate his architraves, and make all his houses in Regent-street look mean and petty.

The Roman Via Nazionale starts virtually from the Piazza dei Termini to the west of and within a very short distance from the colossal ruins of the Baths of Diocletian, and runs straight down, in a south-easterly direction and in splendid length and breadth, nearly to the Forum of the Trajan Column. Just before it arrives there a détour to the west becomes unavoidable; and it is only in a modified form that a continuation of the Via Nazionale strikes the Corso. But it is then only a few minutes' walk from the Roman Forum; and the day will come, I hope, when the Via Nazionale will be prolonged right down to the shore of the Tiber and to the foot of that bridge which leads to that island which has " the shape of a ship," and whereon stood the Temple of Æsculapius. But this is not by any means the only architectural improvement of which New Rome has been the theatre. The number of new hotels which have been built—the Grand, the Quirinale, the Costanza, the Continentale, and many others—is simply astonishing. Then there is the vast and entirely new Piazza dell' Independenza, and nearly the whole of the Esquiline Hill round the Church of Santa Maria Maggiore has been covered with new and stately streets. The Via Carlo Alberto, the Via Principe Umberto, the Via Principe

Eugenio, the Via Principessa Margherita, and the Via Napoleone—yes, there is a Via Napoleone—all speak with eloquent significance of an altered state of things. These are not old streets rechristened, of which there is such a large and melancholy number in ex-Imperial Paris, but brand-new thoroughfares.

I said something just now about stucco. We should not, I take it, bear too heavily on the memory of Nash, nor revile too scornfully façades coated with stucco or with "Roman cement." The Romans have a way of veneering of their own, which is, to say the least, remarkable—covering the fronts, and even the columns of their buildings with very thin slices of stone, artfully laid upon an inner core or surface of "mattone" or bricks. The brickwork is, it must be granted, extremely good, but the veracities have not been entirely preserved, and the bulk of the seemingly stone edifices are in reality ingenious shams. Is there not a considerable quantity of scagliata among the priceless marbles of St. Peter's itself?

The new streets are stretching south-eastward towards the Baths of Titus. They have neared the Coliseum, and are extending towards the Basilica of St. John Lateran. They have invaded the Palatine Hill, and menace, or rather encouragingly approach, the site of the Circus Maximus. Close to the Piazza dell' Independenza has just been completed the truly magnificent edifice of the Ministry of Finance. Magnificent, I mean, as regards size and lavishness of decoration. There are eleven thousand rooms, they say, in the Vatican, and our own Somerset House boasts a tolerably large number of apartments, great and small; our new Foreign Office is considered to be a somewhat extensive pile; while the Parisians are pardonably proud of their rapidly progressing new Hôtel de Ville; the Bruxellois point with justifiable congratulation to their all but completed Palace of Justice; and in the Far West of the American Continent, Civilisation is triumphantly challenged to produce three bigger things in the way of architecture than the Palace Hotel, San Francisco; the New City Hall, Chicago; and the new Mormon Tabernacle at Salt Lake City. The last-named edifice, it is true, is only just rising above its granite basement; but when it is finished it will assuredly be a very big thing indeed. These eyes have gazed upon the colossal structures just named. Yes; and at home I have some old mezzotint engravings of the immeasurable palaces, the boundless terraces, the interminable Babylonian colonnades which, in sombre majesty of chiaroscuro, John Martin loved to paint, but I conscientiously declare that I never beheld a building that looks so large as does the Ministry of Finances at Rome.

In that very old but still popular Porte St. Martin pantomime-spectacle, "Les Pilules du Diable," a very startling effect is produced in a scene which represents the exterior of a many-storeyed lunatic asylum, by all the mad people, strait-waistcoated and white nightcapped, simultaneously popping their heads out of what appear to be hundreds of windows. So, from the seemingly innumerable casements of the Ministério delle Finanze, used I to fancy that I saw protruded the half-lengths of clerks in the Italian Civil Service, derisively shaking bags of specie in the faces of the Public.

A great deal too derisively. Travertine, tufa, pozzolana, bricks, iron, timber, and so forth may enter into the construction of this astounding fiscal barrack, yet I cannot help thinking that, figuratively speaking, the substance which has been most extensively employed as building materials here has been either papier mâché or carton pierre. The Romans themselves are accustomed to say jestingly that, gigantic as are the dimensions of the Ministry of Finance, it is not half large enough to hold the debts of the kingdom of United Italy. More practical critics denounce the entire edifice as one Titanic job. From the foundations to the roof, they declare, these accumulated stones and bricks represent so many corrupt contracts and " concessions," so many occult intrigues and hole-and-corner speculations by means of which needy and unscrupulous adventurers have been enriched at the expense of an overtaxed nation.

Well, you not unfrequently hear precisely identical strictures passed by practical critics on very grand-looking public works in the United States. In the agreeable environs of the pleasant city of Philadelphia they show you a series of palatial mansions, brown stone houses, with marble façades and mansard roofs, inhabited by suddenly enriched business men, who have had something to do with fingering public money. The American critics have christened these imposing structures by the expressive albeit inelegant term of " Thieves' Row." On the many millions of dollars which the carpets, rocking chairs, and spittoons at the City Hall, New York, cost during the reign of the virtuous " Boss" Tweed, I need not dwell. New Rome—if the Romans are to be trusted—has been to some extent as audaciously "financiered" as New York was in the halcyon days of the Tammany Ring.

Yes; the Ministry of Finance continues to bear an uncomfortable resemblance to a palace of papier mâché; and the whole of United Italy still realises with unpleasant literalness Mr. John Hollingshead's remarkable vision of "The City of Unlimited Paper." It happened that I was in Italy in the year 1866, just prior to the breaking out of the war with Austria, from which the Italians gathered the doubtful laurels of Custozza and Lissa, but were subsequently consoled by the cession of Venice, when the inconvertible paper currency was first introduced. The "rag money" had not been in existence eight-and-forty hours ere it was at a discount of 8 per cent. It sank much lower in subsequent years; but at present you are told that the paper notes are very nearly on a par with gold, and that the resumption of cash payments, or what the Americans call "honest money," or "the dollars of our daddies," is imminent.

The statement is simply exasperating. The paper in circulation is to be redeemed by bullion next week, next month, next year, or the year after next, until at last you begin to think that it would be on the safer side to assume that gold and silver will positively make their reappearance on the occurrence of the Greek Kalends. As things stand at present, when you change gold for notes the banker gives you only a few sous premium on your sovereigns or your "marengo"— the still popular name for a twenty-franc piece; and the hotel and shopkeepers give you no premium at all. The greediness with which they clutch at a piece of gold when it is tendered them, and the alacrity with which they hand you ragged, greasy notes in return, is equally edifying and equally irritating.

It is only at the buffet at the Turin Railway Station that the waiters have enough conscience, if you pay in gold, to hand you change in silver. Otherwise you would have to carry a bundle of the unctuous and malodorous chiffons with you through the Mont Cenis Tunnel to Modane, and so across the frontier, where the view taken by French money-changers of the monetary value of Italian paper currency would probably be of a highly facetious kind. There are notes of so low a denomination as fifty centesimi, or fourpence three-farthings, and they are so flimsy in texture and become at last so ragged and rotten that large quantities of them must annually disintegrate and disappear from circulation altogether; a consummation beneficial to the Italian Treasury—inasmuch as the annihilation of these miserable little promises to pay relieves the State of a portion of its indebtedness—but scarcely of a nature to gratify the public. New Rome is a highly imposing metropolis, and Young Italy is a very interesting and promising country; but neither, I am afraid, will attain real prosperity until this curse of an inconvertible paper currency be definitively abrogated.

XX.

THE ROMAN SEASON.

ROME, *December* 2.

"You can always tell when the Roman season is beginning in right earnest," recently said to me a veteran *habitué* of the Piazza di Spagna and the Pincian, "by the numbers of pianos which you see moving in to the hotels." Now, the Roman season properly so called means the arrival in Rome for a period of at least ten weeks of a large contingent of those joys to hotel proprietors and letters of furnished apartments, English and American families, and the settling down of a family of *forestieri*, including in each group two or more young ladies, infers almost as foregone conclusions the retention of so many private *salons*, and the hiring of so many pianofortes. It is true that in all the first-class hotels there is a pianoforte in the ladies' drawing-room, on which instrument the principal performers—save when, now and again, the Cavaliere Maestro Sfracellorecchi of Bergamo, temporarily staying in the hotel, obliges the company with a concerto after the table-d'hôte—are Transatlantic damsels whose harmonic tastes are catholic, and whose agile fingers interpret, now the compositions of Schubert and Gounod, and now the simpler hymn tunes of "Will you come to the beautiful river?" or "Hold the Fort."

But the English families who are as yet scarcely accustomed to what may be called that "Grand Hotel life" which has been borrowed partly from the French and partly from the Americans shrink from exhibiting their pianoforte-playing, or, it may be, their practice in public; and there are, consequently, a greater number of private rooms engaged in the best Roman hotels than in any other city in Europe—London and Paris, of course, always excepted. If I hinted, just now, at "practice," it is for the reason that "the scales" are a by no means unfamiliar sound in a Roman hotel; indeed, as in this winter city there are few days, even in December and January, when you cannot keep your window open for at least eight hours of the twenty-four, you hear "the scales" very frequently during most hours of daylight, to say nothing of fresh young Anglo-Saxon voices carolling the lyrics of Sir Arthur Sullivan and Mr. Frederic Clay. Being a Philistine, I prefer these harmonies to the indigenous ones. Italian vocalism seems to me to be extremely beautiful everywhere save in Italy itself—where singing out of tune and playing out of time seem to be the rule rather than the exception.

In addition to Philistinism, it may be prejudice which has led me to adopt this conclusion. I remember, some years ago, dining with a friend at a *pensione* in Milan, where there were no less than five retired *prime donne assolute*—such, at least, was what my hostess told me. They all sang after dinner; all their voices were hopelessly cracked; and they were unanimous in expressing their opinion that Madame Adelina Patti was a shockingly overrated artiste. It is a curiously instructive exercise, however, when your window at Rome is open, and more or less tuneful sounds, vocal and instrumental, are issuing from so many casements around you, to try to distinguish the nationalities of the different performers; the profound "brumbrum" of the German baritone, the shrill and slightly nasal trilling of the Frenchman, the frenzied shrieking of the Italian, the clear, bird-like notes of the American, and the melodious, tender, but timid and subdued warbling of the young English girl, who, entreat her as her instructor may, obstinately declines to open her mouth when she sings.

There are many other signs of the Roman season having begun besides the migration of pianos—usually "upright grands"—from the ground floors of the music warehouses to the hotels, even to the topmost storeys thereof. Art and letters begin to arouse themselves, for now is their "opening day." There are letters and letters; and the literates who are most hopefully excited by the arrival of the *forestieri* are the professors of Italian. It is often for their sake, quite as much as for that of the pianofortes, that the additional cost of a private room is incurred by "the families." There is, ostensibly, no necessity for any foreign sojourner in a well-managed Roman hotel knowing so much as ten words of Italian. The porter is usually a polyglot individual, and talks to each stranger in his own tongue—that of the porter himself being Pomeranian, Scandinavian, or Moldo-Wallachian. The waiters, whether they be Germans or Italians, devote the stillness of the night season to the study of Ollendorff, and are always ready with assurances in Ollendorffian English that the melted butter of the fried sole will be followed by the mashed potatoes of the broiled cutlet. The *valets de place* speak the jargon of their tribe, and the pages of Murray's handbook, or of Mr. Augustus Hare's "Walks in Rome," now happily enable the intelligent traveller to dispense with the services of a *valet de place* altogether; while, if the travelling Briton wishes to know what is going on in the city itself, and cannot read *Fanfulla* or the *Capitan Fracassa*, he will find all he needs in the columns of the *Italian Times*. Good English, too, is spoken at the principal chemists and druggists, and bad English in the other shops patronised by the *forestieri;* but in the last instance the privilege of hearing a few garbled sentences in your own language is seldom enjoyed without the addition of about thirty per cent. to the cost of the articles which you have purchased.

Moreover, the "families" who encamp in Rome for the season are generally imbued with a vague but wholesome impression that their stay should not be destitute of a slight educational character, for the benefit, at least, of the younger branches. The young ladies may have a taste for *bric-à-brac*, and long to be able to chaffer for bargains in the old curiosity shops in the bye-streets or at the great "omnium gatherum" of picturesque rubbish presented every Wednesday morning in the Campo di Fiori. They may wish to be able to spell through a paragraph or so in an Italian newspaper every morning, or to be able to read Professor Gregorovius' "Tombe dei Papi" in the original. So they must needs take a course of Italian lessons, and at the beginning of the season the hearts of Professore Nasomuffa, of the University of Bologna, and Dottore Macinaparola, of Velletri, leap high within them as they behold the hotel omnibuses quite full within and much baggage piled on their roofs rattling through the stony streets on their way to the hotels most frequented by the *forestieri*. In a week or ten days after the arrival of the "families" you may expect to hear the waiter at breakfast addressed—often in a very nervous, faltering voice—as "Cameriere," and in another fortnight your ear may be so fortunate as to catch inquiries made by the "lingua Italiano in bocca Inglese" for "ove con presciutto" instead of "ham and eggs."

I would that Professore Nasomuffa and Dottore Macinaparola taught their fair pupils among "the families" more assiduously to ask in Italian for the things which they want than to devote wearisome hours, week after week, to the conjugation of irregular verbs, of which they will not have mastered, perhaps, a tithe when the time arrives for leaving Rome altogether. And this observation applies quite as much to male as to female students of Italian. Table-d'hôte life, although in many respects very pleasant—and the Roman tables-d'hôte are certainly the pleasantest in Europe—is apt, after a time, to grow somewhat monotonous; and a most agreeable change therefrom is to breakfast and dine at a native restaurant, and take notes of what the Romans really do eat—how they cook it, and how much is charged for it. Instruction, not unmingled with astonishment, may be derived from such investigations. But how are you to make them when you have no Italian wherein to order your dinner or your breakfast, and instruct the waiter how you wish the meal to be served?

Unless you resort to some system of self-teaching, the worthy Nasomuffa and the excellent Macinaparola will not, I fear, be of much assistance to you. They pin their faith to those exasperating irregular verbs. You may, to be sure, take a conversational vocabulary with you to the *ristorante*, and look out your dishes in English with their Italian equivalents, one by one. The English University Don who tried to dine at an Athenian restaurant carefully looked out the Romaic for beefsteak; but when he desired the waiter to bring him a "mpiphteki" the expression on the face of the servitor was one of blank amazement and perplexity. The gentleman from England was unaware that in the modern Greek alphabet B is pronounced as V; and that the subsitute in Greek for our B are the two letters M P. The gentleman should have asked for a "biphteki" or a "trizola."

"The families," however, can only devote a comparatively short portion of their time to the practice of music and the study of the distractingly irregular verbs "scingere" and "uscire." With the exception of a small majority whom I shall presently mention, the Protestant section of the Anglo-Saxon tourists who come to the Eternal City have just two objects in view—sight-seeing if they are new to Rome; whilst if they be old Romans the desire to exchange the horrors of an English winter or the asperity of an American one for a mild, balmy, sunny climate which gives you, even in the very worst months of the year, an average of five bright days a week. And the general amenity of a Roman winter is the chief promoter of Anglo-Saxon society on the banks of the Tiber. The refugees from frost and fog, darkness and damp, find English or American friends who, like themselves, have escaped from regions of shivering and choking; and from Christmas almost to Easter the Corso comes to resemble Regent Street, and the Pincian the Ladies' Mile; you meet the same people in the Via Condotti and the Piazza di Spagna as you do in Pall Mall or Bond Street, the Piazza del Popolo is metamorphosed into Hyde Park Corner, and the Piazza Colonna into Trafalgar Square.

Thus "five o'clock tea" flourishes exceedingly, and suggests another use for the private rooms at the hotels; dinner parties are frequent; nocturnal receptions more frequent still; the congregations at the Protestant places of worship grow fuller and more fashionable every Sunday; stately British matrons and graceful maidens of the Du Maurier type may be met trooping through the Forum or driving along the Appian Way; the Roman Hounds draw crowded "meets;" and the shopkeepers about the Piazza di Spagna, the Via Sistina, the Via del Babuino, and the Via Frattina, who deal in English pickles, sauces, and condiments, bottled beer, biscuits, stationery, and haberdashery, drive a roaring trade. When I knew Rome first there was only one English tradesman in Rome who dispensed such commodities; at present the wares of the British grocer, biscuit baker, and wine and spirit merchant are to be found in astonishing abundance from one end of the Peninsula to the other.

But the mild climate and society-loving patrons of the Roman season are a very different class from the sightseer, and these again may be divided into two sections. The first I may call the Flying Sightseers, the second the Sedentary ones. The former gallop through the city, so to speak, rushing literally from pillar to post—from St. Peter's to the Lateran, from the Pantheon to St. Paul's without the Walls, from the Coliseum to the Baths of Caracalla, from the Tomb of Cecilia Metella to the Catacombs, from the Forum of Trajan to the Vatican, from the Ponte Molle to the Pyramid of Caius Cestius. "The Capitol," once significantly remarked Pio Nono, in a political harangue, referring to the seizure of Rome by the Italians, "is close to the Tarpeian Rock." The Flying Sightseers "do." the Campidoglio, its museum, the Church of the Ara Cœli, and half a dozen more churches to boot in the course of a single morning; and when you meet them in the evening at the table-d'hôte they enumerate the achievements of the day as though the sights which they had seen were so many scalps ravished by ruthless tomahawks from inimical skulls, and to be dried and hung up as trophies in their lodges in the far distant West.

Other substitutes for scalps do they find in the amazing number of photographs which they purchase. Commercially, I should say that a photograph all the world over is an article which can be produced at the cost of about a penny, and which is sold at from a shilling to eighteen-pence. Somebody must be making a vast fortune every year by the sale of Roman photographs. They beat the Neapolitan ones— those of Pompeii excepted—most signally. The Bay of Naples does not photograph well, and Vesuvius under the sun's pencilling comes out but poorly. The modern architecture of Neapolis is uninteresting; the huge Royal Palace resembles a barrack; the façade of the San Carlo is vast, but not imposing; and the exteriors of the churches are naught. The costume of the people is as deplorably ragged as ever, but it has ceased to be picturesque. But at Rome everything with the exception of the staring brand new houses in the Via Nazionale and the new quarter of Macao is worth photographing. There are said to be eleven thousand rooms in the Vatican; and, could they be all photographed, I have little doubt that customers could be found for prints of every *loggia* and every *stanza*.

It is pleasant to think of so many thousands of these photographs—ruins, churches, palaces, aqueducts, obelisks, fountains, tombs, pictures, and statues going to embellish the apartments of brown-stone houses with marble façades at Chicago or on "Nobs' Hill," San Francisco; but at the same time the artistic sense grows a little wearied when in the most frequented streets of Rome every other shop seems to be one for the sale of photographs. The Romans, however, may with justice plead that photograph selling is extremely profitable. A Roman shawl of brightly-dyed silk, a Roman bronze of the Triumphal Augustus, and Roman jewellery and mosaic work, cannot, I should say, be sold at a profit of more than a hundred and fifty per cent. But a much wider margin of gain is presented by the photographs, which in such astonishing profusion are vended to the flying sightseers.

And the Sedentary ones? They take their sight-seeing soberly, gravely—not sadly, but still slightly educationally from the classical and archæological point of view. They make "experiments solitary" and "experiments in consort," as Bacon puts it in the "Sylva Sylvarum," on Republican, on Imperial and Mediæval Rome—on the Rome of the Cæsars and the Rome of the Popes. The Sedentary sightseers systematically prime and load themselves with note and rubric before they proceed to see or re-see the sights themselves. They look up their Piranesi and their Rossini engravings of Old Rome. They take a morning *douche* of Soubriad Tranquillus, and emerge with memories refreshed on the subject of the Gardens of Messalina, the site of Phaon's villa where Nero died, and the details of the winter dress of Augustus—"a thick toga, four tunics, a shirt, a flannel stomacher, and swathings upon his legs and thighs." They read up their Ampère's "Histoire Romaine à Rome," their Gaston Boissier's "Promenades Archæologiques," and the works of German sages too numerous to mention; and then they sally forth well armed for the fray, well strengthened to wrestle with the dead and dusty past.

They have seen the ruins, trailed the ways, deciphered the inscriptions fifty times before; but the real Roman antiquary is never tired of revisiting the Old. He is always nourishing the hope that, by patience and good fortune combined, he shall be able, some day, to discover the New. For those who have no taste for sitting up till two in the morning poring over archæology or history, or getting up at six a.m. to pursue those edifying studies, there are "experiments in consort" to be made. Classical picnics—antiquarian camp meetings, so to speak—can be organised. The news flies like wildfire round the hotel that some erudite Englishman, such as Mr. Shakespeare Wood, is about "to take a party round" and lecture *in situ* on the history, the antiquities, the manners and customs, of ancient Rome. The ladies are in raptures. It is so pleasant to listen to a lecture—to those who like lectures. You learn something without having been at the pains of acquiring knowledge for yourself. It is more pleasant when the lecture is delivered in the very place of which the exposition treats. So smiling, interested, patient, and never bored or yawning bands of ladies and gentlemen gather round the learned expositor in the Forum or the Capitol, in the Pantheon or the Baths of Diocletian, in the arena of the Coliseum or by the Arch of Septimus Severus, while he holds the rapt ears which they so willingly lend him with the fairy tales of the Rome that once has been and the long result of ruin and decay.

While the perambulatory sightseers are thus pursuing their "experiments solitary" and their "experiments in consort," there is another class of amateurs who are deriving equal gratification from a wholly different branch of inquiry. They do not care two bajocchi about the identification of the true Via Triumphalis, the exact conformation of the Metæ Sudans, the precise distribution of the Palace of the Cæsars, or the real purpose of the rotunda of the Pantheon of Agrippa. The so-called Temple of Vesta might be the Choragic Monument of Lysicrates, at Athens, for what they care. They are picture-hunters. They are seeking after little-known examples of Martino da Udine or Pierino del Vaga. They have heard of an Andrea del Sarto in one of those sacred edifices known as a "chiesa qualunque"—some church or another, the votive saint of which is not very popular, or which, like the Church of Santa Bibiana, is open only once a year. So they are seeking for the *custode* of the "chiesa qualunque," to tempt that aged and snuffy janitor, with hints of lire and centisimi, to show them the supposititious Andrea del Sarto, the rumoured Mantegna, the whispered Cimabue, the reported Bamboccio, the reputed Giovanni Bellini, which very possibly has no existence there whatever. Still the quest is an exciting one.

Little need be said of the Catholics, who, from all parts of the world, come to Rome, in season and out of season, not to study antiquities, not to see sights, not to benefit the shopkeepers and the masters of languages, the jewellers and picture-dealers, the mosaic-workers and shawl-weavers, but simply because it is the City of St. Peter and St. Paul—a Shrine to which they are Pilgrims. You do not see much of them at the hotels frequented by the "families." You do not meet them to any great extent at five o'clock teas and dinner parties or receptions. They have their own *alberghi*, their own society, their own objects and pursuits. And they see a vast deal of inner Roman life utterly and inevitably invisible to the sightseers and the societarians who bring the manners of Mayfair into the Piazza di Spagna, and during twelve weeks or so make the Corso look like a squeezed-up copy of Piccadilly.

There remains only to be noticed in the way of Anglo-Saxon visitors to the Eternal City the small minority at whose existence I have already glanced. They come with tolerable frequency to Rome, because it is Rome; and they stay there month after month until the heat renders it no longer habitable to English people, simply because they like being in Rome. Were you to ask them, with the searching directness which made the son of Sophroniscus such an embarrassing interlocutor to the Athenians of old, what were the grave reasons for their love of Rome, they might, perhaps, be puzzled to give a definite answer. The place suits them; they have been here so many times before, the water is so drinkable, life is so easy, one is never bored, you sleep so well at night, you can get up so early in the morning, the people are so civil, there is no fuss, you can do what you like; existence, if you can speak Italian, is so cheap; something fresh turns up every day; idleness is not accounted a crime; you can dress as you please—does not his Majesty King Umberto appear even in places of fashionable resort in a "pot" hat?—"these, or any other reasons why" may be given, just as they arise to the mind, by the people who come to Rome without any ascertained purpose and remain there without any particular views upon matters in general.

Such explanations might not have satisfied the too exigent son of Sophroniscus; but a quick-witted Italian would at once understand and accept the explanation, however lamely it was given. Rome in the winter time is the place where you can indulge to the very fullest in that most charming of all pursuits, the "dolce far niente;" and it is those who during the greater part of the year work harder than carthorses labour who are most addicted to coming to Rome when they can snatch a holiday, in order, practically, and for a few short but delicious weeks, to exchange their names for that by which Charles Lamb, when he came home for good on his India House pension, declared that, if he had a son, he would christen him "Nothing to Do."

XXI.

IN THE VATICAN.

Rome, *December* 5.

I HAD been but a very few days in the Eternal City when it began to be mournfully apparent to me that I had fallen into evil odour with some of the oldest and most esteemed of my Anglo-Roman friends. In the course of an entire week I had not shown the slightest inclination to revisit the Forum Romanum; nor had I made any inquiries touching the Arch of Constantine or the Baths of Titus. I may voluntarily add to the catalogue of my sins of omission by avowing that I went away from Rome altogether without renewing my acquaintance with the Coliseum and the Baths of Caracalla, and without setting foot in the Catacombs. Even worse than this, I explored but very few churches, and visited even fewer palaces in which there were picture galleries.

The truth is that when one has arrived at a certain period of life, the remainder of that life—it *must* be brief, and may end the next minute—is not long enough for sight-seeing. When, safe at home, you possess your *Murray* and your Francis Wey's "Rome," and Guhl and Kohner's vast antiquarian work; when you have a large stock of photographs, large and small, of the ancient and mediæval monuments of

Roma Urbs; and when, finally, you still retain a tolerably accurate remembrance of the things which you have beheld in the bygone, why should you run the risk of catching a bad cold by sallying out on a wet day to see a pile of old stones, which two thousand years ago was somebody's mausoleum, or to inspect the marble torso of an unclothed gentleman destitute of head, arms, and legs, and representing, as you are informed, "Hercules Reposing after Slaying the Erymanthian Boar"? Why should you be expected to go into hypocritical ecstasies over a picture very possibly painted by Titian or by Domenichino, but which has become so blurred and smirched by time and the smoke of fifty thousand devotional wax tapers, or else has had its handiwork so hopelessly marred by the wretches called "restorers," that it conveys no kind of impression on your mind beyond a dim sensation that you are looking at so much Smudge, and that the Smudge is, both technically and æsthetically, infinitely inferior to the line engraving you have of the now ruined work—an engraving executed when the picture was young, centuries before the wretched restorers were born.

It is my misfortune, if it be not my fault, to fail in the appreciation of relics of antiquity, simply because they are antique. It is possible to be old and ugly. *Experto crede.* When I was at Constantinople a few years since, I bought in the Mosque of St. Sophia, and for the moderate sum of a medjidie, say four shillings, a handful of tiny vitreous cubes, some coloured, some gilt, which were continually falling on the pavement from the disintegrating mosaic work of the cupola. I gave away most of the "tesseræ;" but the residue

I placed for safety in a little cardboard box, which had once been full of gum-arabic jujubes. I opened this cardboard box one day, and was proudly exhibiting one of my vitreous cubes—a dull yellow in hue—when, to my discomfiture, I discovered that I had taken out a little cube of gum-arabic, by mistake. The cubes were so very much alike: only I had bought the bit of gum at a druggist's in Piccadilly the day before yesterday; whereas the little bit of coloured glass had been laid in its bed of cement in the reign of Justinian, and was some fourteen hundred years old.

This apologue touching the mosaic work in the Mosque of St. Sophia is not, I would entreat you to believe, a digression. It naturally recurred to me when a few mornings since I found myself watching with eager interest and curiosity the various processes employed in what I may term "picture-building" in the Royal Pontifical Manufactory of Mosaics in the Vatican. Elsewhere Leo XIII. may be discrowned; but here at least he is King, and in truly regal quarters is his Holiness' mosaic factory installed. My good antiquarian and æsthetic Anglo-Roman friends, who had taken in such dudgeon my neglect of the ordinary round of sightseeing, had laid a kindly trap for me, and baited it with an envelope adorned with a flaming vermilion seal bearing the effigy of a cardinal's hat surmounting a profusely emblazoned scutcheon. The envelope contained a card of admission to the Pontifical Mosaic Manufactory, courteously granted by one of the Eminences of the Sacred College. Such permits were, I was given to understand, very rarely granted, and I should be privileged to see a sight not only interesting but unique.

It took me, however, a considerable time to make up my mind to visit the Vatican and see the mosaics made. There was so much to view and to admire—I use admire in the sense of being astonished—in New Rome. Take the new Post Office, for example. The old one was a gloomy, tumble-down edifice, the rules and regulations of which were as antiquated as the building itself; and owing to the ignorance and stupidity of the officials, and the difficulty which they experienced in deciphering English names, Murray used gravely to recommend his readers to have their letters, for reasons of safety, addressed to the care of a banker or of some respectable hotel. The postage of a letter from Rome to England was fifty-five centimes, and to the United States one franc fifteen centimes. At present all the countries which have entered into the International Postal Convention enjoy the privileges of the reduced tariff of twenty-five centimes, or twopence-farthing and a fraction, for a single letter; and the new Roman Post Office occupies an immense disestablished monastery in a Piazza approached from the Corso by the Via dei Convertiti.

The façade has been made "architechtonically" splendid with that facility for passing off old clothes for new—and what are buildings but the old clothes of Time?—of which the Italians are such wondrous masters. In the interior the old convent garden in the quadrangle has been left pretty much in its former state, and looks pleasantly fresh and green, with a fountain cascading in silvery spray in the middle; but the cloisters surrounding the *cortile* have undergone an astounding transformation.

No more venerable friars with shaven crowns and cowls and

sandalled feet peacefully pacing the marble flags, and rapt in ascetic meditation, or tranquilly perusing the Acts of the Saints or the works of St. Thomas Aquinas, or some other good book. In the place of these holy men the once solemn arcades re-echo now to the tramping of hurried letter-carriers, to the vociferations and laughter of boisterous *contadine* clamorously demanding payment of post-office orders; to the shrill trebles of urchins sent to purchase postage stamps, and to the authoritative tones of ¦travelling Britons, in plaid ulsters and Glengarry bonnets, sternly inquiring after letters addressed to " Signor Giovanni Smith—Monsieur John Smith, you know, Poste Restante, laissez till called for—What the doose does the fellow mean?" The "fellow," otherwise a civil and intelligent post-office employé, has been vainly endeavouring, first in Italian and then in French, to explain to the stern and ultimately exasperated Briton that if he requires a letter addressed to Signor Smith he should ask for it at the window over which is painted the letter "S," and not at the casement in front of which the Briton is now shaking his fist and raging like a lion, and over which is inscribed the letter "P."

The "poste restante" arrangements in the new Roman Post Office are simply admirable, and equally so are the facilities for registering letters, obtaining money-orders, buying postage-stamps and post-cards, and franking books and newspapers. The Central Telegraph Office is in the same building with the Post Office; and the room in which you write your telegrams is provided with comfortable chairs and an ample table. There is another apartment equally comfortable for persons who wish to write letters and post their correspondence there and then. There is, moreover, on the part of the clerks, unvarying civility and a desire to oblige the foreigner. If they, the employés, would only refrain from puffing out volumes of smoke from the most horribly-smoking of conceivable "Cavours," while they are giving you information, I should be disposed to think them about the pleasantest set of post-office clerks that I have ever come in contact with.

Art as well as utility has been well cared for in the new building of the "Regie Poste." The arches of the cloisters and the panelled walls between the windows, looking into what were once the cells of the monks, are luxuriantly and cheerfully painted with arabesques in fresco, reminding you somewhat of the decorations with which nearly forty years ago Mr. Rudolph Sang enriched the arcades of the quadrangle in our Royal Exchange. But a curious exuberance of design marks the achievements of the fresco painter in the transformed monastery. The arabesques designed by Rafaelle and executed chiefly by his pupils in the Loggie of the Vatican, have evidently been the models selected for imitation by the modern painter. You are familiar with the curious little accessories in which, either in caprice or with subtle symbolism, the illustrious Sanzio of Urbino has indulged here and there in the Loggie—the cupids bestriding snails, the nymphs battling with lizards, the owl gravely riding in a chariot drawn by swallows.

But the imagination of the decorator of the Roman post-office arabesques has run riot to even a greater extent than this. Now and again he has out-Heroded Herod in the way of redundant accessories: introducing among his scrolls and acanthus leaves such incongruous objects as parrots, monkeys, squirrels, oysters, lobsters, peaches, figs, tomatoes, and onions. Yes, onions; and with a very fine effect of colour too. The boldest artistic performances of the converted convent are, however, two frescoes flanking one another under the archway of the entrance to the cloisters. One symbolises the "Regie Poste" personified by an athletic female draped in the Italian colours, and apparently sitting on one of the buffers of a huge locomotive, the black funnel of which towers over her head and belches fuliginous fumes into the pure blue sky. At the feet of the sitting figure are mounds of letters, postcards, newspapers, and pamphlets, all painted with really remarkable spirit and realism. I have seen some very strange sights in my time; but I scarcely thought that I should live to see postage-stamps, newspaper-wrappers, and engine-buffers limned in fresco on the wall of a convent at Rome.

The spectacle was perhaps a little too modern to harmonise with even my Philistine spirit. You scarcely care about the sight of a company of Turkish soldiers washing in an antique Roman sarcophagus of porphyry. The whistle of a penny steamer on the Canalazzo at Venice jars upon your nerves somewhat; and it is with difficulty that you reconcile yourself to the spectacle of a hideous old woman plying a sewing machine in that very house close to the Tiber's bank, hard by the Farnesina, at the very window from which, according to tradition, the most bewitching of Bakeresses first cast her eyes on Rafaelle and set his heart and brain on fire. I have beheld these things. But the postage-stamps and newspaper-wrappers, the engine-buffers and funnels in fresco, seemed to "cap the climax" of incongruity. Why? If the Romans had had steam-engines and postage-stamps they would have duly depicted them in fresco or in mosaic. That "plagosus Orbilius" of a schoolmaster at Herculaneum, who was so terribly fond of horsing little boys and thrashing them with eelskins, placidly hung out his sign, on which was graphically depicted the entire process of castigation. In modern times we have gone no farther in this direction than the *graffito* of the Irish schoolmaster, who, according to Thomas Hood, chalked on a board outside his shanty, "Children Taken in to Bate."

Be it as it may, I liked the second fresco better than the Postal one. This pendant was an emblem of Electric Telegraphy. In the middle distance, in a stormy sky, lurid with thunder-clouds, you saw dimly the poles and the wires. But right across the field of vision, her garments tossed in air, her comet-like tresses streaming in the blast, came "flying all abroad" Electra herself—the genuine daughter of Atlas and Pleione—the mother of Dardanus borne "on the wings of all the winds," and carrying Light to the uttermost ends of the earth. The artist had made his Electra a little too muscular, perhaps, and she had a trifle too much of the amplitude of Nana of the "stupendi capelli;" still, the conception was a grand one, grandly carried out. Imagine her Majesty's Postmaster-General commissioning Sir Frederick Leighton to paint a fresco symbolical of the apotheosis of Sir Rowland Hill and the penny postage system for the great hall of St. Martin's-le-Grand, or requesting Mr. Poynter to prepare a cartoon of the Pleiades welcoming Electra for the Telegraph Office in Lothbury.

But that noble figure of the nymph with the "stupendi capelli"—the Italians have not ceased to rave about Nana's torrent of golden hair—put me in a good temper with modern Italian art, and I surrendered myself quite submissively to the brace of trusty and well-beloved but despotic friends who were to be my guides through the Mosaic Manufactory of the Vatican. I have been wandering about the habitable globe during so many years that I have been able to pick up only a smattering of cities. I know most of them slightly, but none thoroughly. Well, there are travellers and travellers. My topographical knowledge is more akin to the lore of a Queen's Messenger than to that of Ulysses. Thus, while I deeply revere, I timorously dread, the man who knows Rome thoroughly. He is sure to be a despot. He frowns upon you darkly when you erroneously mention a particular picture in the Church of San Carlo in Corso, when in reality it is in San Luigi dei Francesi. The Guido in the Palazzo Schiabbi! Stuff and nonsense! It is in the Palazzo Frattaglia. The Via dei Ravenelli? You mean the Via della Bella Pizzicagnola. If you are to make such absurd blunders as that, you had best not come to Rome at all. The friends, however, who conducted me to the Mosaic Factory in the Vatican were not exceptionally hard on me for my ignorance of that particular item of the "Roba di Roma;" since I shrewdly suspect that on the morning when we alighted from our carriage on the Piazza San Pietro they knew as little about Mosaic as I did myself.

A CARDINAL ENTERING THE VATICAN.

We entered the Palace of the Vatican by the Gate of Bronze, which is kept jealously guarded by the "Svizzeri," or Swiss bodyguard of the Pope. In the old days of the Temporal Power there were, I believe, some eight hundred of these "Svizzeri," but since the advent of United Italy their ranks have been sadly decimated. Their maintenance in their former strength would be far too grievous a burden on the Papal Exchequer, and I question whether the Swiss Guard at present numbers so many as fifty men. I was glad to see the historical halberdiers once more, in their quaint mediæval costumes, which make them look half like wasps of abnormal dimensions and half like bellicose harlequins; but the glaring hues of their garb, which jar upon the vision when you are close to them, harmonise and tone down admirably well when they are seen in groups at a distance. I was much struck by the youth and beardlessness of these warriors. The old Swiss Guards were mature and often grizzled soldiers. The Papal gendarmes, of whom a few were scattered about the corridors and staircases, are very fine and athletic-looking men, in handsome but not too showy uniforms.

Our permits were inspected first by the "Svizzero" who was standing sentry, and next by the gendarme on duty, and we had access to the Vatican. Ascending a lofty stone staircase, we seemed to have left Italy a very long way behind us. No "loafers," no brawling newspaper boys, no feverishly disputing politicians. Everything was very still and quiet. Now and again a shovel-hatted priest or a purple-stockinged Monsignore glided by. A "Svizzero," lounging on a bench by the guardhouse door, was reading the orthodox *Osservatore Romano*. I wonder whether he had ever heard of such wicked papers as the *Pungolo*, the *Fanfulla*, and the *Capitan Fracassa*. No; Italy was such a very long way off, and in my mind's eye at every corner I seemed to see a placard addressed to non-clerical Romans, and inscribed "No admission, even on business."

It was from a corridor at an angle of the Court of San Damaso that we entered the "Reale Fabbrica" of mosaics. I had expected to find some scores of art-workmen busily employed; but in the spacious and lofty studio into which we were ushered after passing through a gallery hung with splendid specimens of completed mosaic work, there were only two artists present. One was an elderly gentleman in spectacles, who was busily engaged in copying a noble picture of a Madonna and Child by Rubens. He had been occupied with this labour many months, and would be occupied with it many more. Some of the largest pictures, such as those, for example, which serve as altar-pieces in St. Peter's, have taken from fifteen to twenty years to execute, and each of the boldly-designed and rather roughly-finished series of portraits of the Popes recently completed for the embellishment of the frieze in the basilica of Saint Paul Without the Walls took twelve months to perfect.

The guardian, a most affable old gentleman in a black velvet skull cap, was apparently very anxious to impress on our minds the fact that there were twenty-seven thousand different tints of vitreous enamel kept "in stock" for the purposes of the work. In *Murray* it is stated that there are only ten thousand various shades of glass preserved ready for the hand of the Master Mosaicists; but I have seen the number quoted as being as high as fifty thousand. How many thousands of bits of glass enter into the composition of a mosaic picture as large as the Transfiguration or the Saint Cecilia only the artist can tell—if, indeed, he has cared to keep count; for when the finished picture is finally ground and polished down so as to present a uniformly glossy surface the joints between the smaller "spiculæ" of enamel almost entirely disappear, especially in the flesh tints, and the use of a strong magnifying glass is needed to arrive at the discovery that there were some hundreds of tiny vitreous morsels in the high light in a nose, a chin, or an eye.

The elderly gentleman in the spectacles stood before what appeared to be a painter's easel of unusual size and strength. To his right, about four feet from him, was the Rubens which he was simulating. About three parts of the mosaic picture, which was considerably larger than the model, were finished, the artist having apparently worked downwards. The last quarter or lower part of the picture was, to speak plainly, in a shocking mess, and conveyed to my mind an odd impression that the ingenious craftsman was not only an artist in mosaic, but a layer of bricks and a spreader of mortar, and that there should properly be standing behind him a labourer with a hod. There were great gaps and fissures in the work; there were rows upon rows of unfinished glass brickwork with the mortar, so to speak, plainly visible between them; there was a good deal of dust about, and a good deal more moisture. But I began, by degrees, to understand the process which was being employed, and the guardian in the velvet skull cap came to my aid, when I was at fault, with most courteous explanations. He mentioned incidentally that, in a portrait of Pope Pius V., there were one million seven hundred thousand pieces, each no larger than a grain of millet; but this statement I take to have been mainly guesswork. The enamel, he proceeded to tell me, is a kind of glass, coloured with metallic oxides, and it is so fusible that it can be drawn out into threads, small rods, or oblong sticks of varying degrees of fineness, slightly resembling the type used by compositors. These polychromatic rods are kept in drawers properly numbered, so that the artist knows to which case to repair when he requires a fresh supply of a particular tint or tints.

When the picture is commenced the first step is to place on the easel a slab of marble, copper, or slate of the size fixed upon; and this slab is hollowed out to a depth of about three and a half inches, leaving a flat border all round, which will be on a level with the completed mosaic. The excavated slab is intersected by transverse grooves or channels, so as to hold more tenaciously the cement in which the mounts of enamel will be embedded. Then the hollowed slab is filled in with "gesso," or plaster of Paris, on which the proposed design is accurately traced in outline, and usually in pen and ink. The artist then proceeds to scoop out a small portion of the plaster with a little sharp tool. He fills up the cavity thus made with wet cement or "mastic," and into this mastic he successively thrusts the "spiculæ" or the "tesseræ," as the case may be, according to the pattern at his side. In the broad folds of drapery or in the even shadows of a background or a clear sky, his morsels of enamel may be as large as one of a pair of dice; in the details of lips or eyes or hair, or foliage or flowers, the bits of glass may be no larger than pins' heads. The cement, or mastic, is made, so far as I could gather from my informant, of slaked lime, finely powdered Tiburtine marble and linseed oil, and, when thoroughly dry, is as hard as flint.

Sometimes the mastic which fills the cavity is smoothed and painted in fresco with an exact replica of the pattern, and into this the bits of glass are driven, according to tint, by means of a small wooden mallet. It is obvious that, by this last-named process, a skilled mosaicist could produce a picture "out of his own head," and without having recourse to any pattern at all; and it strikes me that an ingenious novice might make considerable progress in the art by adopting the frescoed mastic way of working, which would simply amount to a continuous series of displacements and replacements, by matching a spot of the frescoed design by a morsel of enamel of exactly the same hue, and thrusting in a bit of hard glass in lieu of the soft mastic. If the effect produced wounds the artist's eye, he can easily amend the defect by withdrawing the offending piece of enamel and driving in another while the cement is still wet; and, by observing proper precautions, it can be kept damp for more than a fortnight. When the work is completed, any tiny crevices which may remain are carefully plugged or "stopped" with pounded marble, or with enamel mixed with wax, and the entire surface of the picture is then ground down to a perfect plane, and finally polished with putty and oil.

Byzantine may be broadly distinguished from Roman mosaic by the circumstance of the surface of the former being left unground and unpolished—save where there is burnished gold—thus leaving an irregularity of surface productive of great vigour of effect. A vitreous picture of the Byzantine style can at once be recognised as a mosaic, even if it be hung at an altitude of a hundred feet from the ground; but a perfected mosaic picture, after the Roman manner, might easily be mistaken, even at a very short distance, for a very elaborately-finished and highly-varnished painting in oils.

WOMEN OF THE CAMPAGNA.

XXII.

WITH THE TRAPPISTS IN THE CAMPAGNA.

ROME, *December* 8.

GONDOMAR, Spanish Ambassador at the Court of James I., who was so grimly instrumental in getting one of the wisest and noblest heads in England—that of Sir Walter Raleigh— cut off, was, on occasion, fond of a joke. "On your arrival at Madrid," he said gravely to a young gentleman of Aragon whom he was sending back to Spain with dispatches, "you will present my compliments to El Señor·Sol, and tell him how delighted I shall be to renew my acquaintance with him. I have not seen him during my residence in this country." This was, very probably, a standing jest at the English climate in Gondomar's time; and it remains a jest to this day.

"El Sol sale a Antequera," say the Spaniards; but Britain, it would seem, is a wholly sunless land. When London is not shrouded by fog it is deluged with rain; and, according to our lively neighbours and critics, the French, so densely impregnated does the watery downpour become with the sooty residuum of our perpetually generating smoke, that when it rains in London it rains ink. When the vivacious *feuilletonniste*, M. Alfred Assolant, constrained for a season to inhabit the dismal region of "Le Soho," wished to replenish the contents of his inkstand he had only, according to his own showing, to open his window and hold forth his *encrier;* and forthwith the sable-weeping heavens filled it with imperishable jet black japan writing fluid. Yes, it is all too true; and continuously recurring fog, rain, and cloudiness, aggravated by smoke, make London the most colourless city in the world.

It may be considered, nevertheless, as equally gratifying and consolatory to wounded English susceptibilities that foreigners have at most times been extremely fond of following English fashions; and in New Rome the rage which exists at present for imitating all things English approaches the proportions of an Anglomania. Three out of every five young Roman ladies wear ulsters and Gainsborough hats; the shop windows are full of "Swanbill corsets" and "kiltings made by steam;" boots, body-linen, hosiery, are all marked "Inglesi" in conspicuous characters; "nonpareil velveteens," warranted of Manchester manufacture, are extensively worn; and Roman gentlemen not only patronise English tailors and trim their hair and whiskers according to our "gilded youth," or "jeunesse stage-doory" pattern, but they are beginning to keep betting-books and bulldogs, to carry "crutch" sticks, and to understand the merits of Apollinaris and Wilhelmsquelle, of English pickles, potted anchovies, and pale ale.

But there is another and less agreeable particular in which during my stay in the capital of King Umberto the aspect of my dear native land was followed with painful fidelity. It rained during nearly the whole time, and the Roman clerk of the weather was apparently a fanatical Anglomane, resolved to prove to the *forestieri* that no efforts on his part should be wanting to make the Corso and the Via Nazionale vie, in the way of colourless dinginess and muddy wretchedness, with the Holborn Viaduct at the beginning of November or Cheapside at the end of February. I thought of Gondomar and his joke about the sun; I thought of M. Alfred Assolant and his sneer about the ink-raining sky in "Le Soho," when, a few mornings since, I started on an expedition into the Campagna of Rome. Perhaps I inwardly chuckled and mentally rubbed my hands. The day was such a curiously accurate reproduction of a London day of the very worst late autumnal kind. It did not rain heavily—no, no; that would have afforded some promise of its "holding up," and of the sun breaking through the leaden veil of the sky. The downcome was a fine, steady, pitiless, conservative drizzle; and it made you less actually wet than generally damp and proportionately miserable. The City of the Cæsars was tinted in a dismal monochrome in its lightest parts akin to the suit of dockyard drab with which they used to indue the old wooden three-deckers laid up in ordinary at Sheerness. In the Corso umbrellas were thicker than, probably, leaves are in Vallombrosa at this season of the year, and the Piazza Colonna was dotted with shiny black groups of Roman citizens enveloped in macintoshes. All out of doors was thoroughly English and thoroughly like London, and I inwardly exulted.

We were bound on a pilgrimage to the historical Abbey of St. Paolo alle Tre Fontane, or of the Three Fountains, the legend of which may be very briefly recited. Three churches are comprised in the actual buildings of the abbatial demesne; the site on which they stand being known to the ancient Romans as the Salvian Waters, or "Massa Aquæ Salviæ," a name given to the district from the unhealthy swampiness of the neighbourhood, which was the property of a noble Roman family, the Salvia "gens." The legend tells that when Nero decreed that the Apostles Saint Peter and Saint Paul should be put to death it was to the Salvian Waters that the Apostle of the Gentiles was conducted, while the Fisherman Saint was made painfully to climb the Heavy Hill of the Janiculum. St. Paul was brought to the Aquæ Salviæ; he was bound to the truncated shaft of a pillar, and at one blow the executioner struck off his head. When separated from the trunk the apostolic head made three successive leaps or bounds; and from each spot where it touched the earth a miraculous fountain instantaneously sprang, and has continued to flow until this day. The water of each of these fountains has, so the pilgrims say, a different flavour. The first is very soft and sweet to the palate, and almost tepid; the second is harder and cooler; and the third is icy cold. After the persecutions had come to an end a church was built over the place of the Three Fountains. At the end of the sixteenth century, the sacred edifice having fallen into 'a hopelessly ruinous condition, it was entirely rebuilt by Cardinal Pietro Aldobrandini.

Close to the edifice which serves as a canopy for the Three Fountains was afterwards erected another to commemorate the martyrdom of St. Zeno, the Tribune who, with the ten thousand two hundred and three Christian legionaries under his command, was put to death at the Aquæ Salviæ during the persecution of Diocletian. The pious legionaries had been in the outset condemned to labour as convicts in the construction of the Baths of Diocletian, but when that vast pile was completed, the Emperor being at a loss to know what to do with such a vast number of Christian captives, had them brought hither and slaughtered *en masse*. Their remains were interred close to a spring which bore then, as it yet bears, the name of " the overflowing rill." The church containing the Zenonian relics is called St. Mary of the Holy Ladder, to perpetuate the memory of a vision of St. Bernard, who, while celebrating a mortuary mass in the church dedicated to the Madonna, saw in a vision a ladder by which angels were conducting redeemed souls from purgatory to paradise.

Finally, to complete this group of sacred fanes, is the early Christian basilica of San Vicenzo and Sant' Anastasio, built in the reign of Honorius in the seventh, and restored by Pope Leo III. in the eighth century. Anastasius was a Persian monk, who, with horrible tortures, was put to death during the persecution of Chosroes III. The body of the martyred saint was sent by the Emperor Heraclius from Constantinople to Rome, together with a carefully-painted portrait of St. Anastasius in his habit as he had lived. This effigy was held in such deep veneration that at the Second Council of Nice it was cited as evidence against the Iconoclasts as a proof of the orthodoxy of a "cultus" of holy pictures. St. Vincent was a Spanish saint, whose bones were brought from the Peninsula to the Salvian Waters. The head of this saint was preserved in the Abbey of Clairvaux in France until 1789;

but during the troubles of the Revolution it altogether vanished. You may ask me why, in this city, which is brimful of the relics of saints and martyrs, I should specially make a pilgrimage to the Abbey of the Three Fountains. I will only answer that my reason for repairing thither lay simply in the fact that the establishment by the Salvian Waters is tenanted by perhaps as interesting, as laborious, and as beneficent a monastic community as can be found anywhere in Christendom.

Prior to the year 1868, when a band of Trappist monks arrived at the Three Fountains, the locality was fatally renowned as the very unhealthiest in the whole Campagna of Rome. It was called emphatically "Il Sepolcro"—the sepulchre. It was the most desolate spot in a Plain of Desolation; and the malaria raged there more furiously than in any other of the fever-stricken environs of the city. The abbot and leader of this party of pioneers was a certain Dom Eutropio who had been prior of the Convent of Gethsemane, and had lived and laboured long in the United States. Returning after many years' absence to the Old World, he sought what he thought would be permanent retreat at the Trappist Abbey of Melleray, in France; but in his sixtieth year, feeling a "mission" within him, he repaired, with the reluctant consent of his superior, to Rome, where he obtained permission from Pio Nono to set up the standard of his Order at the long-deserted monastery attached to the basilica of Saint Anastasius and Saint Vincent, alle Tre Fontane. For ages there had been a community of monks of Citeaux of the Congregation of St. Bernard there; but in the year 1810, two years after Napoleon I. had violently laid hands on the Patrimony of St. Peter and made a prisoner of the Pope, the Abbey of the Three Fountains was placed under the administrative rule of an Imperial French Commissary. About the same time the magnificent silver reliquaries and other precious objects offered by the piety of Charlemagne and succeeding generations of princes, potentates, and cardinals mysteriously disappeared. Much valuable vine and olive land was alienated from the monastery; and the last Superior, Dom Gerardo Giovannini, had the mortification to see the conventual cellarer promoted over his, Dom Gerardo's head to be Abbot, and died of a broken heart.

After the restoration of the States of the Church, Pope Leo XII. paid a visit in state to the Three Fountains. He found no one there to receive him, and was mournfully struck by the wretched condition of dilapidation, neglect, and foulness into which the entire premises had fallen. By a bull shortly afterwards promulgated he deprived the order of Citeaux of all property in the Tre Fontane, and entrusted the custody of the abbey to the Friars Minor of the Observance. The Friars Minor, however, did not care much for their new appanage. It was so horribly unhealthy. For years no service whatsoever was celebrated in the three churches; and the solitary inhabitant of the monastery was a lay brother who in the daytime officiated as a guide to the strangers and pilgrims who came to visit the sanctuaries. But at eventide the discreet lay brother, through fear of the dreadful malaria, took refuge at the adjoining hamlet of San Sebastiano. During the pontificate of Pius VII. a priest came once a week during

the pasturage season to say mass in the Church of the Holy Ladder, and to catechise the children of the shepherds. At length, in 1868, a munificent gentleman, named De Mauligny, having offered to restore the basilica, Pio Nono permitted the Trappists of the Order of Citeaux to take possession once more of the church and monastery which during so many centuries had been theirs.

Nineteen monks were found ready to confront the malarial terrors of the "Agro Romano." During the first years of their residence at the Three Fountains the sufferings of these devoted monks were terrible. Every one of their number was in turn stricken down by the fever, to which many of them succumbed. But fresh contingencies of friars continued to arrive from the central monastery of La Trappe; and eventually the indomitable energy and perseverance of Dom Eutropio and his coadjutors succeeded in vanquishing obstacles which had at the outset appeared insurmountable. There were times when the community was reduced to a feeble band of living skeletons, so to speak, going about their work with half-fevered, half-palsied limbs; but they triumphed at last. The purpose of the Abbot who had been in the United States was not by any means to make of this plague-spot in the Campagna a kind of Thebaïd, where merely anchorites should dwell. Dom Eutropio's object was essentially that which governed the life-long philosophical investigations of Francis of Verulam— that is to say, Fruit. He sought to make this desert fair; this pestiferous swamp sound, and fertile, and healthy. His ultimate aspiration was the reclamation of the whole waste of the Campagna.

As a beginning, the monks began to plant the marshy neighbourhood of the Tre Fontane with the beneficent eucalyptus. By means of this thirstiest of trees, growing as it does with astonishing rapidity, and to an amazing altitude, the stagnant waters over many square acres around the monastery were drained. Mountains of vegetable rubbish were burned or carted away; and then the monks began to break up the ground of the Campagna and plant it with vines, and olives, and corn. But, in many dry places, where the earth had been undisturbed for ages, the soil had become so hard as to defy the action of spade and pick, and the resolute Trappists were fain at last to undermine the obstinate crust and blast the indurated clods bodily with dynamite. They found beneath a virgin soil in which all healthful verdant things would grow and thrive and render fruit in due season. They trenched and channelled, they built an aqueduct to carry off waste water; but all this time they had to fight the fever.

Their allotment of land from the Pontifical Government was but small, but in process of time the eucalypti which they had planted stood their friends. Too poor to consume quinine in adequate quantities, they found in the eucalyptus a providential remedy for fever. They used at first, and with success, a decoction of its leaves, as is the practice in North Africa, on the banks of the Danube, and in other malarious regions, but the inconvenience of this rudimentary preparation eventually led them to the concoction of an Elixir of Eucalyptus, which in their laboratory they are now constantly labouring to perfect. Meanwhile their agricultural labours have resulted in an actual change in the climate of the Tre Fontane. The monks are no longer compelled, as they were during the first year, to reside in Rome during the summer, and leave their cells in the Campagna to solitude and the Demon of the Malaria. During the deadly season they take every day, fasting, a small dose of the Elixir, and repeat it whenever any premonitory symptoms of returning fever are felt. If, in spite of these precautions, absolute fever does make its appearance, the use of the Elixir is preceded by a small dose of sulphate of quinine.

But how, it may be asked, have a small band of Trappist monks, numbering sometimes less than twenty, been able to accomplish all the work of drainage, reclamation, and cultivation which have made their allotment in the Campagna a hale and smiling champaign. I must explain that they have had help. In the last days of the Temporal Power, Monsignor de Mérode, who was Director-General of the Pontifical Prisons, and took great interest in the enterprise of the courageous Trappists · of the Tre Fontane, lent them a numerous gang of galley slaves from the Bagno of Civita Vecchia. The Government at present dominant in Rome did not, I am glad to say, repudiate the wise measures of its predecessors; and the friars of the Tre Fontane continue to enjoy the approval and assistance of the powers that be. They have now, I believe, as many as a hundred or a hundred and fifty convicts employed in building and agricultural work round about the monastery. We met a whole omnibus full of these rogues on the road to the Tre Fontane.

We had driven out of Rome by the gate called Trigemina

or Porta San Paolo, hard by the Pyramid of Caius Cestius and that Protestant Cemetery where the bones of Keats and the ashes of Shelley's heart lie buried, and so along the Ostian Way to the great Basilica of St. Paul without the Walls. I was noticing, curiously, some wooden barriers placed at irregular intervals along the wayside, and reminding one somewhat of the bar in the angle of the wall at a police-station in which delinquents recently "run in" are preliminarily arraigned before the inspector on duty. The driver told us, in answer to our inquiries, that these barriers were for the protection of pedestrians in imminent peril of being overtaken, gored, and tossed by the wild cattle, herds of which still roam over the Campagna. The answer was scarcely satisfactory to me, since the entrances to these barricaded enclosures seemed quite wide enough to admit the wild cattle as well as the wayfarers; and I contemplated with feelings the reverse of pleasant the contingency of being shut up at close quarters with an infuriated buffalo.

All at once, turning a corner of the road we came upon the omnibus or covered van containing a cargo of quite another species of wild cattle. These were convicts. Their dress did not strike me as being intolerably degrading in cut or hue. I have seen convicts in many lands, and I confess it makes me shudder and turn sick when, in their garb, they are made to assume the aspect of gigantic canary birds, or of two-legged zebras, or of polychromatic "pierrots." I do not think, for all that a rascal has richly earned the agony and shame of penal servitude, Society has the right wholly and utterly to obliterate the sign which he should bear on his front: "This is a Man;" and I have been aware of convicts who have looked not like men, but like gorillas, clean shaven and fantastically accoutred, or like kangaroos with their tails cut off. These rascals in the omnibus reminded me of the marsupial Australian quadruped which is hyperbolically asserted to take only four leaps to a mile, in so far as on their villanous-looking heads they wore closely-fitting caps of some dingy brown fur. They were all murderers, I think the driver told us.

We met more convicts as we approached the Fontane, or saw them far off in the fields at work, watched by military guards armed with rifles and swords. Each convict wore a single chain, fastened to a gyve, round one ankle, and held up by a leathern band round his waist. The shackle seemed to me just heavy enough to prevent his scampering away over the Campagna after the manner of the wild cattle, but not so ponderous as to impede his ordinary movements or to torment him while he was working. The poor wretches touched their caps civilly as we drove by, and some of them looked harmless fellows enough. It is not all the rogues that are in gaol and with the "darbies" on. Later in the day, the Scotch mist having developed into drenching rain, the galley-slaves were allowed to knock off work, and were marched to their prison barrack in one of the courts of the vast old monastery. The front gate of the yard was heavily barred, but all and sundry were free to look through the grating and watch the gentlemen in trouble in their cage. In an hour or so the weather mended, and they congregated in groups in the court, in seemingly unrestricted association, prattling and laughing as though with their animal spirits at least there was not much the matter.

There was only a single Trappist father in full monastic panoply of white woollen and one or two lay brethren in brown gaberdines to be seen; and practically we had the Abbey of the Three Fountains to ourselves. It was well worth grave and reverent inspection, and I shall never forget the hours which I passed there. We entered the basilica which Honorius built, and which Leo VII., eleven hundred years before M. de Mauligny's time, restored. It has eight arches on either side, supported by pilasters and ornamented by frescoes of the Apostles, said to have been originally designed by Rafaelle, and executed by his scholars. The pictures at present visible are, however, the most pitiable of imaginable daubs. Through an open door, by the side of the apse, we could see an inner cloister of the monastery, and the entrance to a large refectory. In front of the basilica is a beautifully planted garden, blooming with bright-hued, fragrant shrubs and flowers. All things around spoke of work, and skill, and cheerfulness, and peace; yet one of the friends who accompanied me told me that he could mind the time, a very few years since, when the church and monastery were one hideous laystall, one Malebolgian desert of ruins, and decay, and garbage. No wonder that it was called "Il Sepolcro" till the Trappists and the Eucalyptus came.

XXIII.

FROM NAPLES TO POMPEII.

Naples, December 17.

WITH varying success during the last five weeks, and in twice as many cities of the Continent of Europe, have I been seeking, with the object of making my grateful compliments to him, El Senor Sol. On the whole, my Travels in Search of Sunshine since mid-November can scarcely be said to have yielded a triumphant result; and more than once, shivering with cold, drenched with rain, or choked with fog, in regions which, even at this advanced period of the year, are ordinarily blessed with a sunlit sky and a balmy temperature, I have read with sweet envy the accounts of certain phenomenally luminous sunsets which have recently occurred in England. Still, I have continued to hope for sunshine, and now and again have been blessed with brief snatches of golden bounty.

For example, I have been three days in Naples. All the way from Rome it poured mercilessly. My first Neapolitan day was so cold a one that my energies were mainly devoted to the task of blowing the bellows, and striving with adulatory puffs to coax and flatter the sulky logs in a fireplace not much bigger than a rabbit hutch into a cheerful blaze. Next came a day of gusty and rainy wrath—a day when the Mediterranean, dark and opaque in hue almost as the Black Sea, beat angrily against the parapet of the Chiaia, overleaping it even, sometimes, in spiteful, cat-spitting flakes of foam—a day when the leaden-coloured sky was so murky that the outline of Vesuvius was scarcely discernible. On such a day —the recreation of blowing the bellows having grown somewhat wearisome—the most available means for raising the spirits was to revisit the Museo Nazionale, and once more revel in the view of the Farnese Hercules, the Capuan Psyche, the Wounded Gladiator, and the Callipygian Venus.

But even the contemplation of those marvels of antique art palled after a time, especially when returning from the Museo on foot—it had cleared up a little in the afternoon—and looking in at a few curiosity shops, we were passionately adjured by Giovanni Tascabile from Sorrento, by Edoardo Senzavergogna from Palermo, and by Baruch of Posilipo, to purchase reduced copies of the Hercules, the Psyche, the Gladiator, and the Venus in alabaster, Parian, bronze, ivory, and terra-cotta. But there was a rosy sunset and a rosier afterglow which momentarily converted all the houses on the shore of the bay—from the palatial hotels and villas of the Chiaia to the miserable hovels beyond Santa Lucia—into so many kiosks of pink and gold, fit to be tenanted by the good Caliph Haroun Alraschid. The Night fell a few minutes afterwards—black and sudden like a funeral pall; but a weather-wise friend, well versed in the climate of Naples, confidently predicted the finest of Italian wintry days for the morrow; and on that morrow we determined to drive out along the shore towards Castellammare and lunch at a certain *locanda*, whither I had not been for sixteen years, about fourteen miles from Naples.

We could have gone by rail; but for a dozen reasons at least I preferred the road. There would be no dust—the rain had taken good care of that—and the drive I knew to be one of the most interesting that in any part of the world a traveller anxious to mark the aspect, manners, and customs of a people, and to compare them with the aspect, manners, and customs of their ancestors two thousand years ago, could possibly take. I say their ancestors, for although all manner of races of mankind have successively settled and had sway on the shores of this bay—Phœnicians, Greeks, Romans, Goths, Byzantines, Lombards, Frenchmen, Spaniards, and Germans—and although there are very few remains of ancient architecture in Naples or her immediate neighbourhood, the road from the Chiaia to Castellammare is still, emphatically and distinctly, the road from Neapolis to Stabiæ; from the Greek colony to the Roman city, and, from beginning to end, full of things and people differing very slightly from the things and people which Alma Tadema has, with astonishing force and truth, resuscitated in his pictures of antique Greek and Roman life. I say this seriously and deliberately; and with the full knowledge and remembrance that the people of Neapolis and Stabiæ two thousand years ago did not habitually wear trousers, and had no railways, gas, electric telegraphs and telephones; no printing presses, steamboats, and photographic studios, and that they were the most benighted of pagan idolaters. But the life and surroundings of their descendants are, for all that, in a thousand indelible traits and features the life and surroundings which Alma Tadema has conjured up from the remote past, and transferred to a canvas which almost breathes, and is vascular in its picturesqueness of realism.

I must confess that although the cheerful prognostications of my weatherwise friend as to the fineness of the morrow turned out to be perfectly accurate, I wished him very sincerely at the bottom of the Bay of Naples, when about seven in the morning he began to thump at my bedroom door and bade me get up and see the sunrise. I scarcely think that the Russian family in the next room approved of the thundering summons. I am sure that the Italian lady and baby on the other side were not pleased with the noise; indeed, the *bambino* began to howl in a distressing manner; but English people, when they have been long resident in Italy, always appear to me to have—if I may phrase it so—" weather on the brain." The climate is nominally so exquisitely beautiful that they resent a bad day as a sort of personal grievance; while the remembrance of exceptionally *belle giornate* of unusually lovely skies at sunrise or sunset, are treasured up and affectionately remembered as things of beauty which have become joys for ever.

As for the poorer class of Neapolitans—who form, I should say, at least three-fourths of a population of more than half a million—the sun is their inheritance, and very often their only patrimony. With sunshine and a few centesimi-worth of macaroni they can live and be happy. The sun is to them patron, host, friend, consoler, and physician. " Vieux vagabond, le soleil est à moi!" cries Beranger's beggar, dying in his ditch; and so it is with the Neapolitans, young and old. When it is cold or rainy their very physical aspect changes. They shrink, they wither, they cease to sing, they speak harshly and discordantly. They creep instead of walking. The mendicants forget their eloquence of alms-asking. Even the shopkeepers lose for the time their craft of loquacious lying. You begin to fancy that they are turning into moles and dormice; that, in a really severe winter, and with no foreigners in their midst to be fleeced, they would roll themselves up into balls and hybernate in some hole or corner till fine weather came again. It is only the hope of to-morrow being one of sunshine and the presence of the *forestiere* who in foul or fair weather is always susceptible of being fleeced that keep the Neapolitans wide awake—very wide awake—in winter time.

It was a very splendid sunrise, sure enough. I was constrained to admit that fact, and I had an opportunity as splendid for beholding the harbinger of a *bella giornata*. From the balcony of my chamber the view of the entire sweep of the Bay of Naples is commanded. On my right, westward, stretches the long sea wall and fashionable promenade of the Chiaia, in the direction of Posilipo. To the eastward stretch the unfashionable Chiaia, Santa Lucia, Portici, Resina, Torre del Greco, Torre dell' Annunziata and Castellammare, Vesuvius, with a long white pennon of condensed vapour from its summit floating horizontally across the sky, dominating the whole eastern region. Right in front of my window, and within a stone's throw, the astounding seascape is bisected by a huge mountain of masonry looming in dark grey shadowed in indigo in the clear sea and clearer sky. This is the famous Castel dell' Ovo, so called from the egg-like shape of the islet on which it is built, joined to the mainland at the foot of the hill of the Pizzofalcone behind me by a narrow bridge flanked by two towering stone turrets. Of what materials the Castel dell' Ovo is composed, I hesitate to say. Its structure strikes me, like many things American, as being " a little mixed." Blocks of lava may, for aught I know, be among its component parts. There is also, apparently, a good deal of granite and an immense quantity of brickwork in its frowning walls. Moreover, the stronghold seems to comprise a liberal allowance of rock. The rock appears to have grown into the castle and the castle into the rock, until it becomes a matter of uncertainty as to which portion is natural and which artificial. One of its sides is roughly laminated, as though it had been coated with some thousands of mediæval oyster-shells.

The Castel dell' Ovo has been haunting me day and night for the last fifty-six hours. Vesuvius is the distant mystery. The Castle of the Egg, scowling on the cheerful hill of the Pizzofalcone, is the near mystery, gloomy, occult, and terrible. It was a mystery to Froissart, five hundred years ago, for does not the old chronicler define it as " standing by enchantment on the sea, so that it is impossible to take it but by necromancy or by the help of the devil " ? I have been devoutly wishing that my window were not opposite this haunted fortalice, over and over again; but it has exercised a grim fascination over me. I have never closed the shutters

U

nor drawn the curtains since I first found it confronting me. Were I to shut it out I doubt not but that I should see it in my dreams, or find it lying heavy on my heart, a huge ostrich egg of history—a rocky nightmare. How much poison has been drunk there, I wonder; how many persons in the most picturesque of costumes have languished in its dungeons, have been stabbed in its inner chambers, or have been flung from its battlements into the bay? Yet there may have been merry days and nights, banquets, festivals, masques, merrymakings, and what not in this castellated roc's egg. Lucullus had a villa there, once, some antiquaries maintain. Robert the Wise employed Giotto to paint in the chapel of the castle some long vanished frescoes.

It does not much matter. It is a barrack and a military prison now, the guide-books tell me. But by that information I do not set much store. I prefer the Castel dell' Ovo as a mystery—as an architectural enigma—as a kind of many-chambered Sphynx. I should not like to have an official *permisso* to explore its interior and to find an officer of Bersaglieri reading the *Pungolo* and smoking a "Minghetto" in the apartment where Queen Joanna of Naples may have supped with Sir Otho of Brunswick, or two penitent artillery-men expiating their offences in a cell which may once have been occupied by insubordinate Roman slaves or Saracen pirates. Lares and lemures, necromancers and alchemists, *bravi*, and masked conspirators, cowled capuchins bearing torches and intoning alarming penitential psalms, and beautiful but implacable ladies in black velvet and diamonds, ordering the immediate execution of faithless young gentlemen in purple satin doublets and trunk hose of pearl grey silk—those should be the proper denizens of the Castle of the Egg. I wonder whether the "Vista del Castello" will figure as an "extra" in my bill at the Hotel Vesuvio?

The sun rose in all its splendour, and the vineclad slopes of the mountains, even to the predominant Vesuvius himself, had their blue shadows flecked with rainbow hues; but the Castel dell' Ovo declined to assume anything but a dark and minatory aspect on the field of view. The sky above was now of burnished silver, and the sea around of deepest lapis lazuli, but the grim barrack prison, the Megaris of Pliny, seemed unaffected by the prevailing radiance. An unbidden, unwelcome guest at a gay festival, swarthy, uncult, unkempt, hulking, morose, scowling upon and literally imprecating the surrounding revellers—that is of what this intractable Egg mainly reminded me. I gave the castle up as a bad job, for the nonce at least, and the carriage being ready we rode away, followed by the apparently maniacal adjurations of at least five-and-twenty beggars and the affectionate wishes of the German hotel porter that we should return in time to dine at the table d'hôte.

The Continental hotel porter, embodying, as he does, the aspirations of the head waiter and the proprietor, is evidently of opinion that those only go eventually to the happy hunting grounds who with undeviating punctuality dine at the table d'hôte. Nor in Italy does the German hotel porter very much approve of foreign guests who can speak Italian fluently. He loves them more fondly if they can speak English, and English only. His own days and nights and those of his acquaintances the waiters have been devoted to the study of Ollendorff; but he does not encourage the acquisition of foreign tongues by travellers from the British Isles or from the United States. He will just tolerate a little French; that is all. Colloquial familiarity with Italian or German fosters a dangerous spirit of independence on the part of the *forestiere,* and is detrimental to the interests of the table d'hôte. As for the German hotel porter in Italy himself, it is his business to be multi-tongued. Is not his name in Naples Totila, in Rome Alaric, in Venice Genseric, in Florence Attila, in Milan Vitiges, in Turin Theodoric? The Goths and Vandals, the Huns and the Alemanni are extinct, you may think; the Tedeschi no longer rule in Lombardy and the Dominio Veneto. That may be, historically and politically; but the strong man from beyond the Alps is socially and financially stronger than ever in the Peninsula, and Vitiges and company—Baruch of Posilipo "standing in"—are doing very nicely indeed in modern Italy. The barbarians no longer break up the statues or rase the cities to the ground. On the contrary, they are fond of building villas and collecting works of art; but they still continue to do very nicely indeed in this fat and opulent land, while the miserable natives groan under the pressure of the eternal "mancanza di quattrini"—the lack of pence which vexes the mass of the Italian people.

And so, in the bright, clear, crisp, and gloriously sunny after-breakfast morning, we set forth to make once more the journey that all the travelling world has made since, in the year 1748, a peasant sinking a well in a field near Torre dell' Annunziata came upon a certain painted chamber containing statues and other objects of antiquity. For more than a hundred and thirty years the great army of sightseers has been flocking to that painted chamber and its fellows. I pleased myself, as we rattled along in a shabby-genteel livery-stable landau, drawn by two plucky little steeds which, considering the Rosinante-like development of their osseous structure and their apparent unfamiliarity with oats as an article of diet, did their work very cleverly, and driven by an individual who looked like a decayed schoolmaster, his pantaloons displaying that imperfect state of repair common to the nether garments of so many thousands of his fellow-citizens—I pleased myself, as this modest turnout bore us eastward, with thinking on the hundreds of grandiose equipages drawn by satin-skinned horses of price, driven by coachmen in resplendent liveries, escorted by glittering cuirassiers and hussars, and preceded by dashing outriders, which had travelled over the self-same road, their occupants actuated by no more elevated a motive than that which has guided for generations the Brown, Jones, and Robinson race—the desire to see the most curious Show in the whole world of sights, the disentombment of a long-buried past.

The salt of the earth has savoured this lava-strewn causeway. Tsars and kaisers, kings and queens, princes and archdukes, must have gazed, as we were gazing now, on the marvellous beauty of the scenery and the more amazing dirt and squalor of the people and their dwellings. Not a brougham, not a mail phaeton, not so much as a doctor's gig, met or passed us on the road. The only wheeled vehicles in sight were the universal, and, it would seem, inevitable tram cars; a few market carts full of vegetable produce, on which the ubiquitous municipal taxgatherers kept the sharpest of eyes, darting out upon the wains to claim cess on each load of cabbages, pumpkins, or tomatoes, and armed with long spitlike goads with which to probe suspicious merchandise; and the wondrous little local shandrydans, each conveying a *combinazione* of from nine to eleven country folk, comprising at least two swarthy individuals who, if they had not once been brigands, had certainly been organ-grinders dwelling on Saffron-hill, London, E.C., an old woman bent double, a laughing girl in rags with a large pair of coral and gold earrings, and a plump priest with a red cotton umbrella. Babies do not count in the human cargo of such a shandrydan.

The *bimbi* are thrown in as make-weights, and the load may be completed by a flock mattress, a bundle of salt fish, and a bunch of wild celery; the vehicle being drawn by a single horse, diminutive in size, desperately attenuated, but to all appearance not discontented with his lot. The brazen bells over his collar, which tinkle merrily, are said to drive away the flies, and may keep him in good spirits. Possibly he has never met with any equine friend who, in the intimacy of the stable, has told him of a land where horses, and even mules and asses, are treated with common humanity—at all events, he has got to do his work, and he does it, as his forerunners have done for who shall say how many centuries. The conformation of the shandrydan, moreover, is slightly favourable to the horse. The wheels are very large, the axle-pole is very high, the shafts slant downwards, and altogether the wretched, weedy little "screw" between them seems to be less dragging the cart than pushed along by its own momentum. The private sentiments of the horse on the subject it is obviously impossible to ascertain.

But to think of the sumptuous coaches and the illustrious personages who have made this journey! In my mind's eye I see King Joachim Murat and Caroline Bonaparte his wife —the former all whiskers, moustaches, gold embroidery, and white ostrich plumes; the latter glorious in diamonds and Brussels lace. They are [going to see the Show where the road to Castellammare is quitted at the end of Torre dell' Annunziata, and a *détour* is made to the left. Who is the short florid lady in a velvet pelisse and a great hat and feathers who accompanies the Royal couple? Can it be her Royal Highness Caroline Princess of Wales? Who is that furred and whiskered person in the dickey of the barouche? Can it be a party by the name of Bergami? How far are we from our destination, I hear my companion, who is becoming hungry, ask the coachman. But I am asking myself how far it is to Pizzo on the coast of Calabria, where, in October, 1815, the discrowned King Joachim, captured in a harebrained attempt to recover his lost realm, tried by judges who in the days of his power he had promoted from the meanest of stations, and condemned by virtue of a law which he had himself enacted, was shot to death as a public enemy, crying to the soldiers who were his executioners, " Salvate al viso, mirate al cuore," " Save my face, aim at my heart," and grasping as he fell the miniature of his wife and children? Ay; and the stout lady in the hat and feathers. How far is it to the vault in the church at Brunswick, where, seven years after she had crowned with laurel the bust of King Joachim in the Palazzo Reale at Naples, was laid the coffin of Caroline, Queen of England?

Everybody has been here. Nelson and Lady Hamilton, but with a Bourbon King and Queen; Lord and Lady Blessington, with Count d'Orsay the dandy and Charles James Mathews the actor; Casimir Delavigne, and Edward Bulwer Lytton—all with the same object. To see the Show due to the happy accident which befell the peasant who was sinking a well in a field. When I say "everybody," I am speaking, of course, from the "visiting-list" point of view. I have, of course, been book-hunting during my short stay in Naples, and a very worthy old tradesman offered me, for the modest sum of 150f., what he considered to be an exceptionally interesting collection of autographs, contained in the "Visitors' Book" for the year 1848, formerly belonging to his Royal Highness the Count of Syracuse. Such noble and distinguished autographs! Our Prince Consort, a Prince William of Hesse, Prince George of Cambridge, Thalberg the pianist, Baron Brunnow, Lord Palmerston, Baron Decazes, Prince Joseph Poniatowski, the Duke of Ossuna, the Countess of Montijo, Lablache, Prince Paul of Württemberg and "Jones Arthur Davies." Now you will understand what I meant by everybody.

But to-day there was nobody but the most squalid and poverty-stricken of Neapolitans; in every other face written the proclamation of hopeless indigence—of the "eterna mancanza di quattrini." Everywhere it was the same. From Portici to Torre del Greco handsome villas are scattered along both sides of the road; but this is no time for villa residence, and the noble or wealthy proprietors are in Naples or in Rome, in Paris or in Florence. Only the poor and the little black holes of unglazed shops where the multitudinous but rubbishing needments of the necessitous were vended remained to make up a picture of Neapolitan life. The poor are making purchases all day long, and these are generally for ready-money, although their bargains may not exceed a few farthings. They tell me that here in Naples there are commodities which can be bought for two centesimi, and five of these go to a halfpenny. This continuity of the pettiest commerce leads to an incessant going to and fro, a chattering and gesticulating that never ends, a constant wrangling in doorways and yelling from high-up garret windows, a shaking of fists and throwing-out of extended fingers, a howling of children and barking of dogs, crowing of cocks and cackling of hens, wondrous to see and to hear. The horses tethered to the doors of blacksmiths' forges are "in it," and neigh. The mules and asses exhibit a lively interest in the transactions, which generally end in themselves being overladen and cudgelled with sticks, and they burst into anticipatory braying.

All these things go towards making up what the Neapolitans are so fond of terming the "movimento"—the undying, swaying, surging to and fro of this half million of souls. To make the "movimento" quite complete you should throw in the strumming of a guitar in some anonymous back yard, and the vocalisation of some lean and tattered caitiff, who suffers from the hallucination that he is gifted with a baritone voice and is shouting "Ah! che la Morte" *a tutta gola*. Please also not to forget the unwashable beggars and monstrosities whining at the wheels of the *forestieri*, and whose invocations of the saints are changed with astonishing rapidity to shrill maledictions if they are disappointed in their hopes of obtaining some "piccola moneta." They contribute integrally to the "movimento." Nor cease to bear in mind that this *tohu-bohu* of noisy and mainly penniless humanity is watched every quarter of a mile or so by a little shabby old priest, who stands in the middle of the roadway—it is usually in front of the local *farmacia* that he takes his stand—with his umbrella under his arm, and regaling himself with a leisurely pinch of snuff. He knows all about the "movimento." He has been watching it all his life long. He knows all about the people —their wants, their misery, their secrets—but he is a discreet cleric, and keeps his secrets as carefully as does that huge, grimy Castle dell' Ovo scowling from the sea opposite my window yonder.

We reached our bourne at last, after a two hours' drive, rendered from time to time slightly uncomfortable by the tramsected road and by the somewhat too liberal spattering of lava mud from passing wheels. But we had passed through Portici, Resina, Torre del Greco, and Torre dell' Annunziata. Then we had turned away to the left from the road to Castellammare, and had stopped at the well-remembered inn, about the door of which hung many beggars and monstrosities yelping for alms, and several guides imploring us to make the ascent of Mount Vesuvius, which I have no more intention to do than to make that of the Monte di Pietà. I have other fish to fry. In the inn-parlour we had a very bad and very dear lunch—that is to say, seventeen francs were charged for some very equivocal viands and muddy wine; and the landlord or landlady had the impudence to add, without having asked permission, two francs for the refreshment of the coachman, whose normal wants would be probably three-halfpennyworth of macaroni and a farthing tomato. The plates and the knives and forks were moreover very dirty, and the waiter was certainly not a pattern of cleanliness.

We did not grumble at the meagre and ill-cooked meal. We did not lose our temper at the extortion. It was enough for me—it was enough for my companion to read the inscription painted on the back door of the institution. "Secondo Piano, a Destra." Thus ran the legend. Blithely did we open that back door; nimbly did we ascend to the second floor of the mean inn, and, reaching it, turn to the right. Through a room full of bronzes and painted earthenware, out into the sunny open; a few steps, and then through a turnstile into an avenue, the lava walls of which were crowned by tufts of cactus and prickly pear. We had reached our bourne. A.D. 1883 fled away. We were in A.D. 79. We were at the Sea-Gate of Pompeii.

XXIV.

THE SHOW OF A LONG-BURIED PAST.

NAPLES, *December* 17.

THE esteemed reader will be considerably mistaken should he imagine that, having ascended to the second floor, turned to the right, and entered Pompeii very much as one enters the gardens of the Royal Zoological Society in the Regent's Park, I have the slightest intention of inflicting upon him anything approaching a detailed account of the edifices of the long buried city. Without stirring from your own fireside in London you can make yourself master of all the architectural features of Pompeii—the Forum and the Basilica, the Temples, the Public Baths, the Houses of Diomed, of the Faun, of the Tragic Poet, of Pansa, and of Castor and Pollux; the greater and smaller Theatres, the Stabian Baths, the Exchange, the Amphitheatre, and the Street of the Tombs. Archæological and artistic details in abundance are to be found in the works of Dyer, Gell, and Overbeck; the latest and most accurate description of the excavations has been officially promulgated by Signor Giuseppe Fiorelli, Superintendent of the Researches at Pompeii; while there is little that can be added to the beauty of the embellishments of Pompeii, lately reproduced in chromo-

THE HOUSE OF PANSA AT POMPEII, RESTORED.

lithography by the learned French antiquary, M. Gaston Boissier.

Add to these ample materials a good collection of photographs, which are as easily procurable in London as at Naples; stimulate your imagination by a reading of Lord Lytton's "Last Days of Pompeii," and it strikes me that a very respectable image of a disentombed city might be presented to the untravelled eye; an image definite enough to be further developed by means of a lecture and a magic lantern. But that is not the kind of Pompeii that I wished to see, and that, after a lapse of sixteen years, I have just revisited.

The main purpose which, I apprehend, ought to present itself to the observant mind in coming hither should be something different from, and perhaps I may add something higher than, the mere gratification of curiosity. In the way of sightseeing, indeed, there is, perhaps, an *embarras de richesses* when you have to "do" Pompeii in a day. One street, with its houses, shops, taverns, and pavement rutted by chariot-wheels, should, to the contemplative spirit, suffice for a whole week's interrogation. I say interrogation, since from the moment of your first setting foot in the city to the moment of your quitting it, there should be incessantly presented to you the How? the Who? the Why of these things Pompeian. How were the streets lighted at night? How late did the shops remain open? How did the charioteers contrive to steer their vehicles between the huge blocks of lava which formed stepping-stones between kerb and kerb in rainy weather? How many houses had a story above the ground floor? Had any a second or a third floor? Were the roofs flat or slanting? Was there a covering of tiles to the wooden beams? Where were the stables and coachhouses? And, above all, where did the poor live?

No traces of the habitations of the utterly indigent appear as yet to have been discovered. Were the poor left in a state of slavery which, albeit it was attended by many stripes, gave them at least bread and lodging; or was the highly-fashionable watering-place of Pompeii destitute of any pauper population at all? But a vast tract of the city yet remains to be dug out from the crust of pumice, scoriæ, tufa, and lapilli, with a two-foot vegetable mould above all, in which it is, so to speak, "potted" for the edification of antiquaries, not in the remote, but in the imminent future; for the excavations under the direction of the Cavaliere Fiorelli have been continued without intermission since Italy has been united and free; and although only the modest sum of 60,000 lire, voted by the Legislature, is annually available for the works carried on, wonders have been done within the last few years in the way of discovery.

One of the foremost charms of a visit to Pompeii at the present day is that you are able in your rambles from street to street and from house to house altogether to dispense with the assistance of a guide book; not that I would disparage the archæological and topographical merits of *Murray*, *Baedecker*, and *Harper*. But I would advise you to confine your study of those excellent mentors and of Mr. Rolfe's admirable "Guide to the Museum at Naples" to your studious hours before and after your visit to Pompeii. Bring no handbook whatsoever to the place itself. If you do you will lose, so far as observation is concerned, the sight of one eye, and with the remaining orb you will be little better than parcel-blind.

When the troupe of the Comédie Française first came to London their performances were witnessed by vast numbers of worthy people whose gaze was generally fixed on the copies of Molière which they had brought with them, and who seemed to pay but very scant attention to the actors and actresses on the stage. The same curious phenomenon was observable when the Meiningeners appeared at Drury Lane. A large portion of the audience were intent on conning their English translation of Schiller instead of attending to what Herr Barnay and his fellows were about behind the footlights. Have you not seen lady students in the stalls at the Royal Italian Opera equally assiduous in following the lines of the libretto while Patti was singing? You should not do this kind of thing at Pompeii. If you do you will miss half the sky and be unconscious of half of the subtle play of light and shade among the roofless tenements and the great columns of the temples and the villas. You will be inattentive to the silent monitions of Vesuvius yonder, always present, watchful, mindful of past wickedness—ready, perhaps, to visit fresh sinfulness with the fiery torrent of his wrath.

Bring no guide-book. These fresco-painted walls, these battered pillars, these dried-up fountains, these darkling dungeons in the gladiators' barracks, in which skeletons were found with their leg-bones yet in the shackles; these dreadful vaults beneath the judgment seat of the Prætor in the Basilica—the vaults in which the malefactors lay while their fate was being deliberated upon by the judges above—these should be your teachers. These will help you towards accomplishing the grand result—that of absorbing and drinking in and saturating yourself with Pompeii, until at last the incantation is accomplished, the spell works, the revelation is made, and in your mind the city suddenly ceases to be dead, and leaps up like the armed men in the Valley of Dry Bones—leaps into the life of eighteen hundred years ago—a life that you seem to see, to hear, and to feel. If such be not your object in visiting Pompeii I should respectfully counsel you to stay at home by the fireside diligently consulting Gell and Dyer, the Cavaliere Fiorelli, and M. Gaston Boissier.

For the rest, if laudably anxious to study as much as is possible of the infinite suggestiveness of Pompeian reality, you will leave *Murray*, or *Harper*, or *Baedecker* at your hotel at Naples; you will find a sufficiency of topographical and architectural information supplied to you by the official and living guides. These worthy fellows wear a military uniform and have all been soldiers, being selected for their present duties on account of their good character and general intelligence. They have all been carefully drilled by the Cavaliere Fiorelli, and, when they take you over a notable house, are able to point out with simple exactitude the locality of the " vestibule " or waiting-room, the " atrium " or court, the impluvium in the midst thereof, the " tablinum," the " peristylum," the " viridarium " or garden with its fountain, and the " triclinium " or dining-room. They can direct you to the picture-gallery, the library, the shrine of the household gods, the " cubicula," or bedrooms, the quarters for the gentlemen and those for the ladies, and the staircase which led to the varnished floor above, where the slaves lived.

They are equally accurate indicators of the principal points of interest in the temples and the theatres, the shops and taverns. They tell no lies, and never bore you, and all you have to pay for their services and for the privilege of exploring the ruins is the certainly not exorbitant entrance-fee of two ire, or one shilling and sevenpence sterling. Most of these military guides possess enough English or French to make Pompeii comprehensible to the tourist who is wholly ignorant of Italian. Conspicuous at the gates of entrance are official notifications that the guides are not allowed to receive gratuities from visitors; but there is a showroom of photographs just outside the Sea Gate, and you are permitted to mark your appreciation of an exceptionally intelligent bear-leader by purchasing sun pictures of the ruins, the frescoes, the statues, and the skeletons at a franc apiece.

If I could visit Pompeii every day for, say, six weeks—taking care to avoid lunching at the inn where there is a second floor and a turning to the left—I fancy that I should pass a great deal of my time in the neat little local museum which has been in recent years wisely established within the walls of Pompeii itself, and wherein are deposited a number of objects found in the latest excavations, and possessing, in some instances, which I shall presently point out, a simply enthralling interest. When you are shown specimens of old Pompeian cartwheels, axletrees, cart-shafts, harness for horses, rings for the tethering of bridles, farriers' tools and forges, you at once remember that not half-an-hour ago you saw objects differing not one whit in form from these, in actual use on the road from Portici to Torre dell' Annunziata. You recollect a lanky, sallow baker's boy whom you saw crawling along the main street of Torre del Greco, bending under the burden of a board covered with squat round loaves of bread, somewhat slack-baked in appearance. Here, in a glass case, are rows of precisely the same round squat loaves, like muffins impressed with a rude " rose " pattern, only the red-hot ashes have calcined the loaves to a uniform sable; and these are eighteen hundred years old.

You call to mind the infinity of small wares which crowd the paltry little cavernous shops that line the road from Naples to this place. Everybody has something to sell, but no vendible commodity appears to be worth more than a few quattrini. Look in these cases, or look at the vaster Museum behind at Naples, and you will find all the black "fetches" of the infinity of small wares, all the trumpery marine stores of the Roman seaport town of A.D. 79. I declare that the cattle-bells and the kitchen boilers, the fishhooks and the spits, the bagpipes exactly similar to the modern instrument in use among the Zampognari of the Abruzzi; the metal skillets and pots and pans; the drinking-pots and hot-water urns—the last the very image of Russian *samovars* —the door hinges, the locks and keys, the children's money-boxes, precisely resembling French *tirelires*, the latches, bolts, and screws, the sieves, tongs, and fire shovels, the nails and clamps, interest me far more than do some of the finest bronzes, the most beautiful statues, the richest bas-reliefs, the

DISCOVERY OF LOAVES IN A BAKER'S OVEN AT POMPEII.

choicest mural paintings that ashes-engulphed Pompeii has yielded to the light.

The fact is, that ever since the dawn of the Renaissance—let us say for nearly four hundred years—civilised nations have lived in an atmosphere of more or less sham antiquity of a pictorial, plastic, and structural sort. A comparatively restricted number of masterpieces of Greek and Roman sculpture and architecture, mural decoration and mosaic, have in the course of these four centuries been discovered, to the astonishment and delight of the world. A comparatively limited number of masters, Renaissance and modern, have all but successfully rivalled the great artists of antiquity; but these manifestations of genius are but as exquisite islets glittering in the midst of an immeasurable ocean of mediocrity, plagiarism, and downright fraud. A Doric town hall in the Midland Counties, an Ionic county court in Cornwall, a Corinthian joint-stock bank in Lancashire, a composite hotel in Yorkshire—all these may be duly designed on the lines laid down by Vitruvius, or in accordance with the models discovered in the Campagna of Rome or on the platform of the Acropolis. But do such edifices bring you any nearer to the confronting, to the measuring and probing and diagnosing of antiquity than a kamptulicon doormat with "Cave Canem" or "Salve" inscribed on it; than a coal-scuttle of "classic" design, or a pickle-jar adorned with Etruscan figures executed as the Staffordshire Potteries can do it?

Even the acknowledged masterpieces of antique art have been plagiarised or absolutely forged, over and over again, by the ancients themselves. In the Museum at Naples there are at least half-a-dozen more or less pirated imitations of the Venus de Medicis, and as many of the Crouching Venus. In Pompeii itself the thorough artistic badness of the majority of the fresco paintings is something altogether ludicrous. But that the pictures are so immensely aged you would at once place them in the "penny plain and twopence coloured" category. The paintings which are really gems have long since been removed to Naples. You grow weary of a never-ending procession of Venus and Mars, of allegories of Bacchus, of Hercules delivering Dejanira, of Bacchantes in their cups, of Pan and the Nymphs, of Adonis holding the nest which contains Castor and Pollux just hatched from the eggs of Leda.

Truly, when you contemplate these rubbishing frescoes, clumsily drawn, and in execution "scamped" by some third-rate journeyman house-painter in a provincial town, the conviction is forced upon you that these daubs had their origin in some remote, undiscoverable, and exquisitely beautiful school of Greek art. But the pattern has been lost, no man can tell when; and successive stages of degeneracy have at length brought about the advent of the third, nay, of the tenth-rate journeyman house-painter in the provincial town.

The Pompeian shop-signs are at least honest, and tell you something to the point—the point of understanding the ways and manners of this people; in many respects a sufficiently immoral one. Judge the nobility, gentry, and *bourgeoisie* of Pompeii—of their poor we know, as I have said, nothing—from the pictured and sculptured evidences which they have left us of their daily life, and they appear to have been a community literally wallowing in sensuality. The horrible inscriptions on the ivory pass checks which their wives and daughters had to take as they entered or left the theatres; the abominable paintings on the walls of the tenements which modern lady visitors are not allowed to see; the shameful emblems flaunting in the light of day in the streets, all seem to denote a condition of society altogether depraved, corrupt, and rotten—of patricians and plebeians equally given up to animalism. The baths, the theatres, the exchange, the temples, the basilica, the banqueting-halls, the wine-shops, the gambling dens, the gladiators' haunts, and worse; was there much more than this in the life of a Pompeian gentleman in the year of grace 79?

And yet the patient palæographers in the Naples museum laboriously unrolling, deciphering, and translating the papyri found in the buried city—papyri that had been so blackened by the action of heat that they were at first mistaken for sticks of charcoal and destroyed by the hundred by the ignorant finders—have made legible to modern eyes two books of a "Treatise on Music" containing essays on Music, on Vice and Virtue and on Rhetoric. There were, then, at least some few people in Pompeii who thought decently and lived cleanly lives. How many? That, among the mysteries of Pompeii, has not yet been revealed. Perhaps the homilists on Vice and Virtue preferentially devoted themselves to the composition of edifying works in the days immediately preceding an earthquake or an eruption. For the merriest and most thoughtless among us must needs listen to the preacher sometimes; and the Pompeians had their pulpit in Vesuvius, yonder. Sermons were not frequent, but they were terrible. Penitential psalms of pumice, collects enforced by red-hot scoriæ, litanies of boiling lava, and a Commination Service of sulphur and steam; reminders such as these that there are Days of Wrath for those who live the life of devils upon earth may now and again have made the Pompeians a little serious, and incited the Syrian philosopher, Philodemos, who visited Rome and Pompeii in the time of Horace, to draw up some neat little tracts for the improvement of a population who otherwise seem to have cultivated every vice with an amount of success rarely attained in modern times by any civilised city, lovely and rascally Naples only excepted.

Although corporeally present in the smart little local museum, my mind, while I thought these things, had been wandering over the whole city through which we had been quietly trudging for three mortal hours. The sky was blue, the sun blazed brightly; but we felt neither the heat nor the travail. Who that has an object before him ever grows tired in Pompeii? As I have said, the aspect of the local museum is smart. It glistens, it gleams with its polished oaken fittings and glass cases. The pots and pans, the fishhooks and stirrups, the calcined loaves and fruits and nuts that have almost, but not quite, brought me face to face with the people of A.D. 79, are black from carbonisation, but they are comely. The whole room looks bright and cheerful, yet on every side are there mementoes of Death, sudden, violent, and terrible. Ranged round the walls are skeletons of men, women, infants, horses, mules, dogs, cats, and poultry, all dug from the ruins.

Stay, the little sucking pig yonder, that was found in the baker's oven, escaped a violent end. He had been mercifully stuck to death before they scored and trussed him for the bakehouse. His tender crackling, the gristle of his snout, his ears and eyes have long since been resolved into dust and ashes, but the osseous structure of the tiny creature is yet perfect, even to the bones of the pettitoes and the vertebræ of the once curly tail. Plum sauce and not pumice-stone should have crowned the funereal pyre of that little pig. How brown and shiny he must have been growing, how nice he must have smelt, when the black rain of ashes came down upon him, and covered him up for eighteen centuries.

But the middle of the Museum; what is there in the midst of the Museum? Sudden violent and dreadful death, the aspect of which is almost supernaturally revealed to us, but which bears no appalling look. I have rarely known a civilian who, having once been over a field of battle, say three days after the slaughter, exhibited the slightest desire to make a second time that journey full of horrors. Yet there is nothing shocking, and scarcely anything, indeed, that can be called painful, in the appearance of the images of death ranged at full length on the tables. Take the prostrate figure of the man who, from the aquiline outline of his countenance, is known as the Roman, and who is girt with a money-belt. His death must have been from asphyxiation. His head reposes on one of his arms; the expression of the countenance is one of deeply thoughtful gravity—scarcely sleep, although the eyes are closed, but rather profound meditation. And then the *ragazzo*, the boy of eleven or twelve summers, who has tumbled face foremost on the ground, and died there in a moment. And the *ragazza*, the exquisitely-formed young girl of sixteen or seventeen, her face turned a little on one side, so that you can see her sweet innocent features, and her hair fixed in girlish coquetry.

These images of sudden and violent death are all nude; but when they were stricken down by death they wore the garments of their time and rank—garments which the heated ashes calcined and made to vanish in a moment. But the *aqua bollante*, the boiling vapour permeating the pumice, the scoriæ and the ashes formed round each body a fine paste, which received the imprint of the corpse which it surrounded. This paste, after some days, dried, and became a sharply-defined mould, and then came the eighteen centuries of entombment. The bodies decayed, the bones fell away from ligaments which turned to dust, but the sharp mould remained, retaining every detail of the external form of what had once been human. And one day Cavaliere Fiorelli, superintending the progress of the *scavi*, was told by one of his workmen that with his pickaxe he had struck into a cavity apparently of considerable dimensions. The cavity was sounded, and by-and-by some vestiges of mortality—a vertebra, a bone of a tarsus or a metacarpus was brought to the surface. It instantly occurred to the astute mind of Cavaliere Fiorelli that a human body had once filled that cavity, and that the long-since indurated mass of pumice and ashes had formed a mould which should present an exact imprint of the disintegrated corpse. Liquid plaster of Paris was brought and poured through the aperture of the cavity. The plaster was allowed to harden, and then the surrounding mould was gently removed, and these astonishing transcripts of life suddenly turned into death were revealed.

In only one of these bodies strangely resuscitated—if the paradox can be pardoned—by means of a bucketful of liquefied plaster of Paris, are any signs of acute physical suffering visible. There is a reproduction of the body of a dog which, with a collar round its neck, was found by the side of the vestibule of a patrician's house. The poor dog has died hard, it has rolled over in its agony and lies on its back, its mouth open, its limbs violently contorted. The stretched-out forepaws are crossed almost in an attitude of supplication; and the whole frame is twisted and wrenched in a manner suggestive of fearful pain having been suffered ere the relief of death came.

So up and down the narrow streets and in and out of the roofless houses had we wandered till far into the afternoon. I candidly confess that the main impressions produced in my mind out of the Museum, where, for a moment, the simulacra of death had seemed to live again, were the reverse of a classical or archæological nature. All was very tranquil, very peaceful, and very empty, and Vesuvius in the purple distance looked superb; but that was all. I could not furnish the place in my imagination. I could not people it; and, in spite of all I could do, Pompeii persisted in assuming to me, mentally, a number of unwished-for aspects, kaleidoscopic, but desperately commonplace. I remember, more than twenty years ago, hurrying by railway from Dublin to Queenstown to meet the Cunard steamer bound for Boston, and asking my travelling companion what was the meaning of the lamentably numerous cabins of rough stones visible from the window as we neared Cork—cabins more than three parts in ruins, roofless, the doors and windows mere cavernous holes, unglazed and untimbered. And "Evictions" was all the answer I got to my question. I declare that Pompeii had a generally "evicted" look, on the largest of scales; and in the mood I then was I could more easily have assumed the late tenants of the dismantled tenements to have been peasants in frieze coats and bell-crowned hats, and peasant women of the "Biddy" type, than swarthy Græco-Italians in togas and tunics and sandals.

But the walls of an Irish shebeen from which the tenants have been evicted are not, you may with reason urge, decorated with allegories painted in fresco. Alas! I am only too well aware of that circumstance, but when, staring hard at the allegories, I strove with all my might to dispel the eviction delusion, another quite as incongruous gained the mastery in my mind. Did you ever wander about Vauxhall Gardens by daylight, and long before the performances began? How mean and coarse and shabby looked the pictorial and plastic embellishments which, when the night came, would bear so grandly radiant a sheen under the auspices of "twenty thousand additional lamps!" But the lamplighter had not even begun to do his spiriting, and Vauxhall looked very empty and very dull—the scene-painting coarse, the statues paltry, and the ball-room insignificant, the shell-shaped sounding-board over the orchestra tawdry and gimcrack. You could no more people it with the phantoms of Horace Walpole and his frivolous set of fashionables, and of the Allied Sovereigns and the Prince Regent, who patronised a grand fête at Vauxhall in 1814, than I could people Pompeii with prætors and poets, patricians and parasites, noble ladies and sullen slaves, priests and actors, dancers, mummers, philosophers, and courtesans.

Not so, perhaps, with Vitiges—Vitiges, large of person, luxuriant and blond of hair and beard—Vitiges in a slouched hat, gold-rimmed spectacles, and Byronically turned-down collar, and carrying a bulky note-book in which he ever and anon pencilled matters possibly of deeply earnest moment. I had been aware of him for days—at the hotel, at the Museum —scrutinising things in general with sternly attentive eyes, and from time to time pulling out the big note-book and making entries therein. His hired carriage had closely preceded ours all the way from Naples. With him the gnädige Frau Vitiges, *geborene* Totila, his eldest son Attila, and Fräulein Genseric his niece. A thorough explorer, Vitiges. Speaking Italian quite fluently, albeit with an accent harder than the local lava-blocks, and peppering the guide occasionally with Greek and Latin lore, which that functionary— the quotations not having been included in his course of Pompeian drill—failed to take in very good part. Vitiges evidently means business in the buried city. He is possibly a professor, probably a deeply erudite archæologist, and the next time that I am at Rome and turning over the newest tomes on things antique at Loescher's Library, I shall be but little surprised if I come across Vitiges' latest works: say, "Benützt man Taschentücher in Pompeii?" or "Die

Tragödien des tragischen Dichters, sind sie verloren gegangen?"

We did not at first forgather with the Vitiges and his family. We had our guide and he had his, and a third party of Americans had their guide; and when we chanced to cross each other in the Forum, or the Baths, or the Street of Abundance, or the House of Sallust, we merely exchanged those amiable stares and scowls which form the small change of recognition used by civilised people who have not been introduced to one another. But as the afternoon drew in, and the blue shadows lengthened, and Vesuvius, in the distance, was robed in a darker purple, the scattered groups of pilgrims to this strangest of shrines came more frequently together; and it was about four when we found ourselves gathered in one compact band at the head of the excavations which day by day, Sundays excepted, are being with patient persistence pushed forward, under the direction of the Cavaliere Fiorelli.

It was a strange sight. Picture to yourself a kind of quarry of cold black pumice resembling—well, there is only one simile that will most fitly apply to it. The pumice bank looked exactly like so many piles of Russian caviare, but its summit was rich vegetable mould and bright verdure. A party of some twenty labourers were laying bare the entrails of the Campus Pompeius, undisturbed for eighteen centuries. A group of the soldier-guides were standing on the grassy summit on the verge of the black quarry, chattering to each other in the Neapolitan dialect, which seems to me to be more like Arabic than Italian. Why should they not laugh and chatter? Excavations were no new things to them. They were case-hardened to the sudden revelation of bronzes and marbles, frescoes and gems. But we below, scrambling from hillock to hillock of caviare-looking pumice, or cautiously threading our way over narrow planks which bridged the chasms of excavation, were not so case-hardened, and watched with eager interest every blow of the pick, every movement of the spade. There was a whisper that a fresh house was being unearthed. Straight before me was a shelving mass of inky pumice, say nine feet high. There was a wall behind that mass, they whispered. The workmen stretched out their hands carefully in different directions over the mass. Others came forward with, I suppose, special tools. I cannot tell how it was done; I know not how long it took to do; but all I know is that where had been the mass of inky pumice there suddenly became manifest the wall of a triclinium glowing with roseate and azure hues, surrounded by an elaborately designed decorative border, and having for its central embellishment the figure of an antelope running at full speed.

The image of the graceful creature thus suddenly liberated after eighteen hundred years of sepulture seemed positively to live, positively to bound across the field of vision. Of little moment was it to inquire whose house this was—that of the Pink Philosopher or the Wealthy Money-Lender, the Comic Singer or the Untrustworthy Gladiator. The Cavaliere Fiorelli and Professor Vitiges will settle all those points, in due time. It was enough for me to have witnessed the Resurrection of the Antelope. The inert suddenly became mobile, the mute articulate. The charm worked, the incantation was complete. Pompeii to me was no longer untenanted, no longer roofless. Joyous and riotous, graceful and profligate, mercurial, frivolous, and desperately wicked, the whole life of the destroyed city rose up before me. I heard the rattling of the chariot-wheels, the shouts of the charioteers, the cries of the street-vendors, the oaths of gamblers over their cogged dice in the wine-shops, the falling of the thongs of bull's hide on the shoulders of shrieking slaves, the clamour of the people in the amphitheatre, and the ringing of the gladiators' blades on the bucklers of their antagonists. But for a moment only did the city live again. You had but to look up at Vesuvius the Preacher, darker than ever in its purple bulk against the bright sky, to know that Pompeii was very dead indeed.

XXV.

THE "MOVIMENTO" OF NAPLES.

Naples, *December* 20.

I am in the very midst of the "Movimento," the boiling whirlpool of Neapolitan life. "Il Movimento" is the name neither of a newspaper nor of an opera, nor of a parcels delivery agency, nor a political party, nor a life assurance company. The "Movimento" is simply Naples in its most articulate, audible and characteristic form; and the traveller who has not seen and listened to the "Movimento" of Neapolis will have gained but little by his journey to the shores of Magna Græcia.

Different cities in Italy are distinguished by different sounds, or by the partial absence thereof. Pisa, you know, is very still. Venice, under the Austrian rule, used to be—save only when the band played on St. Mark's Place—one of the quietest of cities: its most conspicuous public sound the plashing of the gondoliers' oars and their warning cries of "Ta-hi!" and cognate monitions, when the *barca* turned a corner on the canal. The quietude of Venice is now marred by the yelping of the newsboys and the sputtering of steam-launches on the Canalazzo. Milan is a gay and festive city, almost as cheerful as Paris once was. It is journalistically, martially, lyrically, and commercially noisy. Rome, in the neighbourhood of the Corso and the Piazza di Spagna, is alive until late at night with all kinds of strange sounds; the Roman small boy is an adept in the art of splitting your ears with an exceptionally shrill and piercing whistle; and about five in the afternoon the gabbling of the *oziosi*, the great tribe of people around the Antonine column with apparently nothing to do save to chatter and gesticulate, and smoke ill-savoured cigars — the *oziosi* are the congeners of the "mooners" on the Puerta del Sol at Madrid—borders on the distracting. The awful silence of Ravenna is, in the night season, supposed to be broken only by the groans of the ghost of Dante and the wailing of the phantoms of inconstant lovers, imprisoned for their sins in the trunks of the dark forest trees of the distant Pineta. Turin is noisily talkative in the harshest of Piedmontese accents. In Florence the voice of the *forestieri* is socially more audible than that of the natives; and all I need say of Genoa is that I never passed through the suburb of San Pier d'Arena without finding the most tumultuous of scolding matches in "full blast." The family of Madame Angot must have been of Genoese extraction. This year it was a discussion between three washerwomen and a vendor of roasted chestnuts; and the uproar was fearful. A journeyman dyer—a brawny brute with arms stained crimson to the elbows, who looked like one of the satellites of Herod of Jewry, fresh from massacring unnumbered Innocents—interposed in the interest of the chestnut vendor; the outlying curs took part in the quarrel, and howled themselves hoarse; but the ear-harrowing shriek of the locomotive whistle suddenly and happily intervened to drown the *vacarme*, as our train rolled past the station; and that is all I saw, last November at least, of San Pier d'Arena, by Genoa.

Still, the most restless of towns in the Enchanting Land have their hours of stillness and repose, yet the "Movimento" of Naples never ceases. The city seems not to rest either by day or by night. You are in your room, reading, very late. Your watch warns you that it is time to throw the last cigar-end behind the last flickering of flame from the crimson embers on the hearth, to close the book, turn off the lamp, and go to bed. Confound it! Just beneath your window somebody is twanging a guitar, and bawling a *canzonetta*, with the usual rhyming of " cuore " and " amore," " forte " and " morte," the usual exordium about " Bella Napoli! " and the usual peroration about " Santa Lucia." Does the minstrel outside think that you will open the window and fling him soldi at two in the morning?

But you retire to your couch, and are up again, say at seven—it is midwinter—to see the sunrise. What is that shrill ululation floating over the Bay of Naples—a sound more discordant than melodious, but yet not altogether unpleasing? Is it the cry of a peacock? But peacocks don't fly about the Mediterranean Sea at seven a.m. It would be safer to surmise that the shrill note may be that of the fabled halcyon. However, you lend your ear more attentively to the note. Upon my word it is the squeak of Punch! Two tattered losels, in red nightcaps and the usual imperfect pantaloons, have rigged up in a boat a Punch's show of the most primitive kind—a bit of ragged blanketing, a stick or two, and a couple of red ochre-smeared puppets—and they are rowing about the bay "performing." May be some liberal Jack-tar from a foreign merchantman in the port will fling the floating Pulcinello a copper or two. The entertainment given by these abnormally matutinal histrionics is, I apprehend, intimately associated with the all-absorbing question of quattrini. Behind "Il Movimento" is "La Miseria." Both are equally dependent and consequent on the other. Idleness, profligacy, thriftlessness, and crime bring about the Movement, and the end of the Movement is misery.

I tried a whole day's experience of the "Movimento," resolving to make no excursions, to visit no churches, picture galleries, or museums—in short, to have done with sightseeing altogether for the nonce, and to devote all my faculties to the study of murmuring, pulsating, breathing, trembling, spasmodic Naples. A friend had dropped me a hint of which I eagerly availed myself. "Try the Law Courts," he remarked, "if you want something in the noise and bustle line." Nor did I fail to note his advice to button up my pockets and keep a firm hold of my umbrella while exploring the domain of Themis. So, with enough small change in an outer breast pocket to suffice for a few hours' needments, I hailed a passing cab and bade the driver take me to the "Tribunali." It would be more strictly correct, perhaps, to say, not that I hailed the cab, but that the cabdriver hailed me. The English provincial name for a cab is a fly, and the Neapolitan hack victorias resemble flies to the extent that the drivers have an irritating habit of crawling after you, very often for half a mile at a time, pulling up when you stop to look in at a shop window, and then driving a little in advance and turning their heads towards you, soliciting you to enter their rickety one-horse chaises. Practically, the charioteer settles upon you as a real fly does in summer time: and, although you may after repeated " Va-te-nes," and the use of even stronger language, succeed in shaking him off, another very soon settles on you, and you continue to be half diverted and half exasperated by the four-wheeled fly nuisance until you reach some street too narrow and too crowded for the Automedon to be able to dawdle about after you.

The Neapolitan cab fares are ridiculously cheap—that is to say, you may ride from one end of the city to the other for a little less than ninepence; but the very cheapness of the locomotion tempts you to ride when you had much better walk: and no sooner have you entered the vehicle than the ragged Jehu, perceiving at one keen glance that you are a *forestiere*, begins to importune you, in mingled and mangled French and English, interspersed with the Neapolitan *patois*, to allow him to take you to San Martino, or some place outside the city boundary; for which journey he can charge an additional fare; or to have the privilege of conducting you to the principal churches, palaces, museums, galleries, and so forth. You have made up your mind only to pay him a little less than ninepence. He has made up *his* mind that you shall pay him at least four francs between the present time and two hours hence; and very often he comes off victorious in the encounter.

But when I bade my flyman drive me to the Tribunali, his countenance fell and assumed a most ruefully dejected and at the same time deferential expression. Evidently he thought there was no likelihood of extracting four francs from a fare who was going to the Tribunali. The Law Courts do not form one of the recognised and stereotyped sights of Naples; and the majority of people who come hitherward to see the sights, and to buy photographs, coral, Sorrento woodwork, terra-cotta models of Diana of the Ephesians and the Farnese Hercules, and terra-cotta statuettes of shovel-hatted priests reading newspapers and peasants' eating macaroni, are very probably quite unaware even of where the Tribunali are situated. I have myself no definite knowledge as to the locality of the Law Courts of Naples. I only know that I told the driver to conduct me thither, and that, winding his wheeled way through a prodigious labyrinth of slums, he deposited me, at about eleven a.m., at the entrance of the Temple of Themis. The main thoroughfare, if one there were, leading to the Palace of Justice, was, to all seeming, temporarily closed to public traffic; since there was a string of agents "della pubblica sicurezza" detailed on foot to turn the stream of vehicles into the officially-appointed course.

That which from a classical standpoint may be regarded as a most agreeable result was thus obtained. In a maze of byelanes not much wider than the streets of Pompeii, wheeled vehicles and pedestrians were crowded together in apparently inextricable confusion. The carriages impinged on the footway, and grazed the very wares exposed in the windowless shops; while the people who should have been trudging along the *marciapiede* walked in the middle of the road. A mounted officer in full uniform, the trooper, his orderly, following him; a handsome brougham with a ducal coronet on the panels; hack victorias by the dozen; a donkey laden with fruit-filled panniers, with a long-legged ragamuffin bestriding almost the last of the patient animal's lumbar vertebræ; a string of ragged little goats and kids, the bells of the *capo-capri* twinkling merrily; monks and priests Sisters of Charity, beggars, soldiers, cripples (the Witch of Endor bent double, Mother Red Cap on crutches), idle varlets swathed in ragged cloaks, pedlars, costermongers, and barefooted wenches with saucy looks, white teeth, and sloe-black eyes—all these needed but a very little alchemy to change the squalor mingled with the splendour of Neapolitan humanity into so much old Roman gold. For a painter's use, I mean. The draperies only needed to be a trifle lighter in hue to be transmuted into togas; the priests and friars were easily convertible into members of the College of Augurs; the mounted officer willingly became a centurion; while but the smallest effort of imagination was necessary to metamorphose the occupant of the aristocratic brougham—a stout nobleman with horse-leech moustaches—into an obese Roman patrician borne aloft by slaves in his ivory litter "full of himself." Lictors, even, were not wanting to complete the classic aspect of the scene—at least, it was permissible to accept as substitutes for the stalwart bearers of the *fasces* a couple of strapping gendarmes or *carabinieri*, their bayonets fixed on their carbines, between whom walked, with gyves upon his wrists, a wretched, ragged, diminutive, shambling creature with an Aztec face, and a complexion of the hue of the bladder which covers a jar of pickled walnuts.

Clearly we were on the right road for the Tribunali. A merry road enough. The mob was, as usual, in high spirits. The street vendors tried to thrust halfpenny bouquets, boxes of lucifer matches, bunches of onions, and *tomaticelli* upon the grandees in the carriages; one attenuated man in a conical hat without a brim, and who was the very "double" and "fetch" of Mr. John Laurence Toole as Bertrand in "Robert Macaire," pursued me for many hundred yards, displaying aloft the printed contents-bill of a London newspaper ten days old. He did not speak, but was content with hanging out his paper banner, regarding me meanwhile with darkly expectant eyes. He deemed, no doubt, that the ten days old contents-bill would "fetch" me. It failed to do so. One of the choicest delights of travelling in search of sunshine is momentarily to forget that there are any such things as English newspapers at all; or, if they are forced upon your notice, to view them with the smiling equanimity with which one may assume that the horse of a cabdriver who has taken out a six days' licence witnesses the hitching up in the shafts of the horse that has to work on Sunday. But, O six days' licensed horse, the Sabbath is so short!

The Tribunali at last. I enter a vast courtyard, surrounded by dark arcades, and the frowning walls of an edifice which may have been in olden times a convent, an hospital, or a palace. A mob, thick, struggling, diversified of colour, predominantly tattered in garb, and subacutely noisy, fills the arcades. There is a tumult around you, and another tumult far off. Always remember that the Neapolitan "Movimento" is of a dual kind. There is the movement of tongues and things close to you—agitated, febrile, strident; but away, away in the distance, there is a dully whirring and tremulous murmur and gurgle of humanity, reminding you of the eternal but subdued resonance of Niagara in the far-off. I have no kind of idea as to the structural distribution of the Tribunali; but, practically, I follow the counsel given by the Rev. Henry Ward Beecher to the Englishman who asked him whereabout in Brooklyn his church was. "Take the ferry and follow the crowd," quoth the reverend gentleman. I had taken the ferry, in the shape of the hack victoria; so now I follow the crowd into an arcade to the right, through a grimy portal, and up a wide wooden staircase of three landings. On each of the three landings there is something to see and to speculate upon.

On the first a row of stalls heaped high with what one may term the rudimentary apparatus of litigation. Reams of stamped paper for petitions, requisitions, affidavits, and pleadings. Symmetrical cylinders of copper coins. Law is amazingly cheap in Naples; and, to judge from the crowded state of the Tribunali, the bulk of the population must spend a good deal of their time in going to law. No lengthened bills of costs, no lynx-eyed taxing-masters here. You buy your law hot and hot, as though it were so much macaroni or fried tomatoes, at a street stall: and pay for it on the nail. A notary will draw you up, for a couple of lire, the statement of a case. An *avvocato* retained to plead the cause of some poor devil laid by the heels for a " delitto di poco momento," will take a fee of four shillings. Oysters in Naples are very small; but they are exceeding plentiful and wondrous cheap. Thus forensic fees are low; but the lawsuits are innumerable. Coppers consequently enter largely into the pursuit of litigation; and threepence three-farthings may come quite handy when a compromise is being effected between a plaintiff and a defendant, or when a hostile witness has to be conciliated or a friendly witness suborned.

On the next landing there is a spacious nest of bookshelves; and at moderate rates you may purchase a compendious library of Italian law, criminal, civil, and commercial; to say nothing of stationery, quill and steel pens, wafers—when do we ever see wafers at home?—sealing-wax, pumice-stone, and pounce. On yet a third landing are stalls devoted to the restoration of the inner man. A vast variety of sausages, smoked meat, and tongue; piles of those round, squat, rosette-patterned loaves that you wot of—their fellows were changed into carbon at Pompeii, A.D. 79—fried fish; flasks, basketwork-encircled, containing cheap black and cheap yellow wine; cheese smelling loud as the sound of a Chaldean trumpet in the new moon, and cut in dice or in parallelograms; decanters of lemonade and sherbet seasoned with flies; greasy puffs and cakes; glass jars of cherry brandy, and sheaves of little, thin, shrivelled cigars, like the dried tails of rats. A touch of brilliance is given to the shabby show of comestibles by here and there a *piatto* of rosy-cheeked apples, a bunch of grapes, or a *mazzo* of light red liliputian tomatoes —edible coral, as it were. And everything almost as cheap as the all-surrounding dirt. Behind one of the stalls I became aware of a winding stone staircase, dark and mysterious in its recesses as that wondrous flight of stairs in Rembrandt's etching. Crouching on the *gradini* I dimly discern the dark figures of men shrouded in heavy mantles who are puffing away at the cigars which look like the dried tails of rats or munching dubious food, or solemnly sipping some equivocal liquid from cups. The Rembrandt-like staircase must be the caffè of the Tribunali. But here, as everywhere else in Naples, the mean is mingled with the magnificent. The edibles and potables displayed on the stalls of the third landing could only find their English analogies in a chandler's shop in Great St. Andrew Street, Seven Dials.

Yet a few steps distant from the Cimmerian staircase caffè I enter a vast hall, lofty and noble in its proportions, its walls and ceiling sumptuously painted in fresco. Evidently the Tribunali were, once upon a time, a palace. The ceiling is panelled, scrolled, embossed, and made gorgeous by bright colour and plenteous gilding: while from the walls, between elaborate frameworks of architectural and decorative design, look down a lengthened series of frescoed effigies of kings and princes, bishops, senators, and judges, loftily serene on their painted pedestals. Who were all these grandees, in their costume, half ancient Roman, half Renaissance? Consuls and Dukes of the Longobardi; paladins and prelates of Roger the Norman; viceroys of the Catholic Kings of Aragon; jurisconsults of the French or the Austrian rulers of Naples? They all look exceedingly grave, noble, puissant, and perfectly content with things as they were. Below their portraits are long-winded panegyrics of their courage, their generosity, their piety, their magnanimity, and their love of justice. What sounds are those which I hear obscurely articulate in the near "Movimento" of this hall? Surely I do not hear anything about "sventurata ragazza," about "omicidio," "furto," about "falsificazione," or about a "bestia sotto sembianza umana." How shocked the frescoed effigies of the princes and prelates, the warriors and judges would be if they could only be made sentient and audient, and hear the things which are being muttered down below! *They* never murdered anybody. They never stole things. They never ground the faces of the people, nor gave the children bread which brake their teeth. They never made law a net to catch ducats, nor religion a gin to snare simpletons!

The press, the jostling, the elbowing, the darting to and fro, the dodging past, the diving forwards, all in a laughingly good-tempered manner, of this motley crew of people, coming nobody could tell whence and going nobody could tell whither, were simply bewildering and astounding. Nearly all the men were smoking the vilest weeds that ever tortured the olfactory nerve; yet the very badness of the tobacco was in itself a small mercy. What would have been the odour of that hall had the people refrained from smoking? I need scarcely hint that, abating the afflictive and yet compensating stench of the dried rat's-tail cigars, I was altogether delighted with what I was seeing and hearing. What a Palace of Justice, and what a Central Hall, to be sure! What a *bella famiglia!* What a merry contrast to our own Law Courts, and to that remarkable edifice in the Strand, with those rows of Gothic arches outside, which support no kind of superstructure; with the Central Hall of Pleas, from which it seems to have been the chief motive of the architect to exclude those who have the best right to be there—the public; with those lovely courts concerning the accommodation provided by which judges, jurymen, counsel, solicitors, and witnesses have been grumbling ever since the Royal Palace of Justice was opened!

In Naples things judicial are managed strictly on democratic principles. Everything is free, easy, and above-board. The different courts open directly into the Hall of Frescoed Magnificoes. The portals are doorless. The judges, the lawyers, the prisoners can hear the "Movimento" near and far away. When the judges deliberate the audience are politely bidden to leave the court; so soon as the decision has been arrived at the many-headed are admitted again; but at all times during the sitting of the Tribunali the Central Hall, with its painted and gilded ceilings and its frescoed walls, is open to Infelice Esposito from the slums, to Giovanni Scroccone from Santa Lucia, to Impiccante Rubatasca, to Sozzo Suddicio—to all the tag, rag, and bobtail of Neapolitan life. The authorities who have the management of our new Law Courts justify the more or less rigidly enforced exclusion of the public at large from the Central Hall on the ground that it is desirable to discourage the indulgence of what is known as "morbid curiosity" among the masses. Here in Naples "morbid curiosity" is wholly unchecked; only it goes by another name. It is a part and parcel of the "Movimento."

Probably not one in ten of the tatterdemalions swaying and surging in this huge *aula* has any real business here. But what does that matter? Infelice Esposito is aware that this morning is coming on in the Sezione Penale the case of Sozzo Sudicio, accused of "furto e ferito di poco momento." He would like personally to ascertain how many days' *carcere* Sozzo Sudicio, whom he hates, and whom he was so very near stabbing the other day on a question of three centesimi, will be sentenced to. See those two graceful, graceless minxes with their touzled black hair, their big gold earrings, their flaring yellow kerchiefs, their exiguous skirts, and their bare, brown feet thrust into yellow slippers, who pass swiftly by, arm in arm, in the direction of one of the criminal courts. They are giggling merrily now, but in the course of a quarter of an hour or so they will be quite as ready to whimper, and even to howl, should it go hard with Patibulo Sparafucile, their *spadacino*, who is in trouble on suspicion of homicide. Impiccante Rubatasca is up to-day for pocket-picking. His mother, his grandmother, his sweetheart, and a crowd of *bimbi* of his blood have come down to the Tribunali to see fair. Why not? The scene is quite classical. The gendarmes look more like lictors than ever. For my part I see very little difference—tobacco smoke of course excepted—between the rabble here and that which I feel certain must have filled every morning the Basilica at Pompeii.

For the folk who really have business at the Tribunali there are provided, on the side next the tall windows of the hall, rows of long, broad tables at right angles to the wall. Thereat sit the *avvocati* and the *notarii* consulting with their clients, taking instructions from them, giving them advice, telling them how many legal legs—if any at all—they have to stand upon, and meanwhile covering quires of stamped paper with inscrutable scribbling. They tell me that the Neapolitan advocates, as a rule, not only speak well but write well. Indeed, on the morning of which I am discoursing, I heard in the courts plenty of sonorous, well-turned oratory bestowed on the argument of the most trumpery cases. It must be borne in mind that education of a really superior character can be obtained in every Italian city for an almost nominal sum; that it is the ambition of almost every well-educated young Italian who does not embrace a military, a medical, or a commercial career to become an *avvocato*, as a stepping-stone to political life; that apprenticeship to the law is brief, and admission to the Bar easy and inexpensive; and that the multitude of intelligent, literate, and eloquent young men who crowd the ranks of the forensic profession makes competition cruelly keen, and is to a certain extent one of the causes of the painful indigence which in Italy bears so heavily, not only on the poor, but on the non-trading and well-educated classes.

A week might with advantage have been devoted to the study of human physiognomy at the long tables where the notaries and advocates sate in consultation with their clients. The stale and accustomed looks of the men of law, now meeting a lengthened statement with a half-approving nod, now marking their appreciation of a downright lie by a mild shrug of the shoulders, were in themselves a liberal education in bye-play. Impudent rascality, humorous cynicism, chronic litigiousness, craft, rapacity, terror, nervous hope, black malice, hatred, and despair were all portrayed in the faces of the clients; but these dark glances were relieved here and there by the jovial *insouciance* of the wealthy suitor, well aware that, come what may, a decision one way or the other would not interfere with his material comforts; or the placid imbecility of the rural litigant, who was content to grin vacantly and to pull out his leathern purse uncomplainingly when he was bidden to disburse more lire and centesimi, and who was altogether, in the hands of his lawyer, as clay in the hands of the potter.

Strangest of all was it to see the men of law and their clients steadfastly, anxiously, hungrily, and, as I thought, ominously watched by groups of dusky men hanging round the tables, and with beetling brows almost stooping over the shoulders of those engaged in interminable scribblings on stamped paper. Who were these swarthy hangers-on, these whisperers to each other behind the palms of grimy hands, these lowering watchers? Witnesses waiting to be interrogated, or to be hired? Philanthropists of the genus of that long-since extinct race of benefactors of distressed debtors who were wont to perambulate Westminster Hall with straws in their shoes, and were ready to take any number of oaths at half-a-crown apiece, money down? Or were these watchful men with beetling brows affiliated to the mysterious and terrible Camorra? In vain I looked round for an answer. I might as well have asked the Sphinx for her secret or the moon for warmth. Only in the indefinable distance there continued to rumble the tremulous resounding, the muffled roar of the human Niagara —the whispered thunder of the "Movimento." It is the unquiet muttering of the Human Vesuvius.

XXVI.

IN THE SHADE.

NAPLES, *December* 21.

I AM in "Napoli senza sole"—in the Naples where it is always shade. Surely, you may point out, it is somewhat illogical for a traveller who has come abroad avowedly in search of sunshine, and who has sought the Lord of the Silver Bow as assiduously as the Knight of La Mancha wooed the transcendant Dulcinea del Toboso, to plunge deliberately into a region where notoriously the sun never shines at all, and where what light there is found to glimmer is but a faint reflection, or rather refraction, from far-off sunlit spots. Yet a moment's reflection should suffice to convince the critic that when one has found the sun it is not very prudent to be continually basking in its rays. It is a charming thing to have a bathroom attached to your sleeping apartment; but your medical attendant might warn you against incessantly parboiling or macerating yourself. If a kind friend sends you, at Christmas time, a *pâté de foie gras*, you don't eat up the luscious delicacy at one sitting, do you? No; "il faut boire à petits coups," the gently wise Béranger tells us. Even too much of Spenser's "Faerie Queene" at one sitting is apt to pall on the intellectual appetite; and if the criminal cited by Macaulay, and the relation of whose apocryphal story has done so much harm to the study of Italian history by Englishmen, had not been a fool, he would have taken his Guicciardini in intermittent doses, a little at a time. Then he would not have sickened ere he got to the "War of Pisa," and preferred to go back to the galleys to reading any more. He would have learned properly to appreciate a highly valuable and interesting work.

I enjoyed four days of glorious sunshine in Naples; but, being commonly prudent, I occasionally kept out of the sun There were umbrageous halls in the Museo Nazionale. There were shady nooks at Pompeii, notably in the Baths and in the House of the Tragic Poet. The Caffè Strasburgo at Naples is a very cool and well-tempered resort, with a pretty garden around it, where you can have something else to eat besides the eternal fried soles, "rosbif," veal and mutton cutlets, and badly mashed and worse sauté potatoes which they offer you at the hotels. The modern Italian *cuisine* is poor enough, goodness knows; but it boasts at least a few palatable dishes. At Rome the hotel-keepers have some common sense of a culinary kind; and the fare at such houses as the Albergo d'Inghilterra in the Bocca di Leone, the Louvre, and the Londra, is varied and excellent. In other tourist-frequented Italian cities the table d'hôte is usually a feeble and attenuated imitation of a second-rate Parisian dinner; and the bill of fare for luncheon is, as I have it set down, fried fish, lean and tough mutton, beef, or veal, with the dismal alternative of cold fowl like pasteboard and cold tongue like leather. The head waiter always seems to labour under the persuasion that the dishes mentioned above are the only ones of which you

A NEAPOLITAN MACARONI SELLER.

ever partake at home; that this is the first time in your life that you have ever come abroad, and that you have never heard of such edibles as macaroni and "risotto," as "ravioli," and "stuffato," as "gnocchi" and "uccellini." I wonder what he would say if a foreigner asked for a porringer of "polenta"? It is mainly our fault. We have taught foreigners to believe that we bring with us to the Continent a whole pack of insurmountable British prejudices in the matter of diet; and to those prejudices the foreigner continues deferentially to minister, although many of the most preposterous of their number have long since passed away.

It was difficult—nay, almost impossible—to eliminate culinary considerations from the mind when, with malice aforethought to lose myself and see what came of it, I came away from the Tribunali, and, taking the first turning to anywhere,—for verily it did not much matter in the thick of this great city which was your right hand and which your left—plunged into the midst of sunless Naples. Although you were in presence of a dense population the greater part of whom looked as though they had not, habitually, enough to eat, the sound and smell of cooking were ubiquitous. The bubbling of potatoes in their boiling oil; the spluttering of sardines in the frying-pan; the seething of leeks, the broiling of tomatoes, and the simmering of macaroni in the cauldron saluted you at every turn; and odours of rancid fat, reeking fish, and high-toned cheese stalked, as on stilts, through the dark lanes or blew in warm gusts through the blind alleys. The ways were sunless for the simple reason that the houses, which seem almost to shake hands from the opposite sides of the narrow lanes which you thread, are all as lofty as those of which the Old Town of Edinburgh was once so proud. Goodness knows how many storeys there may be to one of these towering Neapolitan tenements; but storey succeeds storey, each more successful than its predecessor in shutting out any possible rays of the orb of day, until at length, very far above your head, you discern just one narrow strip of deepest blue sky. Whatever may be the state of the temperature, there is always mud and there are always puddles in the footways; and so still and intensely blue is the sky overhead, that you feel tempted to look for the reflection of the stars in the pools beneath, even as you see them reflected in that quiet lake among the crags, in Sweden.

There must be splendid radiance and a glorious view of the bay and of Vesuvius from the roofs of these tall hives of humanity; but the dwellers in the exalted attics do not trouble themselves much or often, I am inclined to think, about the beauties of the surrounding scenery. Not more, perhaps, than did those who lived at the top of the tenement houses about the Five Points at New York—that whilom filthy district has been of late years exemplarily swept and garnished, they tell me—or do those who, with surroundings of train oil, cabbage soup, sour black bread, salted cucumbers, corn brandy, reeking sheepskin *touloupes*, and general filth and discomfort, seethe in the upper hutches of those tenement houses at St. Petersburg and Moscow, which harbour their five to eight hundred miserables apiece. From their eyries near the Five Points the Transatlantic indigents may enjoy a ravishing prospect of Manhattan and its beauteous bay; and noble and stately, from the high-up garrets of Petropolis and of Moscow, must be the spectacle of the Neva and the Moskva, St. Izaak's and the Kremlin, the golden domes, the vast palaces, the broad squares and terraces of the old and the new capitals of Russia.

In poverty-stricken Naples do those whose lot it is to suffer concern themselves to any great extent with the fascinating effect of the sunlight on the dancing waters of the Mediterranean, or with the enchanting play of golden light and purple shadow in the distant mountains? Not much more, I fancy, than does the impecunious New Yorker, high up in the garret, from which he is apprehensive of being turned out for lack of means to pay the rent, feel inclined to expatiate on the picturesque amenities of the Hudson River, or Jersey City, or Brooklyn Bridge. Not much more, perhaps, do Ivan Ivanovich and his callow brood of hungry children feel any incitement to be enraptured with the charms of a Russian summer sunset, when the rays of the sinking luminary bathe dome and cupola, spire and belfry, in wondrously shifting hues of cobalt and ultramarine, of crimson and aureolin and apple green. The "afterglow" at Naples, even in winter time, is perfectly lovely in its luminous ruddiness; but what is the "afterglow" to a man who does not see his way towards having any supper? There is plenty to eat at every street corner; for the incessant needs perennial provision of small eatables is made: but the purchasing power is not always concurrent with the willingness to sell. It is an affair of quattrini; and of those quattrini there is oftentimes "una mancanza assoluta."

Thus the indifference to the surrounding beauties of nature is easily comprehensible. It is the people who have plenty of money or whose business it is to paint pictures for the wealthy who revel in all the grand sights. The eyes of the vast majority of the eyrie dwellers are bent mainly on the rags which they wear, and on the forms, emaciated by privation and disease, of those whom they love. As for their thoughts, they can tend but in one direction—how to get sufficient dimes, kopecks, soldi for the day's sustenance. That is where the shoe pinches; there, most noble, right honourable, and right reverend philanthropists, who after tolerating the existence of the London slums—tolerating them with complacent indifference for so many generations—are now prating so volubly about the necessity for improving the dwellings of the poor and "encouraging them in habits of thrift;" there is the real difficulty, the real problem, the real *crux*. The lack of dimes, the absence of kopecks, the "mancanza assoluta di quattrini," the desperate need, not of pounds and shillings, but of pence for the day's bread; while you are rolling in golden coaches, wearing diamonds in your epaulettes and diamonds in your spurs, or watering railway stock, or "cornering" pork and grain, or robbing the State in order to be able to build marble palaces on Fifth Avenue and commission pictures from Meissonnier, or statues from Storey.

The case of "Napoli senza sole" would be precisely that of Seven Dials, of Chatham Street, of the rookeries of St. Petersburg and Moscow, but for one noteworthy circumstance. The Neapolitan miserables do not get drunk. When the weather is fine—and it is nearly always fine in this earthly paradise, inhabited chiefly by beggars and *ruffiani*—the penniless creep into the open to bask; and it is only with the sun and noisy chatter that they intoxicate themselves. The moody wretch in the ragged red flannel shirt in Manhattan yonder solaces himself with poisoned whiskey or rum; the *moujik* in his entozoa-haunted sheepskin, when he can catch at any kopecks, spends often on *vodka* what he should spend on bread; he drinks that he may forget his misery; the crapulous creature in St. Giles's or Seven Dials when he has pence flies for the self-same motive to the ginshop, where he finds light, warmth, comrades glad to see him, and such comfort as he cannot hope to obtain in the obscene den which is his only home: but the Neapolitan tatterdemalion, in a city where wine is almost as cheap as water, is habitually abstemious. Is he one whit the happier for his sobriety? Come hither, teetotal fanatics; come hither and ascertain and judge for yourselves. Does temperance make Girolamo Esposito or Sozzo Sudicio clean, industrious, honest, truthful, and manly? Yet he is thrifty, too, after a fashion. He hoards his coppers, when he can light on any, to back a number in the next *estrazione* in the lottery—a number chosen because in the lottery office book it corresponds with the circumstance of his having dreamed that his brother has been hanged, that he himself has had the small-pox, or of his having seen a mule cast a shoe opposite a wine shop or a white cat asleep in a wheelbarrow.

But to hoard in order to risk one's hoardings on the hazard of the wheel of fortune is the very feeblest kind of thrift, you will say. Gambling is one of the worst of human evils. The lottery in Italy is one of the most pernicious gangrenes which affect that fair land. Of course it is; and what, if you please, is the market price of Turks and Egyptians? and when you speculate for the "rise" or the "fall" of such and such stocks, what are you doing but staking your money—or the money which you have stolen from other people—upon the hazard of fortune's wheel? The only material difference that I can discern between the Neapolitan Lazarus who gambles in the lottery and the great Exchange operator is that the former, having perhaps saved eighteenpence for gambling purposes—and eighteenpence will not keep one in macaroni and tomatoes for more than a week—risks his *totum* in the hope of winning four hundred pounds; whereas Dives, on the Bourse or the Stock-Exchange, who has already enough money to keep him and his family in honourable competence all the days of their lives, risks his *totum* in the hope of winning a million sterling, of which he may lose every farthing the very next day in some great crash.

Drunkenness is a fearful curse, and the cause of much crime, no doubt; the judges, the parsons, the philanthropists, the moralists, all concur in telling us so. But is not hunger—is not the misery arising from the perhaps inevitably unequal distribution of wealth—the most fearful curse of all? Come hither, and ascertain and judge for yourselves. This city, beautiful, picturesque, and gay, is one of the most miserable and one of the wickedest in the world. Invitations to vice of the most hideous kind meet you, in broad daylight, at every turn. The mass of the population are sunk in the most abject misery. The rulers of the land are doing their

A WATER VENDOR'S STALL AT NAPLES.

very utmost to ameliorate and to regenerate it. The laws are equitable, the press and the people are free. It is pleasant to see the little children with their satchels by their sides trooping in their thousands to and from school. In some parts of the Peninsula factories are springing up apace. Everywhere economists are striving—now by savings' banks, now by agricultural associations, now by sanitary organisations—to make the people self-reliant, moral, healthy, and strong.

That there are hordes of mendicants, and idlers, and vagabonds in Naples one must be blind and deaf to deny. Still, the *lazzaroni* who, in their thousands, under the Bourbon rule formed a race apart—a distinct mischief, nuisance, and peril to society—may be said to be extinct. There is an immense deal of laborious toil, as well as an immense amount of vicious exertion, or of mere idleness, in Naples. The boatmen, the hack-drivers; the fishermen, the fruit-sellers, the hawkers of all kinds of petty wares, the itinerant tinkers and cutlers, and the followers of five hundred kinds of small industries, all seem to be indefatigably laborious in their several callings; but it is the wretchedly insufficient pittance which after much striving they are able to earn that keeps them poor and leaves them poor. The hunger is chronic, and naturally is one of the chief factors of crime.

The hungry man, hitherto imperfectly educated, and sunk in the grossest superstition, grows weary at last of toiling for an inadequate wage. He sees a way towards earning more by doing nothing but what is bad. From Esposito or Sudicio he practically changes his name to Sparafucile or Spadacino. He consorts with the vilest of the vile. He becomes at last the downcast, tattered felon with the half-smoked meerschaum-pipe countenance, or that other, with complexion like the bladder covering a pickle-jar, whom I met this morning handcuffed between the two *carabinieri*, and whose congeners I subsequently saw arraigned on wearisomely similar indictments, thefts *di poco momento*, in one criminal tribunal after another. In one case, where the act of larceny was brought straight home to the accused, a gaunt hobbledehoy of seventeen, with the smallest amount of coat on him that I ever saw—at least it lacked one sleeve, one tail, and a lapel, and was split up the back, and, but for the dignity of the thing, he might as well have gone in his shirt sleeves; only they were, I fear, as imperfect as his coat—his advocate pleaded that although the *delitto* might have been proven, it was evil and cruel policy to expose such a *giovanotto* to the contamination of a gaol. The judges put their heads together for a few minutes, and then concurred in a verdict of "assolto"—acquitted. The gaunt hobbledehoy forthwith slipped out of the dock grinning a very unlovely grin, and was forthwith acclaimed by a band of ragamuffins, male and female, his kindred and acquaintances, who had, I suppose, mustered up between them the few lire required for the advocate's fee. The legal gentleman, who had really spoken with much force and fervour, had, during his address to the court, worn a gown of rusty black stuff; but, so soon as his exculpatory harangue had come to an end, he was approached by the usher of the court, who very composedly disrobed him, and folding up the forensic toga put it away in a cupboard. Was there only a solitary gown, then, for the Tribunal of this entire Sessione Criminale? The advocate, well pleased with his success, turned to leave the court. An unshaven, shabbily-clad gentleman was he; and, if there be anything in facial expression, he was as hungry as his client.

SPRING-TIME IN PARIS.

I.

A CONTINENTAL SUNDAY.

PARIS, *May 26.*

IF the " Rive Droite," or right bank of the Seine, did not smell so very strongly of pitch, the Delightful City, rendered more enjoyable by the delicious weather which glorified and made beautiful there the latter days of May, would as amply fill up the measure of the idea of an earthly paradise as does Andalusia in early spring and the Valley of Mexico—abating only the rainy season—all the year round. Here, in Paris, you are all encompassed about by flowers the loveliest to see and scent, and the rarest to name by the name. It is for others to pay from twenty to a hundred francs each for the prodigious floral trophies which fill with rainbows so many *vitrines* on the fashionable boulevards, and which make a highway of roses by the northern side of the Madeleine. You are not asked to buy those bouquets of price. You may obtain a very pretty button-hole for three sous, from the beggar-woman slinking round the corner. The grand bouquets are for the "raout," to-night, of Madame la Marquise de Tulipano; for the marriage, to-morrow, at the Church of St. Germain l'Auxerrois of M. le Baron Roguet de la Poguerie, that distinguished Bonapartist deputy, to Mademoiselle de

Crac, the daughter of one of the most exalted notabilities of *la haute finance*. But the costly flowers, the big fish, and the colossal asparagus at Chevet's, Potel's, and Chabot's, the miraculous bonnets in the milliners' shops of the Chaussée d'Antin and the Rue St. Honoré, the diamonds at the jewellers' in the Palais Royal and the Rue de la Paix, the bronzes and artistic furniture in the Avenue de l'Opéra, the pictures and bric-à-brac in the Rue Lepelletier and the Rue Drouot, the china and glass, the gilt and enamelled gewgaws of the Passages, the thousand and one glittering, sparkling, radiant trifles of this city, in which "la Bagatelle" has more socially dynamic power than a whole battery of hundred-ton guns, are all yours to ponder over, to expatiate upon, to revel in, free, gratis, and for nothing.

Are not analogous spectacles as varied, as abundant, as attractive, and as cheap, accessible to you in London? Is not Regent Street a mart full of glasses of fashion and moulds of form? Is not Bond Street one long highway of art? Is Piccadilly to be contemned, or are the shopping attractions of the Strand to be ignored? I answer emphatically that the attractions which the very gayest of our thoroughfares and the most brilliant of our shops present, even at the height of the season, are tame and cheerless in comparison with the aspect offered by the boulevards of Paris in a highly sunny and balmy spring-time. Somehow, if you are poor, it does not seem to you that you have any property, not even the ghostliest of contingent remainders, in the pretty things which fill the London shop-windows. You are afraid, even while you gaze upon them, that a tall young man dressed all in black will step out from the shop and ask you severely if you intend to buy anything.

Now, in the *étalage* of a shop on the Paris boulevards I fancy that I discern a kind of tacit recognition of the right of the impecunious public to stare without purchasing. It is as though the proprietors were saying compassionately, and not contemptuously, " We know that you are mostly *des pauvres diables*. It is the lot of the bulk of humanity to be so. A *friture* of gudgeons is more in your line than the big salmon or the choice trout at Chevet's. Nevertheless, come and stare, and welcome. See, there are truffles—truffles black and truffles white. The consideration of those esculents to the well-constituted mind will render the degustation of the halfpennyworth of fried potatoes from the *fruitière's* in the back street more appetising. Admire this snowy Camembert; follow the delicate marbling, the subtle tints of this Gorgonzola; and you may find your morsel of *fromage de Brie* more appetising. A thing of beauty is a joy for ever, but the joy is doubled when the beauteous thing is eleemosynary. Buy? Of course you cannot buy, but you can look. All these brave things are as much your property as are the Column of the Place Vendôme, the Arch of Triumph, the Marly Horses, the façade of the Louvre, and the Porte St. Denis. Look, then, your fill. The sunshine is yours. Bask and be satisfied."

There is another circumstance which tends to make Springtime in Paris an enchanting season. There is no law, written or unwritten, against walking about the streets at as slow a pace as ever you choose to adopt. You may creep, you may crawl, you may prowl, and no man—nor policeman—shall say you nay. I maintain that in a fashionable street in London, when the season is high, your mode of locomotion as a pedestrian is necessarily hurried. Just as in the case of table-turning it is the involuntary muscular action of the persons seated round that makes the table revolve, so in the perpetual up-and-down flowing of the crowd in a London thoroughfare, however slow and measured your step may to yourself seem to be, it is imperceptibly accelerated by the pressure of those behind you and at your sides. You have really no command over your locomotive muscles, and are practically advancing in a desperate hurry when, to your own private thinking, you are strolling along in a most leisurely manner.

When "Japanese Tommy," one of the earliest observers of Anglo-Saxon manners, wrote to his friends at Yokohama a description of his first walk down Broadway, New York, he made mention of "tall men armed with huge clubs, dragging women by their arms with furiously indecent gestures along the public pavement." That which "Japanese Tommy" saw in reality was only a succession of well-bred American gentlemen, with walking-sticks or umbrellas, politely offering their arms to ladies as they escorted them along the side-walk. We should "see ourselves as ithers see us," not only morally but physically; but, to realise the rapidity of Anglo-Saxon pedestrianism, we should either be a noble Redskin—where is the noble Redskin?—or a sententious Arab of the desert, wrapped in his buffalo robe or his burnous, and stalking along in a traditionally slow and dignified manner. But, granting our enjoyment of those ethnological conditions, we should probably, ere we had stalked a hundred yards in Bond-street or the Strand on a fine day towards the end of May, be jostled against the wall or elbowed into the gutter, or tripped up, to the peril of the integrity of our nose, by the involuntary and unconsciously heaving, surging, and "madding" crowd of well-dressed people. It would be better, perhaps, to survey the scene from the secure point of vantage of the car of a captive balloon.

On the Paris boulevards, both by day and by night, you can and you do, both by necessity and from choice, lag and halt and prowl. If the Parisian be in a hurry he hails a hack carriage, the driver of which dashes through thick and thin, "washes the wheels of other carriages," and vituperates their Jehus; yells out "Gare!" after, and not before, he has all but run over people crossing the road: and conducting you "tant bien que mal"—very often worse than better—at last shoots you out of his trap, and dumps you on the side-walk, as the Americans say, in a more or less shaken and dislocated condition of body and mind. But, when you are on foot, you make up your mind to take things easily, and fifty thousand people behind and fifty thousand people in front of you have made up their minds in a similar intent. The good things of Paris are on either side, to peer at, to dawdle over, and to digest. You are not obstructing the thoroughfare by moving along *piano;* for the reason that the pace of everybody else is *piano;* and consequently, as regards the circulation, it is *sano;* and "chi va sano va lontano"—that is to say, the progress, although slow, is sure! and if you desire to "do" the "totality of the boulevard"—to the old Parisian there

A A

can only be one line of boulevards—you will, starting from the Madeleine with a healthy determination to take stock of the contents of every shopwindow, to give eyes to every kiosque, to give ear to every quack, to take note of every pretty girl, of every hideous old woman, of every loiterer under every *porte cochère*—you will reach the Rue Montmartre at last. On the upper boulevards, as far as the remote regions of the Place de la Bastille and the Barrière du Trône, people are allowed to be in a hurry and to walk fast. But what *flâneur* ever dreams of travelling to the Barrière du Trône save when the *foire aux jambons* or a great public festival is on foot?

On the Boulevards de la Madeleine, des Italiens, and des Capucines people do not walk, they dawdle; and the only individuals to whom it is permissible to show the slightest symptoms of hurry are, first, the cocked-hatted and blue-coated *garçons de bureau* of the banks and *comptoirs d'escompte*, with their leathern portfolios stuffed with bills for acceptance, bills for payment, and other valuable securities, fastened by light, strong steel chains to their waists; and next the bare-headed work-girls who, generally arm in arm, troop out between half-past eleven and noon from the houses of business where they are employed. Their ostensible errand is breakfast. They find the pursuit of that pleasant quest compatible with treading on your toes—with an airy and wholly harmless pressure—giggling in your face, and indulging in many criticisms on the fashion of your watchguard, your waistcoat, your whiskers, and your nose. So was it when my life began; so was it when I was a man; so is it now when I am old. They say that the *grisette* is dead! that Lisette is an extinct biped; that Frétillon has become a fable and Rigolette a myth; but I rejoice in the conviction that there is no diminution in the eel-like agility and adroitness with which the bare-headed work-girl wriggles and insinuates her way between the serried files of *flâneurs* on the boulevards at noontide, and that there is to all appearance not the slightest surcease of her graceful, good-tempered, and invincible impudence of mien. She is not the sister of the extant Gavroche, that pallid, paper-smoking, purulent varlet. She is the daughter of Bouffé, the "gamin de Paris," in the days when *gaminerie* meant frank, merry sauciness, and not depraved *polissonnerie*.

It has been for a long time obvious to me that—as is the case with most proverbs—there is a double edge of signification to the saying which warns you that "you may go farther and fare worse." I take the locution to be a caveat not only against desponding adversity, but against restless desire of greater things in prosperity. "Rest and be thankful" might indeed be the complement of the counsel to abide where you are instead of going farther at the risk of faring worse. For example, the last Saturday I passed in London was the most magnificent of May days of the old-fashioned type. It was a day so gloriously and equally sunny as to make the elderly mind revert to the halcyon period when you could walk down the shady side of Pall Mall in white trousers, without the risk of being derisively howled at by the small boys. The exquisite beauty of the afternoon made me think—ill-conditioned ingrate!—of how much more beautiful the weather would probably be in Paris. I pined to revel in the unbridled licence of the "Continental Sunday," which to me means not much more than the privilege of sitting at a little table outside a café on the boulevards over a *bavaroise* or a *mazagran* from eight in the morning until long past midnight, if I so please, without the fear of the Middlesex magistrates and the licensing laws being perpetually before my eyes.

Yes, I had an unholy longing for the Concert des Champs Elysées and a hankering after the flesh-pots of the Café Anglais on Sunday. How large the asparagus and the strawberries would be at the Paris restaurants on Sunday; and how unconscionably you would be robbed by the purveyors of those delicacies at the boulevard dining rooms! And the picture galleries that would be open, and the trim *demoiselles de magasin* that would be afoot luxuriating in the sinful recreation of the *promenade*. And the facilities for buying newspapers all day long. And the theatres and balls that would be open in the evening. And the grimly humorous pleasure of watching crowds of English people, who at home wear the conventional downhearted and dolorous look, and who seem to be thinking—between church and chapel hours —of nothing less than of the dire necessity that will arise for the hanging of their cat on Monday for killing of a mouse on Sunday; of watching these worthy folk crowding the *perron* and the courtyard of the Grand Hôtel, gossipping and flirting in the vestibules of the Continental, dashing forth in barouches on their way to Vincennes or St. Cloud, and, in fine, entering into all the spirit of the Continental Sunday, for all the world as though they were rational beings.

"I will go over to Paris," I said. "There will be a light train and a light boat; for Wednesday will be the Derby Day, and the sight-seeing classes will be more inclined to coming home than to going abroad this particular Saturday evening." This was, on my part, blunder number one. I had entirely forgotten that Saturday was the eve of the French Derby, run at Chantilly, and that consequently we should have a heavily-laden train from Charing Cross to Dover and a boat as heavily laden from Dover to Calais. To the traveller who neither owns nor bets on racehorses, and to whom a race means little beyond a minimum of fun with a maximum of dust, drought, unsavoury companionship, lavish expenditure on utter superfluities, and general discomfort, followed by an uneasy sensation of mortified repentance over time and money wasted, the apparition on a brief continental trip of the surroundings of English sporting life is little less than the ugliest of nightmares.

I like the Derby when I am at Epsom, and the Cup when I am at Ascot, and the St. Leger when I am at Doncaster; and, although I could hardly rise to the height of sporting sentimentality of the lady who told me that she could never see the parti-coloured satin jerkin of a jockey hanging over the wire-blind of a tradesman in St. James's Street without an inclination to shed tears, I think that a race, just before and while it is being run, is one of the very prettiest spectacles that the world can offer. But I confess that I do not care much for the sight of the deck of a Channel steamer crowded with individuals almost exclusively of the sterner sex, with pallid flat faces, small eyes, square jowls, and crania of the bullet conformation, either clean-shaven or with closely-cropped whiskers, in garments very exiguous about the hips and very tight about the legs, generally with horse-shoe pins in their neckerchiefs, and short sticks or hunting-crops in their buckskin-gloved hands, and whose conversation is an impartial mixture of citations of the odds, slang, and downright blasphemy. If the English sporting fraternity, jockeys, trainers, bookmakers, and all, could only travel to and from the Continent in balloons! But that is a consummation which, however devoutly it may be wished, will scarcely be realised in our time.

By the time I reached Amiens I had come, very much against my will, to know a great deal more about horseflesh than I had been aware of for several years past; but I am happy to say that the impression made on my memory by the suddenly and reluctantly acquired lore was of the most fleeting nature, and that when we reached the Gare du Nord, and had gone through the very mild ordeal of the Paris *douane*—they tell me that there will be fearsome tribulations at the English custom-house when we return—I had entirely forgotten that the French Derby was to be run at Chantilly that very afternoon. My flat-faced acquaintances with the horse-shoe breastpins were straightway absorbed in the immensity of Paris; while I was with equal suddenness altogether engulfed in the contemplation of a scene which I have gazed upon, these five-and-forty years syne, hundreds of times, but which seems as new and strange and interesting to me as though the Rue de Lafayette were the high street of some city in the Mountains of the Moon, and I were treading the pavement—if pavement there be—of that high street for the first time in my life. It is only Paris at early morning.

It is just a quarter to six a.m., and upon my word here is a young damsel of some eighteen summers with her hair faultlessly adjusted, with a collar and cuffs immaculately snowy and irreproachably starched, and whose neatness about the feet and ankles should be a pride to herself and a stern example to all who are slatternly, who, in front of an establishment for the sale of *denrées coloniales*, is apparently taking a spell of penal toil at the crank. Hard labour, and by one of the softer sex, so close upon sunrise, and upon a Sunday morning, too! There was shame in the very thought of such an outrage. But the young lady, as she turns and turns the handle, has a beaming smile on her slightly pug-nosed but otherwise comely countenance. She is only winding up the iron shutters of the establishment for the sale of *denrées coloniales*. Presently the stock-in-trade of the *magasin* is revealed in all its varied richness. A treasure-house of what may be termed the quack groceries of the epoch. Miraculous cocoas, phenomenal tapiocas, world-famous sagos, life-preserving linseed, and a wilderness of macaroni. The private and exclusive coffee of the Veuve de Malabar, and the dried prunes which have been crowned in successive international exhibitions with nineteen medals and innumerable honourable mentions. The Tonkin tea, the Black Flags chocolat de santé, the Khroumir's biscuits, the *haricots blancs* of the Isthmus of Suez.

And the clock is just striking six this Sunday morning. The *patron* and the *patronne* will be down presently.

Adolphe, the shopboy—who ought to have wound up the shutters, by the by—has gone round to a neighbouring *coiffeur* to have his hair curled; for Adolphe, you may rest assured, is bound to be a visitor at a suburban ball this afternoon. As to Mademoiselle, the trim damsel, released from her toil at the ostensible crank, she sits quietly down in front of the shop in the Rue de Lafayette to read the last number of *Le Voleur* or *La Vie Populaire*. As the customers drop in she will sell to them such articles as they need; then she will go to mass. She will return to the midday meal, and if it be her Sunday *de sortie* she will go for a walk with her young man, and dine at a barrier *guinguette*, and go to the play or to a ball in the evening. If it be not her "Sunday out," she will continue during the whole afternoon, and until eight or nine in the evening, to serve behind the counter, or to occupy the stool outside the shop, reading cheap periodicals or gossipping with similarly circumstanced shop-boys and shop-girls, her neighbours. If she be of country extraction and *dévote*, she may trot away before sunset to vespers, while a withered old *bonne* minds the shop for her.

And what, I wonder, would the Metropolitan Shop Hours League say to this kind of thing? I fancy that the Parisians themselves, were they interrogated on the subject, would answer, with a shrug, "C'est comme ça." They do as their fathers and their grandfathers, and their remote ancestors, did before them. As with the grocer so with the *charcutier*—as with him so with the butcher, the baker, and the candlestick maker. The fruiterer will not put up her shutters again till late at night; the *rôtisseur's* spits are heavy with fowls and joints; the coal and coke dealer ceases not to supply his wares; the druggist is, of course, continually on hand. But whatever can the bookseller, the goldsmith and jeweller, and the old curiosity dealer want with their shutters down before seven o'clock on a Sunday morning? I pass scores of such shops ere I reach the hotel in the Rue St. Honoré where I alight. Once, however, arrived in that quarter, and of that of the great boulevards, you will find that, although the shopkeepers who supply the necessaries of life continue their trade as usual, Sunday closing of the most rigorous kind is the rule with the establishments which purvey the costlier articles of luxury.

But be not led astray by this apparent growth of reverence for the sanctity of the Sabbath. The great shopkeepers of the foreigners' quarter of the Rue de la Paix, the Rue du Quatre Septembre, the Avenue de l'Opéra, the Rue Royale, and, to a great extent, the Rues de Richelieu and Vivienne, forswear trading on Sunday, for the simple and sufficing reason that they have no trade to transact. On the first day of the week their clients, who are chiefly aliens, utterly and entirely desert them; so the shutters are hermetically sealed, and the shopkeepers and their assistants betake themselves— whither? Why, to the pursuit of pleasure, to be sure. M. le Patron before eleven has struck will be smoking his cigar and sipping something alcoholic in front of a café, or playing dominos or piquet in the interior thereof. Madame la Patronne, between mass and breakfast time, will be visiting her female acquaintances or bedizening herself in view of the entertainments of the afternoon. The young *calicots*, or assistants, are scattered about the *estaminets* and *brasseries* of the quarter, and the clicking of billiard-balls and the puffing of cigarettes or of briar-wood pipes are incessant. To-day everybody who has any money—and you must be a good many days in Paris, on each recurring visit, before you begin to light upon the people who have no money—means to go to the races at Chantilly. Is not to-day the French Derby run?

The answer comes between eleven and noon in peal after peal of thunder and then in a violent downpour of rain. " It will clear up," cries Auguste, hopefully, as he peeps from the *estaminet* door. The sky changes from the hue of zinc to that of lead and thence to a plumbago tint, and a fresh deluge of rain descends, vertical, implacable, and as it strikes the pavement ricochetting in the most alarming splashes. " Ha!" cries a cynical journeyman house-painter, who is compelled to lay by his brush and descend from the ladder, perched on the higher rungs of which he was decorating the frontage of a newly-established *marchand de vins*, " this will slake the lime on the faces of the *belles petites* at Chantilly." But the tempest affects other things besides the *belles petites*. I was " caught in the rain," as the saying is, in the Place du Palais Royal, and was fortunate enough to reach the shelter of the arcades of the Galerie de Valois ere the storm reached its height. Now, the Palais Royal has become, of all places on the Rive Droite, the one where the edifying but, so far as Paris is concerned, deceptive rule of Sunday closing is most strictly observed. Even the money-changers have taken to shutting up shop on the Sabbath. The cheap tailors no longer vaunt the excellence of their wares, and Albert Smith's Mr. Ledbury and his friend Jack Johnson would be puzzled to find the emporia where were vended the celebrated twenty franc "Cachemir Indian" shawl dressing gown, and the equally renowned "habillement complet" for thirty francs—the money to be unhesitatingly returned should the garments in question have "ceased to please."

I had passed through the Palais Royal about ten, and had found it a wilderness of closed shutters. Nobody in the Galerie d'Orléans, and only one elderly couple—provincials evidently, for Monsieur was reading the *Constitutionnel*, and Madame was knitting—at the Café de la Rotonde. But when the thunder began to peal and the rain to come down in torrents, the deserted arcades began to teem with surprising suddenness with life. Such life! Miserable, discomfited, disappointed, dripping, and draggle-tailed Paris. I declare that it was pitiable to watch the almost tearful glances which the poor holiday-making work girls cast behind them at their soaked frills and furbelows, their splashed stockings and muddied *bottines*. "The heart of man," says the grim old Patristic writer, "is no great matter; it is barely enough for a kite's dinner; yet the whole world is not large enough to satisfy its lust, its greed, and its ambition." It was not so very large a world that the heart of the poor wet-through little Parisiennes coveted. Their ambition, it may be, did not extend even so far as the racecourse at Chantilly. A long walk, a *bock*, a few sous worth of *galette*, an orange, and the innocent pleasure of looking without envy at the fine clothes and carriages and houses of people richer than themselves, were, perchance, all that they had promised themselves on their "Sunday out;" and now the cruel rain had come and spoilt everything.

But Auguste's prophecy, in the end, was verified. It did clear up at last into a gloriously warm and sunny afternoon; and, but for the omnipresent odour of pitch on the boulevards, where they were repairing in innumerable places the asphalte pavement, my first day of Spring-time in Paris would have been one of unqualified pleasure.

II.

"TO ALL THE GLORIES OF FRANCE."

PARIS, *May* 30.

Is anything of the nature of an apology required when I state that until Wednesday, the 28th May, 1884, I had never been to Versailles? Well, I have never seen Kenilworth, nor Haddon Hall, nor Knole, nor Chatsworth. Mine eyes have never gazed on Plymouth nor on Exeter; and, although I have been frequently and contumeliously bidden to "go to Bath," I have never been there. It was on a very hot day in the month of August, 1839, that I first arrived in the Rue Jean Jacques Rousseau, Paris, whither one of the diligences of MM. Laffite et Caillard had transported me from Boulogne-sur-Mer. I mind the hour as having been just before noon; for as twelve o'clock struck I heard a dull, distant detonation, which was due, I was informed, to the discharge, through the agency of the sun and a burning-glass, of a cannon in the garden of the Palais Royal. It was a broiling-hot day; there were few broad thoroughfares away from the boulevards in the Paris of those times; and the narrow streets, crossed at intervals by cords sustaining the *réverbères*, or oil lamps—there was gas only in the boulevard and in the Rues de la Paix and de Rivoli—were all in pleasant shade, and smelt delightfully of melons, peaches, celery, *fromage de Brie*, and fried potatoes. Even the swollen torrent of the kennel, plashing down the middle of the execrably paved street, had to my ears a soothing murmur; and, as one could with difficulty discern the tribute of dead cats, old shoes, and saucepans past service which it was bearing to reward the more vigilant quest of the *chiffonniers*, the gutter-music was enchanting as that of the Fountain of Trevi.

I had been met by a "big brother," resident in Paris, whose mission it was to conduct me to school. I remember that before we began our journey to the Rue de Courcelles, in the Faubourg du Roule, where the *pension* to which I was bound was situated, and after I had partaken of a great deal too much gingerbread and many more grapes than were good for me, to say nothing of two goblets of *coco* from the pagoda of an itinerant vendor of that sweetly frothing preparation of liquorice water, I impetuously demanded to be taken to Versailles. Possibly I had just been reading in the pages of some magazine an article called "Meditations at Versailles," which was to be reprinted in the following year in "The Paris Sketch Book," by one Michael Angelo Titmarsh; or, it may be, I had gathered some Versailles lore from a wonderful book entitled "The French Revolution: A History," by Thomas Carlyle, published in 1837. At all events I was frantic to see Versailles, the Jeu de Paume, the Cour d'Honneur, the Galérie des Glaces, and, especially, the Œil de Bœuf, which last, in my youthful cranium—of which the sutures were scarcely closed, so to speak—may have possessed some remote but pleasing association with bulls'-eyes.

But my "big brother" gravely informed me that Versailles was a long way off; that I must be very tired; that the day was very hot, and that he had it in charge not to allow me to overheat myself; that my schoolmaster—O! word of fear—at the Pension Hénon, Rue de Courcelles, Faubourg du Roule—was waiting for me; and, finally, that, before I undertook any excursions of a recreative character, it would be requisite that I should be—well—washed. We diligence travellers had been twenty-two hours on the dusty road between Boulogne and Paris. So, just as I was beginning to enjoy the unwonted spectacle of a regiment of little creatures with the fiercest-looking moustaches that I had ever seen, with yellow epaulettes and red legs, headed by drums beating like mad, marching across the Place des Victoires, I was bundled into a hackney carriage called a *dame blanche*, and conveyed to the far-off Faubourg du Roule.

The mills of the gods grind slowly, but they grind exceeding small. I went for a walk to the Rue de Courcelles the other day, and was elated to find that my old school had been pulled down long years ago, and that not a trace or vestige of it remained. Let it pass away, with the memory of its musty haricots and sour *vin ordinaire*, its too much work and too little play, its pedantic *répétiteurs* and umbrageous *pions*, and its horde of ill-conditioned louts who used to pinch and pull the hair of a lonely English boy for the reason that it was Marshal Blucher and not General Grouchy who arrived in time to turn the scale of victory at Waterloo, and because Sir Hudson Lowe at St. Helena persisted in calling the Emperor Napoleon "General Bonaparte."

The remembrance of that high noon in August, 1839, started up vividly before me when, on a latter day in May, 1884, I cooled my heels in the Salle des Pas Perdus of the St. Lazare railway station, waiting for the eleven o'clock express to Versailles. Nearly five-and-forty years had passed by since I first contemplated a visit to the town and palace created by the Roi Soleil; and, somehow or another, I had never been there. Schönbrunn and Potsdam, the Escorial and the Buen Retiro, the Alhambra and the Alcazar, the Winter Palace and the Hermitage, the Kremlin and the Old Seraglio, the Palace of Cortes and the White House at Washington had all been visited and revisited; but on the pile built by Mansard and Bernini, on the saloons decorated by Lebrun, on the gardens designed by Lenôtre, I had never set eyes. I have watched—at far too short a distance to be personally agreeable to a non-combatant spectator—the breaking out and consummation of three great revolutions in Paris: the toppling off his throne of Louis Philippe in February, 1848; the *Coup d'Etat* in December, 1851; the collapse of the Second Empire in September, 1870; but none of these tremendous political convulsions had made it necessary that I should visit Versailles.

Perhaps the absence of necessity has been the real reason why in the course of so many years I left this famous historic shrine unvisited. The pastrycook's young lady assistant abhors, it is said, jam tarts, and cannot look upon Bath buns without aversion. The porter at the Mausoleum Club, Pall Mall, when he was asked what he thought of the architecture of the newly-built Sarcophagus Club next door, replied that he had no opinion whatsoever to offer on the subject, inasmuch as the Sarcophagus was not on his way home ; thus he whose business it has been during nearly three decades to wander up and down the world to see and describe Pomps and Vanities may not have recognised the necessity for repairing to a great show house which he had never in the course of business been "told off" to describe. François Cramer, who during so many years led the orchestra for the ballet at Her Majesty's Theatre, had nothing to say about the respective choregraphic merits of Taglioni and Fanny Ellsler, Cerito and Duvernay. His business was to supervise his fiddlers, and not to look at the dancing. I was never bidden to go to Versailles, and so I never went there, until a friend who happened to be spending a few weeks *en villegiature* at the *annexe* of the Hôtel des Réservoirs asked me to come to breakfast with him on a given Wednesday. We were to have a drive afterwards, and return by an early afternoon train to Paris, where he had business. I should not be bored, he added, by having to go over the palace and gardens. He had no country cousins with him; and, of course, I knew both palace and gardens "like a book." Did I ? All that I really knew about them was from books.

The jaunt by express from the St Lazare station to Versailles is, on a fine day, pleasant enough. The name of every station mildly "wakes you up," and fills you with amiable memories. The landscape tries its very best to be pretty ; and, aided on this particular Wednesday by brilliant sunshine and abundant verdure, it very nearly succeeded in being beautiful. So attractive, indeed, did the country look at Ville d'Avray that had the train made a halt there I am very much afraid that I should have alighted, and sought out Les Jardies, and striven to conjure up the ghost, not of the recent Gambetta, but of Honoré de Balzac and his long-since-demolished villa. The train did stop at St. Cloud, and I had really a hard struggle to desist from getting out and making an expedition to the park and the ruined château; but fortunately a trifling circumstance intervened to conduce towards my keeping my seat in the train and my engagement at Versailles into the bargain.

My only companions in the compartment were a lady and gentleman, presumably married, and their son, a gawky *moutard*, aged about eight. The gentleman was young, disagreeably good-looking, and the roots of his hair were distant not much more than an inch and a half from his eyebrows. He was much given to sucking the top of his cane. The lady was middle-aged, in features equine, and in demeanour effusive. They were evidently a Constant Couple, a decorous couple, a model couple belonging to the *haute bourgeoisie*. The boy was a Fiend Child. The upper part of his body was clothed in a ghastly caricature of nautical costume, and he had "Tonkin" in gilt letters on the band of his broad-brimmed, low-crowned hat. His lower half was in knickerbockers, and his legs were bare. I should much have liked to draw the attention of a certain raven of my acquaintance, residing at a livery stable in Guilford Street, Russell Square, to the lower extremities of the Fiend Child in the Versailles railway carriage. I have been aware of this raven fully half my life. His age must be immense; but he still looks remarkably strong about the beak. I fancy that he would have made some impression on the Fiend Child—I could make none. The imp plunged and dived and thrust half his body out of the open window to the terror of his parents, almost incessantly. He was interested in my watch-chain, at which he "grabbed"; in my boots, on which he "stomped"; in my hat, which he temporarily annexed. He curled himself up into a ball on the cushions, and then threw out his arms and legs at random, as though he had been a windmill gone mad.

In his brief intervals of quiescence his papa and mamma half smothered him with caresses. They fed him with *brioche* and barley-sugar, and called him Loulou. Horrible little ogre! Whenever the gaze of his fond parents was averted I made the most hideous faces at him that my muscles could muster up; and I was able to perceive with gratification that he was just beginning to whimper with affright when the train drew up at St. Cloud, and he, his papa, and mamma left the carriage. I did not follow them. I felt inclined to hope that they would lose Loulou before the day was over, and that he would be found by the gipsies, or the cannibals, or by Monsieur and Madame Croquemitaine. And yet, I dare say, his parents were the worthiest of folk, and loved this unlicked cub as the apple of their eye. How distressed, how indignant they would have been had they detected me in making faces at the disagreeable little urchin, to them only a flower on whom inexhaustible tenderness was to be lavished!

Most of us, childful or childless, have our Loulous. You do not like to hear a stranger allude to your charmingly ugly dog as "a nasty, snarling little beast;" and when you have given four pounds fifteen shillings for a deliciously scarce little cookery-book of Queen Anne's time, you are apt to be out of temper with the domestic censor who rebukes you for wasting your money on "another rubbishing old book." And it smells so strong, too! the censor adds. The dog, the book, to you may be Loulou. So it was in a more tolerant frame of mind, I trust, that, when the Fiend Child and his parents had disappeared at St. Cloud, I sped towards Versailles; to alight in due time at the station in the Rue Duplessis, Boulevard de la Reine. I was, at the same time, not quite at my ease mentally. Would my friends believe me when I told them that I had never been at Versailles before, and should I have the opportunity of obtaining so much as a peep at the palace and gardens?

I approached the subject when I reached the *annexe* of the Hôtel des Réservoirs, delicately and timorously. I was informed that the grand suite of apartments into which I was inducted formed part of a mansion occupying the site of a house once occupied by Madame de Pompadour. Then the conversation naturally turned on Madame Dubarri, on Madame Campan, on the Princess de Lamballe, and on Marie Antoinette—at least, I tried my hardest to make our talk turn on those topics. But my host seemed much more disposed to discourse on M. Alphonse Daudet's new novel of "Sapho," on a new piece called "Le Député de Bombignac," to be produced that very evening at the Français, on the Salon, and the exhibition of Meissonier's pictures. He even made incidental mention of the Congo Treaty, of the Divorce debate in the Senate, and of the Soudan. My hostess was eloquent concerning the plenitude of flowers, the succulence of the asparagus, the waywardness of French servants, and the difficulty of obtaining a really tender *filet* of beef. Was it for this that I had come to Versailles? Well, from the old friendship point of view it was. From the historical point of view it certainly was not.

At length I took the bull by the horns, and, pleading that this was the first time in my life that I had ever been to Versailles, I begged to be taken to the palace as impetuously as I had begged my big brother to take me thither in the month of August, 1839. My entreaty was met by a glance of quite amiable, perfectly courteous, but altogether invincible incredulity. I was convinced that my friends did not believe a word that I was saying; that they believed me not one whit more when, after a long and delightful afternoon spent in the château and the gardens, and a merry dinner, I bade them farewell; and I am afraid that they do not believe me now, and never will. At all events, directly lunch was over we started for the palace, my host remarking, with gentle irony, that, after I had seen the palace I might like to visit the Grand and the Petit Trianon and the Hameau Suisse, with Marie Antoinette's Dairy, and the Maison du Bailli, and the Bridge, the Windmill, the Tour de Malbrouck, and all the rest of it. 'Twas he who said "all the rest of it," not I. It was part of his condition of mind,—of invincible unbelief.

We went. I saw; and I was not conquered. I am not about to do so foolish a thing as to attempt even the faintest outline of description of a palace which to the vast majority of people who have been to Paris—and who does not go to Paris nowadays?—must be as familiar as Windsor or Hampton Court, as the Painted Hall at Greenwich or as Kew Gardens. I only intend to record the impression which the interior of the palace made on me. It was an impression of extreme weariness and utter disappointment. A similar impression has been made on some travellers by the interior of the Basilica of St. Paul's Without the Walls and even of St. Peter's at Rome. The greater part of the first-named structure, although the apse and its mosaics are of immense antiquity, is really brand-new. The last-named edifice has been, internally, so sedulously swept and garnished, so sedulously kept in repair, that it looks too new. Versailles looks too new. When the First Revolution came to a close the deserted palace had fallen into such a lamentable state of abandonment and degradation that its demolition was seriously contemplated by authority; but Napoleon, while preferring St. Cloud as an Imperial residence, spent many millions of francs on the conversion of Versailles into a great gallery, where his celebrated drama of "Blood and Glory," with its unequalled spectacular effects, could be splendidly advertised. The politic Louis Philippe, who with regard to the Napoleonic legend resorted to the untradesmanlike device of saying that Imperialism was "the same concern" with Orleanism, only with Peace substituted for Blood, lavished yet more millions on the pictorial and plastic embellishments of the palace, which—always in the truest spirit of advertising—he dedicated to "Toutes les Gloires de la France."

The result has been grandiose, but, to my thinking, disappointing and even distressing. Your eyes and your brain are made literally to ache by the parade of these acres upon acres of quite modern canvas, crowded with battle-scenes, full of turgid compositions painted in the most glaring colours, and illustrating now the *fasti* of the Bonapartes, now those of Orleanism, now momentous scenes from the remoter history of France. Although the chapel, the Œil de Bœuf, the Galerie des Glaces, and the bed-chamber of Louis Quatorze remain to remind you of the *ancien régime*, the reminiscences are but vague and dim. The monstrous peruke of St. Simon, thatching as it did a skull full of scandal and leasing-making; the laced ruffles of M. de Buffon, dressing in gala dress every morning in order to write his zoological exercitations " on the knees of Nature;" the brocaded coat of Dangeau, the silver-hilted rapier of Bussy-Rabutin, the austerely crimped *tour* of Madame de Maintenon; the high-heeled shoes on the soles of which the Dutchman Vandermeulen painted, to be royally trodden under foot, the victories of his royal patron; the fans and tea-services that Boucher and Fragonard adorned for the Pompadour and the Dubarri, Marie Antoinette's hoop and powdered tresses; and the worsted stockings of Dr. Benjamin Franklin, which created so great a sensation among the courtiers, all these are practically hustled and elbowed and shouldered out of sight by the huge scene-paintings of the Napoleonic campaigns, and such enormous panoramas as that by Horace Vernet of the capture of the Smala of Abd-el-Kader.

Even the pictures of acknowledged and abiding value and interest are engulfed and absorbed in this great ocean of paint.

The famous tableau by David of the "Sacre"—the Coronation of Napoleon the Great—is a work before which an entire day might be well spent. Therein you may read the gist of Madame de Rémusat's Memoirs writ very large indeed. You might study for an hour together the countenance of that placid old Pope Pius VII., looking—ah!—so mild and so benignant, so affably content that the Emperor and King shall himself place on his head the Imperial diadem which the Supreme Pontiff has blessed; content that Josephine should be crowned, not by the Pontifex Maximus, but by her Imperial Lord; content, in fine, to take most things amiably and easily, but not without a touch of Italian shrewdness and astuteness in his features, not without an indication that he, the venerable Barnabo Chiaromonti, who has crossed the Alps to sanctify the enthronisation of this very queer Eldest Son of the Church, will be prepared to defend with inflexible tenacity the claims of his Church and his rights as a Temporal Prince, even if the struggle goes so far as his having to pronounce the major excommunication against the Church's very equivocal Eldest Son. The "Sacre" is to me a simply fascinating picture, unrolling, as it does, a whole Bayeux tapestry record of successful ambition, bravery, intrigue, and fraud: the whole surveyed and inwardly commented upon by Talleyrand with a knavish grin; while the phantom of the actor Talma seems to flit across the scene, explaining in dumb show how he has designed the grand robes of "Jupiter Scapin," and taught this prodigious posse of heroes and swindlers, jurisconsults and legislators, philosophers and mountebanks, and brazen-faced rascals of both sexes how they should properly wear their fine clothes and put on coronation manners.

But such pictures as the "Sacre" at Versailles are swallowed up, and their personalty is mainly obliterated, by the turbulent canvases of Vernet and Yvon, of Raffet and Bellangé. David, all melodramatic and empirically classic as he is, gives you, after all, something approaching a definite image of the First Napoleon—as a splendid "fraud," a superlative charlatan, a greater comedian than Nero, an actor who could play the conqueror and the despot on the stage of history even better than his friend Talma could impersonate such characters on the boards of the Comédie Française. But at Versailles such a picture as the "Sacre" is jostled, and to a certain extent its effect is negatived, by big saltpetre-and-Cirque-Franconi-smelling battle-pictures painted long after the Conqueror and Captive of the Earth had died his miserable death at Longwood; and the rat—while the doctors were making the autopsy of dead Cæsar—had striven to run away with the heart that had throbbed with the lust of universal empire.

III.

LE ROI SOLEIL AND LA BELLE BOURBONNAISE.

PARIS, May 31.

THERE is, as all the world knows, a large and splendid theatre or opera house in the palace of Versailles, which, in very recent times, was converted into the Hall of Session of the French Legislature, but which possesses far greater interest to the student of history as having been the scene of an entertainment which had the result of knocking one of the last of the nails into the coffin of the French monarchy. You will remember that in September, 1789, when the Régiment de Flandre came into garrison at Versailles, there was conceived the unfortunate idea of inducing the officers of that regiment to fraternise with the Gardes du Corps, with which intent a grand banquet was given by the latter on the stage of the palace theatre, the boxes being filled with the *élite* of the Court. Madame Campan has told us, in her Memoirs, how, when the orchestra played the air of " Oh, Richard, oh, mon Roi ! " enthusiastic shouts rent the roof ; and how, when her young nieces, who, by the Queen's command, occupied one of the boxes, were screaming " Vive le Roi ! " with all their might, a scowling Deputy of the Third Estate, who was in the next box, sternly rebuked them, telling them that he was ashamed to see young and handsome Frenchwomen brought up in such servile habits, and bawling outrageously for the life of one man, and that worthy American women would look with contempt on Frenchwomen "thus corrupted from their earliest infancy."

The scowling Deputy of the Third Estate "got his answer" —and a tolerably spirited one it was—from the young ladies whom he had scolded, and Madame Campan followed suit by bidding him mind his own business; when, to the horror of that discreet duenna, to whom the Queen had promised that she would remain in her own apartments during the banquet, the King, the Queen, and the Dauphin made their appearance on the stage. Forthwith the orchestra struck up the air from "The Deserter," "Can we grieve those we love?" Then either white cockades were distributed, or some young men belonging to the National Guard of Versailles turned the white linings of their tricoloured cockades outwards. There was a tremendous hurly-burly of loyalty. Embraces were interchanged, tears were shed, and innumerable glasses were emptied. The officers conducted in procession their Majesties back to their apartments; the lightest-hearted of the Gardes du Corps danced under the King's windows; and a soldier of the Régiment de Flandre climbed up to the balcony of his Majesty's bedchamber in order that his shouts of "Vive le Roi!" might come nearer the Royal ears. This enthusiastic loyalist, it was subsequently ascertained, was one of the most active and most dangerous of the mutineers in the riots of the following October. The scowling Deputy of the Tiers Etat who had scolded Madame Campan's poor little nieces took careful note, I have no doubt, of all these *faits et gestes*.

I was not able to see the theatre, which is being fitted up for the legislative conference about to be held in view of the Revision of the Constitution. I regretted the deprivation, for to me long-disused theatres present a strange charm. Do you know that wonderful old ramshackle structure in the Palazzo Farnese at Parma, the first theatre, we are told, in which boxes were introduced, and which was built full two hundred and fifty years ago? What a wildernesss of cobwebs and rotting timbers it is! But there is another and older dramatic temple at Vicenza, the Teatro Olimpico of Palladio, constructed scrupulously on the lines of Vitruvius, with its fixed scenery solidly built out from the piazza of the proscenium in three diverging streets which, in the foreground, are of a natural elevation, but which artificially diminish in height, while the ground plane as artificially rises as the scene recedes. From the porch of the central street kings and queens, when old Greek tragedies and comedies were played here, used to emerge. From the street to the right entered soldiers and citizens; from that to the left slaves.

Remembering that antique hall I was at once consoled for my inability to visit the theatre where the Régiment de Flandre were entertained by the Gardes du Corps. Why, the whole of this Palace of Versailles is one enormous Teatro Olimpico. Pray observe the permanent scenery, solidly built out, and in the very shammest of sham perspective. From that central archway strode majestically the Great King, toweringly periwigged, amazingly high-heeled, starred, ribboned, painted, perfumed. From the portal to the right streamed prelates and courtiers. And from the left? Well, from the plebeian door there may glide, smilingly, Boehmer, the jeweller, with his famous Diamond Necklace in a casket under his arm—the pretty glittering gaud, for which he only asks a trifle of four hundred thousand francs. Then comes sidling in on her way from the Chaussée d'Antin to the closet of her Majesty, Mademoiselle Bertin, prime revolutionist of the dress of the French ladies. Mademoiselle Bertin is a great artist. She devises headdresses of which the superstructures in gauze, in feathers, and in flowers are so lofty that the ladies cannot find carriages high enough to admit their *coiffures*, and may often be seen stooping as they ride in their grand gilt coaches, or holding their heads out of the windows. Others kneel on the floor of the carriage so that the holy headdress shall not be knocked off by contact with the roof. The historian tells us that when the Queen took Mademoiselle Bertin into her confidence and made dress her principal occupation, all wished instantly to have the same costume as her Majesty's. "The expenditure of the younger ladies was necessarily much increased; mothers and husbands murmured at it; some few giddy women contracted debts; unpleasant domestic scenes occurred; in many families coldness or quarrels arose; and the general opinion was that the Queen would be the ruin of the French ladies." So Mademoiselle Bertin had her small share in knocking a nail—with a beautiful gilt head—into the French monarchical coffin.

At Versailles I found the Olympian theatre moulded on the most colossal scale—Vitruvius and Palladio revised and settled, improved, exaggerated, and distorted by Mansard and Bernini; but where were the actors in the wondrous comedies and tragedies that have been played on this highly glorified stage? To my dulled sense they were invisible and mute. Obviously it would have been in the highest degree indecorous to lie down at full length on the floor of one of those tremendously Olympian saloons, and, with one ear prone to the polished oak, strive to listen to the echoes of the past. Fine-Ear, in the Comtesse d'Aulnoy's fairy-tale, could hear the grass and the very wool on the sheep's backs grow. How I longed for the attributes of Fortunio's gifted servant. I listened for the voice of the Grand Monarque, now tender and beguiling, as he utters soft perfidies to Mademoiselle de la Vallière; now condescendingly affable as he lays his hand on Molière's arm, and, pointing to the ridiculous M. de Soyecourt, Grand Huntsman, bids the dramatist mark an original whom he has not yet copied; now more benignant still, and to the raging envy, terror, and amazement of the great courtiers, bidding the modest author of "Tartuffe" take his place at the Royal table, and share the Royal *en cas de nuit*.

I listen and listen, but can hear no such Louis. Nay, nor the passionate accents of the offended monarch who, on receiving an impertinent answer from a Grand Seigneur, flings his gold-headed cane out of window, crying, "Heaven forbid that I should use my stick to strike a gentleman;" nor the lofty compliment which he pays to the great Condé, as the warrior, old and broken, comes painfully creeping up the grand staircase: "My cousin, you bend under the weight of your laurels;" nor the still nobler compliment which he offers to the rough Jack Tar hero, Jean Bart, who comes to Versailles, and is lionised, and has a stool allotted to him on which he sits whilst he narrates the incidents of his last cruise against the English. "My flagship led the way into action," he begins, "and I ordered the Victory to follow me." "And she obeyed you," interrupts Louis le Grand, with the gracefullest inclination of his periwig and the most benignant of smiles on his countenance. But I can neither see nor hear him now. I try to picture him at the apogee of his pomp and pride, enthroned in the Galérie des Glaces—the Dauphin, the Duc de Maine, the Duc de Chartres, and the Comte de Toulouse around him—receiving with haughty courtesy the humbled Doge of Genoa, and, with just as much sublime serenity as he might have displayed in flinging a marrow-bone to a dog which he had just kicked, presenting the crushed potentate with a portrait of his conqueror, set with diamonds, and a whole bale of sumptuous tapestry from the Gobelins. But the spirit of the Doge of Genoa declines to be called from the vasty deep of the Versailles past.

Again; we are in the sleeping apartment of the Invincible Louis. There is the very bed—a prodigious four-poster, all carving and gilding and brocade—in which he died. Surely, the genius of the place should inspire me here, if anywhere, in this deserted Babel. It is eight in the morning, I endeavour to fancy. The *garçons de chambre* have softly opened the windows and removed the *en cas de nuit*—usually a cold chicken and a flask of Burgundy; the *mortier*, a little silver basin full of water, in which had floated, during the night, a cake of yellow wax with a rude wick—our Charles the First had just such another night-light at St. James's, the night before his execution—and the *lit de veille,* on which, spread on the floor, the first *valet de chambre* had slept. Then the surgeon and physician-in-chief, and the old woman who nursed the King when he was an infant, enter the presence. The old nurse embraces him. There is at least one touch of nature in this vast Comedy of Shams. The *premier valet de chambre,* cautiously opening the bed curtains, hands the Invincible his wig, and then as cautiously closes the drapery. Without that peruke the Invincible must not be seen by meaner mortals. At a quarter-past nine the Grand Chamberlain and the courtiers entitled to the *grandes entrées* make their obeisances. The Invincible is still in bed, bewigged. Holy water is presented to the Invincible by a Court chaplain. The great courtiers who want anything— they are always wanting something, and it is generally something belonging to somebody else that they want—now mumble their petitions through the curtains. Another set of courtiers are then introduced who are privileged to behold the Invincible in the act of dressing himself. He puts on his stockings "with grace and address." We have St. Simon's word for it. Every other day, "with ease and agility," he shaves himself. On the days when he takes physic he receives in bed; but his wig, on those occasions, is a short one.

Being dressed, his Majesty says his prayers, kneeling at his bed's foot. All clerical persons who are present fall on their knees. The laity remain standing, with their heads bent down. Then his Majesty repairs to his cabinet, whither he is followed by a great mob of courtiers and State functionaries, to whom he gives his orders for the day. These dignitaries depart, and there remain only with the Invincible his natural children and their governors. Usually about this time his Majesty gives audience to Mansard, his architect. In the Great Gallery there is a crowd of courtiers. At the door of the Royal cabinet, the Captain of the Guard keeps watch. Presently he proclaims that his Majesty is going to mass; and the Invincible repairs to the chapel. His private pew, or rather balcony, is on the same elevation as the gallery and his bed-chamber; and it is a long way down to the pavement of the sacred edifice. Immediately after mass the foreign ambassadors are received in public audience. Then the King and his Ministers hold a council, which is sometimes prolonged until half an hour after noon.

At one, the Invincible dines, *à petit couvert;* alone at a square table. When he wishes for a moderate repast, or when his physicians insist that it should be moderate, the *officier de bouche* is commanded in the morning to serve *le très petit couvert;* but even this last consists of three courses and a dessert. As a rule, the Invincible eats enormously. And he never suffers from indigestion. Sometimes the Dauphin and later Monsieur le Duc are permitted to stand behind their Royal parent's chair during dinner; but he never asks them to sit down. But when the Duc d'Orléans takes the place of the Grand Chamberlain, and, with napkin on his arm, brings the dishes, the Invincible asks his brother if he would not like to sit down. Monsieur makes a profound bow, and a low *tabouret* is brought for his accommodation.

It is placed at the back of the Royal chair. No lady ever makes her appearance at the *petit couvert*, with the exception of the Maréchale de Lamothe, who is admitted by right of her post as governess of the Children of France. The physician-in-chief "assists" in a remote corner at the repast; but there is no need for his services.

The Invincible continues to gorge daily until he is seventy-seven years of age, without bursting. Then he breaks up very completely indeed. He feels poorly one chilly morning in May. A report gets wind that he is seriously ill; and the foreign ambassadors hasten to send couriers with the tidings to their respective Courts. The Great King is enraged to think that he should be even suspected of mortality. He holds a grand review of his household. For the last time that his aged eyes shall behold them the gendarmes and the *chevaux-légers* defile before the terrace at Marly, and they march past the Invincible, who is splendidly arrayed and mounted on a superb Arabian charger. He is four hours in the saddle. The next day he has a slight attack of fever. But on the morrow, which is the eve of his Saint's day, he feels better, orders a concert to be got ready, and convenes the fiddlers at his bedside. Still the fever returns, not to be chased away on this side the grave. The fiddlers are dismissed, and the doctors and the priests have things all their own way.

It is a mortification which has seized one of his legs, and the gangrene keeps mounting and mounting. The Invincible makes a tolerably dignified end of it; he naively tells two *garçons de chambre* whom, reflected in the mirror opposite his bed, he has espied weeping, that they are foolish to think him immortal, and "that, for his part, he never thought so;" but in his parting words to Madame de Maintenon his old, his sovereign, his supreme selfishness flashes up with a wondrous brightness. "Madame," he says, with solemn politeness, after scolding her for having made him wait so long for her coming, whereupon she excuses herself by saying that she has been praying for him with her boarding-school girls at St. Cyr, "all that which consoles me in my dying moments is that it cannot be long before we rejoin each other." She is three years older than the august patient, and is consequently furious at being reminded of her age. "A fine rendezvous he has given me," Bois-le-Duc the apothecary hears her say as she sweeps from the room. And the gangrene continues to mount.

Of course, as the final moment approaches, the charlatan with the nostrum turns up. He has turned up at the death-bed of our Edward VI., he will turn up with some oil of hartshorn at the deathbed of William Pitt. The Versailles quack is a man from Marseilles, who brings a little bottle containing an elixir infallible in cases of gangrene. At first Fagon and the rest of the King's physicians propose to kick the man from Marseilles downstairs. Sir Walter Farquhar and Sir William Herberden were of pretty much the same mind as regarded the well-meaning gentleman who posted to Putney with his little bottle. But the charlatan over-persuades the faculty; and at last they suffer him to administer a dose of his potion in a goblet of wine of Alicant to the dying man. For the moment the elixir seems to do him some slight good. The dose is repeated; but he grows worse and worse, and two days afterwards he dies. I could have lingered much longer at the carved and gilt balustrades in front of that prodigious four-poster than might have suited the convenience of my good friend's conductors. The bed on which so much pride and pomp and vanity, so much selfishness and meanness, so much profligacy and tyranny had paid the common debt was about the most eloquent thing with which I had yet met in this great Desolation of Painted and Silent Emptiness.

There was a civil *gardien*, with the stereotyped vocal twang of palace-guides all over the world, who conducted us through the private apartments of Marie Antoinette, in which praiseworthy efforts have been made to bring together some handsomely illustrative specimens of the furniture and decorative work of the period. We came to the dressing-room of the unhappy Queen whom the Paris mob made the heroine of the grimly grotesque song of "La Belle Bourbonnaise:"

>La Belle Bourbonnaise,
>La maîtresse de Blaise,
>Est très mal à son aise,
>Elle est sur le grabat.

This song was applied to Marie Antoinette in the early days of her unpopularity caused by the affair of the Diamond Necklace. The *poissardes* and the *forts de la Halle*, who roared the senseless ditty—written by the Chevalier de Boufflers, it is said, so far back as 1768—with its pretty tune, recked little that its concluding stanza contained a darkly-terrible prophecy. "The Pauvre Bourbonnaise," sings the ballad-writer, "finishes her life without a shroud and without a bier."

> La Pauvre Bourbonnaise
> Va dormir à son aise,
> Sans fauteuil et sans chaise,
> Sans lit et sans sofa.

See here. We are in the *cabinet de toilette*. The *gardien*, with the stereotyped twang in his voice, is telling his hackneyed tale; but my memories run faster than does hi bald talk. The peerless Queen stands encircled by her *dames d'honneur* and her *dames d'atours*, her *femmes de chambre*, and her ordinary women. This hands the skirt; that puts on the gown. A *dame d'honneur* pours out the water for the Royal hands to wash in. If a Princess of the Blood be present, the *dame d'honneur* must hand the fine linen to a *femme de chambre*, who hands it to the Princess, who hands it to the Queen. When her Majesty's head is dressed, she curtseys to all the ladies in the chamber, and followed only by her own women, goes into her closet, where her milliner, Mademoiselle Bertin, awaits her. Mademoiselle calls her dress-patterns her " specimens of negotiations with her Majesty."

But with a vengeance does the scene change, although we are still in the private apartments. It is half-past four in the morning. The *poissardes* and the *forts de la Halle* have marched from Paris. They are at Chaville. They are at Versailles, bellowing and shrieking in the Cour d'Honneur. The mob have entered the antechamber of the Great Guard Room. One of the Gardes du Corps is holding his musket across the door, the crowd striking at him till his face is covered with blood. The Queen is in bed. A lady awakens her crying:

"Get up, Madame; don't stop to dress yourself; fly to the King's apartment." She throws herself out of bed: they put a petticoat upon her, without tying it. Two ladies hurry her towards the Œil de Bœuf. At length, after many hairbreadth scapes, she reaches the King's apartments, to go with him to Paris, to the Tuileries, to Varennes, to the Temple, to bid him farewell there, and, after a time to continue her woful progress to the Conciergerie, to the tumbril and the bloody scaffold in the Place de la Révolution.

"La Belle Bourbonnaise!" "La Pauvre Bourbonnaise!" I declare that it was the remembrance of the melody which they used to sing to me when I was a child that woke up all Versailles to me; that made the inanimate vascular, and the dry bones of history live. "La Belle Bourbonnaise!" Behold her beautiful, smiling, radiant in the Swedish painter Werthmüller's picture. She is there as Edmund Burke, in undying language, has described her. But for the "Pauvre Bourbonnaise" of the last stanza of the Chevalier de Boufflers' unconsciously prophetic song, you must seek, not in Paul Delaroche's splendidly dramatic picture of Marie Antoinette passing after sentence from the Revolutionary Tribunal—for she is there, all grey and discrowned as she is, queen-like in her extremity and magnificent in her misery—but in an appalling little pen-and-ink sketch made by David, a copy of which from the original in the Soulavie collection is now in the Bibliothèque Nationale. David—the painter of the "Sacre," but otherwise known as "David of the blood-stained brush," whom the gentle-hearted Flaxman, when he visited Paris, resolutely refused to visit—was at an open window with the Citoyenne Julien, wife of a representative of the people, when the death-cart with Marie Antoinette in her squalid gown and coarse mob cap and her arms tied behind her, as we see her in Lord Ronald Gower's statue, rolled by on its way to the guillotine.

In David's sketch, executed, no doubt, to the intense delight of the Citoyenne Julien, we see the Queen seemingly in a kind of lethargy, the *rigor mortis* stealing over her face, cadaverous, ignoble, ugly. Yet a few touches would transform this dreadful profile into a face of exceeding loveliness. Was the man with the "blood-stained brush"—he who lived to be a Baron and to portray all the courtezans of the Imperial Court—faithful to his art when he made this hideous draught? Well, at all events, "La Pauvre Bourbonnaise" was going "to sleep at her ease"—without a throne, without a sofa, without a chair, without a shroud, without a bier, and with no bed save a heap of quicklime.

IV.

A QUEEN'S PLAYTHING.

PARIS, *June* 1

I BADE farewell to the Stone Colossus, to the Niagara of painted canvas, to the earthly paradise made by the Grand Monarque out of a sandy desert. A precious earthly paradise, upon my word! The stones of the Palace of Versailles are cemented with the blood and sweat of thousands of Frenchmen. While the enormous monument of pride and selfishness was a-building thirty-six thousand men and six thousand horses toiled night and day at it. It was not only Coleridge's Kubla Khan that could "decree" a Pleasure Dome in Xanadu. Louis decreed one here, and bade a palace as big as a town grow up in a waste, and water flow where all before had been arid. Many of the workmen employed were young soldiers, crowds of whom died from the exhalations of the incessantly excavated earth. It was forbidden, under the severest penalties, to speak in the camp established at Maintenon of such a thing as sickness; yet every night, according to Madame de Sévigné, whole wagon-loads of dead and dying men left Versailles.

It is almost a matter for astonishment, when we remember the continuous and wanton waste of human life, not only in works of war but in works of peace, during the long, splendid and maleficent reign of Louis Quatorze, that when in the fulness of time—when Blenheim and Malplaquet had been fought; when thousands of virtuous and industrious Protestants had been driven out of the kingdom by the Revocation of the Edict of Nantes; when thousands more, including women and children, had been slaughtered, outraged, tortured in the *dragonnades;* when the plague had decimated the population of Provence, and famine had swept over the land and so wrung the vitals of the wretched peasantry that they were fain to swill broth made of boiled grass and weeds, and eat bread made of draff and husks—one almost wonders, I say, that when the earth was relieved of the presence of this Moloch Grand Monarque there should have been, with the exception of *grands seigneurs* and *petites maîtresses*, priests, monks, nuns, parasites, opera dancers, hairdressers, tailors, milliners, play actors, lawyers, fiddlers, and hangmen, any French people left in France.

Yet there were plenty left—between twenty-five and thirty millions, possibly. There was a whole nation left to groan under the tyranny of the *gabelle*, to be mercilessly squeezed by the tax-gatherers when, at the accession of Louis Quinze, the "droit du joyeux avènement" was collected from the miserables—the nobles and clergy paying not one *rouge liard*. There were people enough to throng the gardens of Versailles on a holiday when a great courtier, taking the baby Louis from the arms of his nurse, held him up on the terrace so that he might see the multitude below, and said to him, "Behold, my King, all those people belong to You." There were left scribes enow of low degree to teach the boy monarch to write, and to set him that famous text which you may see in the copybook preserved in the Palace at St. Petersburg, "Kings do as they please; their peoples obey them." There were people enough left to make food for powder in a hundred useless battles and sieges; to make and paint, for a few livres a month, the pottery for which china-maniacs will now willingly give a hundred guineas the square inch; there were mothers enough left to have their children stolen by the arch-pander Lebel for his Majesty's seraglio at the Parc aux Cerfs; there were people enough left for the *Fermiers-Généraux* to plunder for yet three generations more; for the priests and monks to fatten upon; for the *bourreau* of the Châtelet to hang, to rack, to scourge, to brand, and to break on the wheel. "None but those," remarked Talleyrand in his old age, "who had lived in France at the time immediately preceding the Revolution could form any idea of the singular sweetness which then pervaded society." Well, does not Clarendon, at the beginning of his history, assert that England, just before the breaking out of the Civil wars, was the happiest country under the sun? "And, for a complement of all these blessings, they were enjoyed by, and under the protection of, a King of the most harmless disposition, and the most exemplary piety—the greatest example of sobriety, chastity, and mercy that any prince hath ever been endowed with." "Les beaux esprits se rencontrent."

It was a slow train, dragging its lazy length along for the best part of an hour, that bore me back to Paris; yet had the journey occupied thrice the time that it did I should not have

murmured. The truth is that my head was full of
Versailles, and is so, now. Not of the Palace. I dismissed
it as a vision of Chaos—as an ugly nightmare of which one
was well rid. The air of the "Belle Bourbonnaise" drifted
into the harsher notes of the "Ça Ira!" the air of which is
that of a once fashionable *contredanse* which Marie Antoinette
was fond of playing on her harpsichord. The mob in the
Place de la Révolution howled the "Ça Ira!" as the Queen
climbed the steps of the scaffold. I bade the Satanic tune
get behind me; but it vanished only to give place to the
ferocious "Carmagnole,"

>Madame Véto avait promis
>De faire égorger tout Paris.

Were more horrible words ever set to a spirited air which
troops can march to at the double-quick, and which is said to
have been borrowed from the *répertoire* of some peaceful
Savoyard bagpiper? I strove to stamp it out of my mind,
together with the nobler "Marseillaise" and the "Chant du
Départ." Napoleon I. sternly prohibited the playing of any
one of these airs; but retributive justice overtook him in the
matter of melody. The First Empire produced no national
hymn; and when, at the beginning of the Hundred Days, the
troops of Louis XVIII. and of the Adventurer escaped from
Elba came face to face, the Bonapartists could make no better
lyrical reply to the Bourbonists whose bands were playing
"Vive Henri Quatre" and "La Belle Gabrielle" than by
striking up "Partant pour la Syrie," the pale and namby-
pamby air composed by Queen Hortense—or her German
music-master. Yet Napoleon had his own favourite warlike

chant, which he was accustomed to hum—villanously out of tune—as he vaulted into his saddle at the beginning of a campaign. His war song was "Malbrouck s'en va-t-en guerre." He had not forgotten it at St. Helena, when, alluding to the old song, he remarked to Las Casas, " See how ridicule can stigmatise all things, even victory."

So odd and capricious is the association of ideas that my pleasantest and most enjoyable remembrances of Versailles will always be associated with "Malbrouck s'en va-t-en guerre," the merry melody of which was, as most people know, appropriated by Beaumarchais for Chérubin's song in the "Mariage de Figaro," and which has long been convivially popular with us as "It's a way we have in the Army, A way we have in the Navy." Now mark this. One of the edifices in the pretty toy Swiss village at the Petit Trianon is called "La Tour de Malbrouck." Many thousands of English and American pilgrims to Versailles have possibly wondered what connection there could be between this architectural trifle and John Churchill, Duke of Marlborough. The connection is a very curious one. The victor of Blenheim had been dead sixty years when a good woman, named, appropriately enough, Madame Poitrine, was fetched from the East of France to act as wet-nurse to the infant Dauphin, son of Louis XVI. She was heard to sing by the child's cradle an absurd ballad with a catching tune. It was, "Malbrouck s'en va-t-en guerre," composed originally, perhaps, by some wandering minstrel who had followed the camp of Boufflers and Villars.

"Malbrouck s'en va-t-en guerre" speedily became the rage at the Court of Versailles; and the vogue of the song became universally contagious. Everybody took to humming the absurd burden, "Mironton, mironton, mirontaine." The stanzas of the ballad were illustrated by paintings on fans and firescreens; and in 1783 "Malbrouck" was produced as a grand pantomime, at the Théâtre Nicolet. Marie Antoinette must needs have a "Tour de Malbrouck" built in her toy "Hameau Suisse." It is to the top of her tower, you will remember, in the song, that Madame de Malbrouck ascends when, from afar off, she espies the page, all clad in black, who is speeding with the woful tidings of the death and burial of her husband. It needed but this encouragement of a popular whim by a young and sprightly Queen to give a most moving historic interest to one at least of her group of mimic *châlets* at the Petit Trianon; but it should not be forgotten that M. de Chateaubriand afterwards declared that he had heard the air of "Malbrouck s'en va-t-en guerre" during his travels in the East, which led him gravely to surmise that the tune had been brought to France by the Crusaders. That it is identified with the little tower at the Petit Trianon is enough for me.

The immense gardens of the palace were, I confess, a little too powerful to be taken in at a single draught. As old Dr. Lister, the physician, said of this wonderful pleasaunce, nearly two hundred years ago, "it is less a garden than a whole country laid out into alleys and walks, groves of trees, canals and fountains, everywhere adorned with statues, ancient and modern, and innumerable vases, with all Æsop's Fables in waterworks *in usum Delphini*." For the rest, the super-abundance of splendour in these gardens puzzles and distresses you. Whither shall you wander first? To the Fountains of Diana or to the Thicket of Flora; to the Tapis Vert, or the Lawn of Latona, or the Basin of the Mirror? Altogether you grow dazed and dizzy with vast vistas of gravel and marble margins of huge water-basins, with Normandy poplars and box-edgings and clipped conical yews, planted in depressing geometrical patterns, relieved only here and there by groves of horse-chestnut. As for the statuary, magnificent as it is, there is so much of it, and there is such an astounding conflict of attitude and gesture, that you are reminded of nothing so much as of Lemprière, Tooke's Pantheon, and Dr. William Smith's Dictionary of Mythology, all made plastic and gone mad.

The Gardens of the Grand Trianon have been described on very high authority as "extensive, angular, and cheerless;" but some interest attaches to the *remise*, full of old state carriages used in the reigns of the First and the Third Napoleon, of Louis XVIII., Charles X., and Louis Philippe. These disestablished coaches are mostly hideous in design; still they are as gaudy as carving and gilding, scarlet cloth, and velvet and heraldic blazonry can render them, and make a sufficiently brave appearance. In a corner, slightly disregarded, is an old Sedan chair, the panels beautifully painted, which was used by Marie Antoinette. I dare say that there are many English admirers of the "Pauvre Bourbonnaise" who would eagerly give a thousand pounds for this *chaise-à-porteurs*. But the most charming and the least melancholy of the monuments of the hapless Queen are in the gardens of Le Petit Trianon. Arthur Young, who came hither just two years before '89, speaks with a qualified kind of approbation of what he calls the Queen's " jardin Anglais." He describes it as " disposed in the taste of what we read of in books on Chinese gardening;" and adds that " there is more in it of Sir William Chambers than of Mr. Brown—more effort than nature and more expense than taste." On the other hand, the critic admits that " it is not easy to conceive anything that art can introduce in a garden that is not here—woods, rocks, lawns, lakes, islands, cascades, grottoes, walks, temples, and even villages. The Temple of Love is truly elegant."

The Temple of Love, with all its elegance, may go to Hong Kong for me. Give me the Hameau Suisse. Here you escape from the immensity of Euclid's problems demonstrated in gravel and verdure by M. Le Nôtre, who has been so highly successful in robbing Nature of almost every grace which she possesses. Alexis Soyer, the cook, when Marshal Pélissier and his staff came to lunch with him before Sebastopol, took the liberty of improving upon Nature by painting the parched Crimean sward before his hut a lively emerald green; but Le Nôtre, had he had the power, would have done more. He would have ribbed the arch of the empyrean with festoons of flowers, and encircled the stars with borders of neatly-trimmed box. He was happily dead when Marie Antoinette laid out her hundred acres of English garden at the Petit Trianon. The villa itself is no great matter. It was built by Louis Quinze for the Dubarri; and here Louis himself sickened of the small-pox, of which he was to die at Versailles. His successor gave the Petit Trianon to Marie Antoinette, who, when she repaired to it, very philosophically slept in the Dubarri's bed. She was accused of a wish to call her new acquisition "Le Petit Schönbrunn," or "La Petite Vienne." She laughed. Ah! if she could only have continued to laugh in this enchanting spot! Her gardeners made quiet and refreshingly verdant glades for her, with a tiny streamlet picturesquely meandering through them, a *pièce d'eau;* and her architects this coquettish little Swiss village, with its Maison du Bailli, its dainty Windmill, its Tour de Malbrouck, and its Dairy. The *bailli*, the miller, the beadle were princes of the Blood Royal of France. The head dairywoman was the Queen. Her dairymaids were the Princesse de Lamballe and the Comtesse Jules de Polignac. If these grand personages could only have been permitted to play at being poor and industrious people to the end of the chapter! The world would have been all the better for so much more butter and cheese and French rolls, and so much less bloodshed, rapine, poverty, and immeasurable anguish and despair.

I was glad that the doors of the little buildings of the Hameau Suisse were all securely locked, and I would scarcely even have thanked a franc-expecting *gardien* had he offered to show us the rooms. It was so much more interesting to peep through the window of the dairy and fancy that you saw the Queen and her dairymaids busy with their churns and their butter-moulds. If you come across a doll's house, and are grown up, you shrink from making the entire façade swing open on its hinges and brutally reveal the mysteries of the basement and the upper floors. You peep discreetly through the windows, and in imagination try to fill the different rooms with real little people. Have you not done the same when you have peered through the stern cabins of the model of a ship of war, or into the interior of the model of a carriage? Models are usually among the most attractive features in every industrial exhibition. Why are they so attractive? Because, so it seems to me, we are unconsciously fond of gazing upon Lilliputian representations of our belongings, and of peopling them in fancy with Lilliputian representations of ourselves. He must be over-wise or over-foolish who does not yield to strange fascination when he gazes on the field of a camera obscura.

THE END.

42, Catherine Street, Strand,
December, 1884.

VIZETELLY & CO.'S NEW BOOKS, AND NEW EDITIONS.

In Demy 8vo, cloth gilt, price 12s. 6d.

A JOURNEY DUE SOUTH;

TRAVELS IN SEARCH OF SUNSHINE.

By GEORGE AUGUSTUS SALA.

ILLUSTRATED WITH 16 FULL-PAGE ENGRAVINGS BY VARIOUS ARTISTS

CONTENTS —

I.—A Few Hours in the Delightful City.
II.—Life at Marseilles.
III.—Southern Fare and Bouillabaisse.
IV.—Nice and its Nefarious Neighbour.
V.—Quite Another Nice.
VI.—From Nice to Bastia.
VII.—On Shore at Bastia.
VIII.—The Diligence come to Life again.
IX.—Sunday at Ajaccio.
X.—The Hotel too soon.
XI.—The House in St. Charles Street, Ajaccio.
XII.—A Winter City.
XIII.—Genoa the Superb: the City of the Leaning Tower
XIV.—Austere Bologna.
XV.—A Day of the Dead.
XVI.—Venice Preserved.
XVII.—The Two Romes. I. The Old.
XVIII.—The Two Romes. II. The New.
XIX.—The Two Romes. II. The New (*cont.*).
XX.—The Roman Season.
XXI.—In the Vatican: Mosaics.
XXII.—With the Trappists in the Campagna.
XXIII.—From Naples to Pompeii.
XXIV.—The Show of a Long-Buried Past.
XXV.—The "Movimento" of Naples.
XXVI.—In the Shade.
XXVII.—Spring Time in Paris.
XXVIII.—"To All the Glories of France."
XXIX.—Le Roi Soleil and La Belle Bourbonnaise.
XXX.—A Queen's Plaything.

VIZETELLY & CO.'S RECENT PUBLICATIONS.

IMPORTANT NEW WORK BY THE AUTHOR OF "SIDE LIGHTS ON ENGLISH SOCIETY."

Two Vols. large Post 8vo, attractively bound, price 25s.

UNDER THE LENS:
SOCIAL PHOTOGRAPHS.
By E. C. GRENVILLE-MURRAY.

ILLUSTRATED WITH ABOUT 300 ENGRAVINGS BY WELL-KNOWN ARTISTS.

CONTENTS OF VOL. I.

JILTS:—Mrs. Pinkerton—A Western County Belle—Zoe, Lady Tryon—An Inconsolable Jilt—A Jilted Drysalter—Love and Pickles—An Entr'acte—Mrs. Prago and Miss Daisy Caunter—A Widow with a Nice Little Estate—An Unmercenary Pair of Jilts.

ADVENTURERS AND ADVENTURESSES:—Of the Genus Generally—Matrimonial Adventurers—The Joint Stock Company Chairman—A Financial Adventurer—A Professional Greek—The Countess D'Orenbarre—Lady Goldsworth—Mirabel Hildacourse—Lily Gore—Bella Martingale—Pious Mrs. Palmhold—Mrs. Decoy—Mrs. Lawkins.

PUBLIC SCHOOLBOYS AND UNDERGRADUATES:—Drawbacks of Eton—Of Various Eton Boys—Rugby and Rugbeians—Harrow, Winchester, Westminster—Oxford Undergraduates—University Discipline—Sporting and Athletic Undergraduates—Reading and Religious Undergraduates.

CONTENTS OF VOL. II.

SPENDTHRIFTS:—Prefatory—The Gambletons—Lord Charles Innynges—Lord Luke Poer—Lord Rottenham—Lord Barker—The Marquis of Malplaquet—The Lords Lumber—Sir Culling Earley—Tommy Dabble—Dicky Duff.

HONORABLE GENTLEMEN (M.P.'s):— Preliminary — Erudite Members — Crotchety Members — Free Lances — The Irish Contingent—Very Noble M.P.'s—Money Bags—Beery M.P.'s—Workingmen M.P.'s—Party Leaders—A Seatless Member.

SOME WOMEN I HAVE KNOWN:—An Ex-Beauty—Miss Jenny—Mademoiselle Sylvie—Miss Rose—Madame de l'Esbrouffe-Tourbillon.

ROUGHS OF HIGH AND LOW DEGREE:—How Roughs are Made—The Nobleman Rough—The Foreign Garrison Rough—The Clerical Rough—The Legal Rough—Medical Roughs—The Rough Flirt—The Wife-Beating Rough—Vandal Roughs—The Tourist Rough—The Nautical Rough—The Professional Bruiser—The Low-Class Rough—Women Roughs.

THE MISSES D'ORENBARRE EXHIBIT THEIR AVERSION TO FAT MEN AND SMOKERS: *from* "*UNDER THE LENS.*"

VIZETELLY'S ONE-VOLUME NOVELS.

BY ENGLISH AND FOREIGN AUTHORS OF REPUTE.

In Crown 8vo, good readable type, and attractive binding, price 6s. each.

NEW VOLUMES.

A MUMMER'S WIFE.

A REALISTIC NOVEL. BY GEORGE MOORE,
AUTHOR OF "A MODERN LOVER."

PRINCE SERGE PANINE.

BY GEORGES OHNET,
AUTHOR OF "THE IRONMASTER."

TRANSLATED, WITHOUT ABRIDGMENT, from the 110TH FRENCH EDITION.

COUNTESS SARAH.

BY GEORGES OHNET,
AUTHOR OF "THE IRONMASTER."

TRANSLATED WITHOUT ABRIDGMENT FROM THE 118TH FRENCH EDITION.

NUMA ROUMESTAN; OR, JOY ABROAD AND GRIEF AT HOME.

BY ALPHONSE DAUDET.

TRANSLATED BY MRS. J. G. LAYARD.

"'Numa Roumestan' is a masterpiece; it is really a perfect work; it has no fault, no weakness. It is a compact and harmonious whole."—MR. HENRY JAMES.

The following One-Volume Novels will be published during January.

MR. BUTLER'S WARD.

BY MABEL ROBINSON.

THE CORSARS; OR, LOVE AND LUCRE.

BY JOHN HILL,
AUTHOR OF "THE WATERS OF MARAH," "SALLY," &c.

BETWEEN MIDNIGHT AND DAWN.

BY INA L. CASSILIS,
AUTHOR OF "SOCIETY'S QUEEN," "STRANGELY WOOED: STRANGELY WON," &c.

In Large Crown 8vo, beautifully printed on toned paper, and handsomely bound, with gilt edges, price 7s. 6d., suitable in every way for a present,

AN ILLUSTRATED EDITION OF

M. GEORGES OHNET'S CELEBRATED NOVEL,

THE IRONMASTER; OR, LOVE AND PRIDE.

TRANSLATED FROM THE 146th FRENCH EDITION AND CONTAINING 42 FULL-PAGE ENGRAVINGS BY FRENCH ARTISTS, PRINTED SEPARATE FROM THE TEXT.

"Le Maître de Forges" of M. Georges Ohnet has proved the greatest literary success in any language of recent times, the author having already realised £12,000 from it. It is a story of admirably sustained interest, skilfully told in graceful yet forcible language; and, unlike the general run of French novels, it conveys a sound moral. It chastises the malice which is born of envy, establishes the folly of that selfish pride which blinds its possessor to all consideration for the commoner clay of humanity, and enforces in convincing language the oft-repeated lesson, that a woman should never trifle with the affection of the man to whom she is mated for life.

An Edition of the above Work is published without the Illustrations in small 8vo, price 3s. 6d.

In Large Post 8vo, with Frontispiece and Vignette, cloth gilt, price 9s.

HIGH LIFE IN FRANCE UNDER THE REPUBLIC:

SOCIAL AND SATIRICAL SKETCHES IN PARIS AND THE PROVINCES.

BY E. C. GRENVILLE-MURRAY,

AUTHOR OF "SIDE LIGHTS ON ENGLISH SOCIETY," &c.

" Take this book as it stands, with the limitations imposed upon its author by circumstances, and it will be found very enjoyable. . . . The volume is studded with shrewd observations on French life at the present day."—*Spectator.*

" A very clever and entertaining series of social and satirical sketches, almost French in their point and vivacity."—*Contemporary Review.*

" Mr. Grenville-Murray's Pistache is capital, and so is Gredon, who gets adopted and befooled, despite his Yankee training, by the *soi-disant* Duke of Pontbrizé . . . The whole story of Timoleon Tartine, winding up with the commission agent's episode, is excellent."—*Graphic.*

" Mr. Grenville-Murray's sketches are light and pointed, and are full of that particular humour in which Frenchmen are supposed to be such adepts."—*Scotsman.*

In Large Post 8vo, cloth gilt, price 9s.

IMPRISONED IN A SPANISH CONVENT:

AN ENGLISH GIRL'S EXPERIENCES.

BY E. C. GRENVILLE-MURRAY.

ILLUSTRATED WITH PAGE AND OTHER ENGRAVINGS.

Fourth Edition, in Post 8vo, handsomely bound, price 7s. 6d.

SIDE-LIGHTS ON ENGLISH SOCIETY:

Sketches from Life, Social and Satirical.

By E. C. GRENVILLE-MURRAY.

ILLUSTRATED WITH NEARLY 300 CHARACTERISTIC ENGRAVINGS.

CONTENTS:

I. FLIRTS:—Born Flirts—The Flirt who has Plain Sisters—The Flirt in the London Season—The Ecclesiastical Flirt—The Regimental Flirt on Home and Foreign Service—The Town and Country House Flirt—The Seaside Flirt—The Flirt on her Travels—The Sentimental Flirt—The Studious Flirt.

II. ON HER BRITANNIC MAJESTY'S SERVICE:—Ambassadors—Envoys Extraordinary—Secretaries of Embassy—Secretaries of Legation—Attachés—Consuls-General—Consuls—Vice-Consuls—Queen's Messengers—Interpreters—Ambassadresses.

III. SEMI-DETACHED WIVES:—Authoresses and Actresses—Separated by Mutual Consent—Candidates for a Decree Nisi—A very virtuous Semi-Detached Wife—Ulysses and Penelope.

IV. NOBLE LORDS:—The Millionnaire Duke—Political Peers—Noble Old Fogies—Spiritual Peers—The Sabbatarian Peer—The Philanthropist Peer—Coaching Peers—Sporting Peers—Spendthrift Peers—Peers without Rent-rolls—Virtuoso Lords—Mad and Miserly Peers—Stock Exchange and Literary Lords.

V. YOUNG WIDOWS:—Interesting Widows—Gay Young Widows—Young Widows of Good Estate—Young Widows who take Boarders—Young Widows who want Situations—Great Men's Young Widows—Widows under a Cloud.

VI. OUR SILVERED YOUTH, OR NOBLE OLD BOYS:—Political Old Boys—Horsey Old Boys—An M. F. H.—Theatrical Old Boys—The Old Boy Cricketer—The Agricultural Old Boy—The Wicked Old Boy—The Shabby Old Boy—The Recluse Old Boy—The Clerical Old Boy—A Curiosity—An Old Courtier.

"This is a startling book. The volume is expensively and elaborately got up; the writing is bitter, unsparing, and extremely clever."—*Vanity Fair*.

"Mr. Grenville-Murray sparkles very steadily throughout the present volume, and puts to excellent use his incomparable knowledge of life and manners, of men and cities, of appearances and facts. Of his several descants upon English types, I shall only remark that they are brilliantly and dashingly written, curious as to their matter, and admirably readable."—*Truth*.

"No one can question the brilliancy of the sketches, nor affirm that 'Side-Lights' is aught but a fascinating book ...... The book is destined to make a great noise in the world."—*Whitehall Review*.

VIZETELLY & CO.'S RECENT PUBLICATIONS

THE RICH WIDOW (reduced from the original engraving).

Second Edition, in large 8vo, handsomely bound, with gilt edges, price 10s. 6d.

PEOPLE I HAVE MET.

By E. C. GRENVILLE-MURRAY.

Illustrated with 54 tinted Page Engravings, from Designs by FRED. BARNARD.

CONTENTS:—

The Old Earl.	The Rector.	The Doctor.	The Bachelor.
The Dowager.	The Curate.	The Retired Colonel.	The Younger Son.
The Family Solicitor.	The Governess.	The Chaperon.	The Grandmother.
The College Don.	The Tutor.	The Usurer.	The Newspaper Editor.
The Rich Widow.	The Promising Son.	The Spendthrift.	The Butler.
The Ornamental Director.	The Favourite Daughter.	Le Nouveau Riche.	The Devotee.
The Old Maid.	The Squire.	The Maiden Aunt.	

"Mr. Grenville-Murray's pages sparkle with cleverness and with a shrewd wit, caustic or cynical at times, but by no means excluding a due appreciation of the softer virtues of women and the sterner excellences of men. The talent of the artist (Mr. Barnard) is akin to that of the author, and the result of the combination is a book that, once taken up, can hardly be laid down until the last page is perused."—*Spectator.*

"All are strongly accentuated portraits. 'The Promising Son' is perhaps the best, though the most melancholy of the series. From first to last, as might be expected, the book is well written."—*Standard.*

"Mr. Grenville-Murray's sketches are genuine studies, and are the best things of the kind that have been published since 'Sketches by Boz,' to which they are superior in the sense in which artistically executed character-portraits are superior to caricatures."—*St. James's Gazette.*

"All of Mr. Grenville-Murray's portraits are clever and life-like, and some of them are not unworthy of a model who was more before the author's eyes than Addison—namely Thackeray."—*Truth.*

An Edition of "PEOPLE I HAVE MET" is published in small 8vo, with Sixteen Illustrations, price 6s.

A BUCK OF THE REGENCY: *from "DUTCH PICTURES."*

"Mr. Sala's best work has in it something of Montaigne, a great deal of Charles Lamb—made deeper and broader—and not a little of Lamb's model, the accomplished and quaint Sir Thomas Brown. These 'Dutch Pictures' and 'Pictures Done With a Quill' should be placed alongside Oliver Wendell Holmes's inimitable budgets of friendly gossip and Thackeray's 'Roundabout Papers.' They display to perfection the quick eye, good taste, and ready hand of the born essayist—they are never tiresome."—*Daily Telegraph*

In Crown 8vo, price 5s.

DUTCH PICTURES, and PICTURES DONE WITH A QUILL.

Illustrated with a Frontispiece and other Page Engravings.

FORMING THE FIRST VOLUME OF THE

CHOICER MISCELLANEOUS WORKS OF GEORGE AUGUSTUS SALA

A SMALL NUMBER OF COPIES OF THE ABOVE WORK HAVE BEEN PRINTED IN DEMY OCTAVO, ON HAND-MADE PAPER, WITH THE ILLUSTRATIONS ON INDIA PAPER MOUNTED.

The Graphic remarks: "We have received a sumptuous new edition of Mr. G. A. Sala's well-known 'Dutch Pictures.' It is printed on rough paper, and is enriched with many admirable illustrations."

In preparation, uniform with the above Volume,

UNDER THE SUN.

ESSAYS MAINLY WRITTEN IN HOT COUNTRIES.

By GEORGE AUGUSTUS SALA.

Illustrated with an etched Portrait of the Author, and various Page Engravings.

In One Volume, Demy 8vo, 560 pages, price 12s., the FIFTH EDITION *of*

AMERICA REVISITED,

From the Bay of New York to the Gulf of Mexico, and from Lake Michigan to the Pacific;

INCLUDING A SOJOURN AMONG THE MORMONS IN SALT LAKE CITY.

By GEORGE AUGUSTUS SALA.

ILLUSTRATED WITH NEARLY 400 ENGRAVINGS.

CONTENTS.

Outward Bound.
Thanksgiving Day in New York.
Transformation of New York.
All the Fun of the Fair.
A Morning with Justice.
On the Cars.
Fashion and Food in New York.
The Monumental City.
Baltimore come to Life again.
The Great Grant "Boom."
A Philadelphian Babel.
At the Continental.
Christmas and the New Year.
On to Richmond.
Still on to Richmond.
In Richmond.
Genial Richmond.
In the Tombs—and out of them.
Prosperous Augusta.
The City of many Cows.
A Pantomime in the South.
Arrogant Atlanta.
The Crescent City.
On Canal Street.
In Jackson Square.
A Southern Parliament.
Sunday in New Orleans.
The Carnival Booming.
The Carnival Booms.
Going West.
The Wonderful Prairie City.
The Home of the Setting Sun.
At Omaha.
The Road to Eldorado.
Still on the Road to Eldorado.
At Last.
Aspects of 'Frisco.
China Town.
The Drama in China Town.
Scenes in China Town.
China Town by Night.
From 'Frisco to Salt Lake City.
Down among the Mormons.
The Stock-yards of Chicago.

"It was like your imperence to come smouchin' round here, looking after de white folks' washin.'"

"In 'America Revisited' Mr. Sala is seen at his very best; better even than in his Paris book, more evenly genial and gay, and with a fresher subject to handle."—*World.*

"Mr. Sala's good stories lie thick as plums in a pudding throughout this handsome work."—*Pall Mall Gazette.*

"A new book of travel by Mr. Sala is sure to be welcome. He possesses the happy knack of adorning whatever he touches, and of finding something worth telling when traversing beaten ground."—*Athenæum.*

"A pleasant day may be spent with this book. Open where you will you find kindly chat and pleasant description. The illustrations are admirable."—*Vanity Fair.*

"As for the style of this entertaining and lively book, it is exactly what we should have expected. The writer is full of life, observation, and swiftness to seize upon salient and characteristic points. His description of the Chinese quarter of San Francisco may be strongly commended."—*Saturday Review.*

"This brilliant work possesses an irresistible charm, difficult to define indeed, but none the less delightful. Reading it is like listening to a good talker—the usual slightly wearisome sense of reading is effaced by the vivaciousness of the style in which the cleverest *feuilletoniste* of the day has narrated his experiences on the occasion of his last visit to America."—*Morning Post.*

"'America Revisited' is bright, lively, and amusing. We doubt whether Mr. Sala could be dull even if he tried."—*Globe.*

VIZETELLY & CO.'S RECENT PUBLICATIONS.

Seventh Edition, in Crown 8vo, 558 pages, attractively bound, price 3s. 6d., or gilt at the side and with gilt edges, 5s.

PARIS HERSELF AGAIN.

By GEORGE AUGUSTUS SALA.

WITH 350 CHARACTERISTIC ILLUSTRATIONS BY FRENCH ARTISTS.

"The author's 'round-about' chapters are as animated as they are varied and sympathetic, for few Englishmen have the French *verve* like Mr. Sala, or so light a touch on congenial subjects. He has stores of out-of-the-way information, a very many-sided gift of appreciation, with a singularly tenacious memory, and on subjects like those in his present work he is at his best."—*The Times.*

"Most amusing letters they are, with clever little pictures scattered so profusely through the solid volume that it would be difficult to prick the edges with a pin at any point without coming upon one or more. Few writers can rival Mr. Sala's fertility of illustration and ever ready command of lively comment."—*Daily News.*

"'Paris Herself Again' furnishes a happy illustration of the attractiveness of Mr. Sala's style and the fertility of his resources. For those who do and those who do not know Paris these volumes contain a fund of instruction and amusement."—*Saturday Review.*

"This book is one of the most readable that has appeared for many a day. Few Englishmen know so much of old and modern Paris as Mr. Sala. Endowed with a facility to extract humour from every phase of the world's stage, and blessed with a wondrous store of recondite lore, he outdoes himself when he deals with a city like Paris that he knows so well, and that affords such an opportunity for his pen."—*Truth.*

"'Paris Herself Again' is infinitely more amusing than most novels, and will give you information which you can turn to advantage, and innumerable anecdotes for the dinner-table and the smoking-room. There is no style so chatty and so unwearying as that of which Mr. Sala is a master."—*The World.*

ZOLA'S POWERFUL REALISTIC NOVELS.

Uniform with NANA *and* THE "ASSOMMOIR." *In Crown 8vo, price 6s.*

PIPING HOT!
("POT-BOUILLE.")
By EMILE ZOLA.

Unabridged Translation from the 63rd French edition. Illustrated with Sixteen Tinted Page Engravings by French Artists.

In Crown 8vo, handsomely bound, price 6s.

NANA:
A REALISTIC NOVEL. BY EMILE ZOLA.

TRANSLATED WITHOUT ABRIDGMENT FROM THE 127TH FRENCH EDITION.

A New Edition. Illustrated with Twenty-Four Tinted Page Engravings, from Designs by Bellenger, Clairin, and André Gill.

Mr. HENRY JAMES on "NANA."

"A novelist with a system, a passionate conviction, a great plan—incontestable attributes of M. Zola—is not now to be easily found in England or the United States, where the story-teller's art is almost exclusively feminine, is mainly in the hands of timid (even when very accomplished) women, whose acquaintance with life is severely restricted, and who are not conspicuous for general views. The novel, moreover, among ourselves, is almost always addressed to young unmarried ladies, or at least always assumes them to be a large part of the novelist's public.

"This fact, to a French story-teller, appears, of course, a damnable restriction, and M. Zola would probably decline to take *au sérieux* any work produced under such unnatural conditions. Half of life is a sealed book to young unmarried ladies, and how can a novel be worth anything that deals only with half of life? How can a portrait be painted (in any way to be recognizable) of half a face? It is not in one eye, but in the two eyes together that the expression resides, and it is the combination of features that constitutes the human identity. These objections are perfectly valid, and it may be said that our English system is a good thing for virgins and boys, and a bad thing for the novel itself, when the novel is regarded as something more than a simple *jeu d'esprit*, and considered as a composition that treats of life at large and helps us to *know*."

In Crown 8vo, uniform with "NANA," *price 6s.*

THE "ASSOMMOIR;"
(The Prelude to "NANA.")
A REALISTIC NOVEL. BY EMILE ZOLA.

TRANSLATED WITHOUT ABRIDGMENT FROM THE 97TH FRENCH EDITION.

Illustrated with Sixteen Tinted Page Engravings, by Bellenger, Clairin, André Gill, Leloir, Rosé and Vierge.

"After reading Zola's novels it seems as if in all others, even in the truest, there were a veil between the reader and the things described, and there is present to our minds the same difference as exists between the representations of human faces on canvas and the reflection of the same faces in a mirror. It is like finding truth for the first time.

"Zola is one of the most moral novelists in France, and it is really astonishing how anyone can doubt this. He makes us note the smell of vice, not its perfume: his nude figures are those of the anatomical table, which do not inspire the slightest immoral thought; there is not one of his books, not even the crudest, that does not leave behind it pure, firm, and unmistakable aversion, or scorn, for the base passions of which he treats. Brutally, pitilessly, and without hypocrisy he strips vice naked and holds it up to ridicule. Forced by his hand it is vice itself that says, 'Detest me and pass by!' His novels, as he himself says, are really 'morals in action.'"—*Signor de Amicis on the "Assommoir."*

All the above are published without the Illustrations, price 5s.

THE ARRIVAL OF THE ELEVEN YOUNG MEN AT NANA'S EVENING PARTY

In Crown 8vo, handsomely bound and gilt, price 6s., the Third and Completely Revised Edition of

THE STORY OF
THE DIAMOND NECKLACE,

COMPRISING A SKETCH OF THE LIFE OF THE COUNTESS DE LA MOTTE, PRETENDED CONFIDANTE OF MARIE-ANTOINETTE, WITH PARTICULARS OF THE CAREERS OF THE OTHER ACTORS IN THIS REMARKABLE DRAMA.

By HENRY VIZETELLY.

AUTHOR OF "BERLIN UNDER THE NEW EMPIRE," "PARIS IN PERIL," &c.

Illustrated with an Exact Representation of the Diamond Necklace, from a contemporary Drawing, and a Portrait of the Countess de la Motte, engraved on Steel.

"Mr. Vizetelly's tale has all the interest of a romance which is too strange not to be true. . . . . His summing up of the evidence, both negative and positive, which exculpates Marie-Antoinette from any complicity whatever with the scandalous intrigue in which she was represented as bearing a part, is admirable."—*Saturday Review.*

"We can, without fear of contradiction, describe Mr. Henry Vizetelly's 'Story of the Diamond Necklace' as a book of thrilling interest. He has not only executed his task with skill and faithfulness, but also with tact and delicacy."—*Standard.*

"Had the most daring of our sensational novelists put forth the present plain unvarnished statement of facts as a work of fiction, it would have been denounced as so violating all probabilities as to be a positive insult to the common sense of the reader. Yet strange, startling, incomprehensible as is the narrative which the author has here evolved, every word of it is true."—*Notes and Queries.*

In Large Crown 8vo, handsomely printed and bound, price 6s.

THE AMUSING
ADVENTURES OF GUZMAN OF ALFARAQUE.

A SPANISH NOVEL. TRANSLATED BY EDWARD LOWDELL.

ILLUSTRATED WITH HIGHLY-FINISHED ENGRAVINGS ON STEEL FROM DESIGNS BY STAHL.

"The wit, vivacity and variety of this masterpiece cannot be over-estimated."—*Morning Post.*

"A very well executed translation of a famous, 'Rogue's Progress.'"—*Spectator.*

"The story is infinitely amusing, and illustrated as it is with several excellent designs on steel, it will be acceptable to a good many readers."—*Scotsman.*

In Post 8vo, price 2s. 6d.

THE CHILDISHNESS AND BRUTALITY OF THE TIME:

SOME PLAIN TRUTHS IN PLAIN LANGUAGE.

Supplemented by sundry discursive Essays and Narratives.

By HARGRAVE JENNINGS, Author of "The Rosicrucians," &c

"Mr. Jennings has a knack of writing in good, racy, trenchant style. His sketch of behind the scenes of the Opera, and his story of a mutiny on board an Indiaman of the old time, are penned with surprising freshness and spirit."—*Daily News.*

In Crown 8vo, attractively bound, price 3s. 6d.

THE RED CROSS, AND OTHER STORIES.
By LUIGI.

"The short stories are the best—Luigi is in places tender and pathetic."—*Athenæum.*

"The plans of the tales are excellent. Many of the incidents are admirable, and there is a good deal of pathos in the writing."—*Scotsman.*

"Pleasant and bright if somewhat sensational, dealing with the old world and the new, and offering a welcome variety of style, these tales may be recommended to the lovers of fiction."—*Literary World.*

In Two Volumes, post 8vo, price 10s. 6d.

SOCIETY NOVELETTES.

By F. C. BURNAND, H. SAVILE CLARKE, R. E. FRANCILLON, JOSEPH HATTON, RICHARD JEFFERIES, the Author of "A French Heiress in her own Château," &c. &c.

ILLUSTRATED WITH NUMEROUS PAGE AND OTHER ENGRAVINGS,

FROM DESIGNS BY R. CALDECOTT, LINLEY SAMBOURNE, M. E. EDWARDS, F. DADD, &c.

"The reader will not be disappointed in the hopes raised by Messrs. Vizetelly's pleasing volumes.... There is much that is original and clever in these 'Society' tales."—*Athenæum.*

"Many of the stories are of the greatest merit; and indeed with such contributors, the reader might be sure of the unusual interest and amusement which these volumes supply."—*Daily Telegraph.*

"We strongly advise the reader to begin with 'How one Ghost was laid,' and to follow it up with 'Jack's Wife,' with whom, by the way, as portrayed both by artist and author, he cannot fail to fall in love. These two graceful little extravaganzas will put him into so excellent a temper that he will thoroughly enjoy the good things that follow."—*Life.*

"The two volumes contain a large amount of capital reading. The stories are of all kinds excepting unpleasant kinds."—*Scotsman.*

In Crown 8vo, price 3s. 6d.

A NEW EDITION, COMPRISING MUCH ADDITIONAL MATTER, OF

IN STRANGE COMPANY.
By JAMES GREENWOOD (the "Amateur Casual").

ILLUSTRATED WITH A PORTRAIT OF THE AUTHOR, ENGRAVED ON STEEL.

VIZETELLY & CO.'S RECENT PUBLICATIONS.

In Demy 4to, handsomely printed and bound, with gilt edges, price 12s.

A HISTORY OF CHAMPAGNE;
WITH NOTES ON THE OTHER SPARKLING WINES OF FRANCE.

By HENRY VIZETELLY,

CHEVALIER OF THE ORDER OF FRANZ-JOSEF.

WINE JUROR FOR GREAT BRITAIN AT THE VIENNA AND PARIS EXHIBITIONS OF 1873 AND 1878.

Illustrated with 350 Engravings,

FROM ORIGINAL SKETCHES AND PHOTOGRAPHS, ANCIENT MSS., EARLY PRINTED BOOKS, RARE PRINTS, CARICATURES, ETC.

"A very agreeable medley of history, anecdote, geographical description, and such like matter, distinguished by an accuracy not often found in such medleys, and illustrated in the most abundant and pleasingly miscellaneous fashion."—*Daily News.*

"Mr. Henry Vizetelly's handsome book about Champagne and other sparkling wines of France is full of curious information and amusement. It should be widely read and appreciated."—*Saturday Review.*

"Mr. Henry Vizetelly has written a quarto volume on the 'History of Champagne,' in which he has collected a large number of facts, many of them very curious and interesting. Many of the woodcuts are excellent."—*Athenæum.*

"How competent the author was for his task is to be inferred from the functions he has discharged, and from the exceptional opportunities he enjoyed."—*Illustrated London News.*

In square 8vo, cloth gilt, price 3s. 6d.

LAYS OF THE SAINTLY;
OR, THE NEW GOLDEN LEGEND.

By the LONDON HERMIT (W. PARKE),

Author of "Les Manteaux Noirs."

WITH HUMOROUS ILLUSTRATIONS BY J. LEITCH.

"Lovers of laughter, raillery, and things ludicrous would do well to become possessed of this volume of humorous poems levelled against the absurd though amusing superstitions of the Middle Ages."—*Newcastle Chronicle.*

In large imperial 8vo, price 6d.

THE SOCIAL ZOO;

SATIRICAL, SOCIAL, AND HUMOROUS SKETCHES BY THE BEST WRITERS.

Copiously Illustrated in Many Styles by well-known Artists.

NOW READY.

OUR GILDED YOUTH. By E. C. GRENVILLE-MURRAY——NICE GIRLS. By R. MOUNTENEY JEPHSON——NOBLE LORDS. By E. C. GRENVILLE-MURRAY ——FLIRTS. By E. C. GRENVILLE-MURRAY——OUR SILVERED YOUTH. By E. C. GRENVILLE-MURRAY——MILITARY MEN AS THEY WERE. By E. DYNE FENTON.

VIZETELLY & CO.'S RECENT PUBLICATIONS. 17

In ornamental covers, 1s. 6d. each; posted, 1s. 9d.

GABORIAU'S SENSATIONAL NOVELS.
THE FAVOURITE READING OF PRINCE BISMARCK.

> "Ah, friend, how many and many a while
> They've made the slow time fleetly flow,
> And solaced pain and charmed exile,
> Miss Braddon and Gaboriau!"
> *Ballade of Railway Novels in "Longman's Magazine."*

IN PERIL OF HIS LIFE.
"A story of thrilling interest and admirably translated."—*Sunday Times.*

"Hardly ever has a more ingenious circumstantial case been imagined than that which puts the hero in peril of his life, and the manner in which the proof of his innocence is finally brought about is scarcely less skilful."—*Illustrated Sporting and Dramatic News.*

THE LEROUGE CASE.
"M. Gaboriau is a skilful and brilliant writer, capable of so diverting the attention and interest of his readers that not one word or line in his book will be skipped or read carelessly."—*Hampshire Advertiser.*

OTHER PEOPLE'S MONEY.
"The interest is kept up throughout, and the story is told graphically and with a good deal of art."—*London Figaro.*

LECOQ THE DETECTIVE. Two vols.
"In the art of forging a tangled chain of complicated incidents involved and inexplicable until the last link is reached and the whole made clear, Mr. Wilkie Collins is equalled, if not excelled, by M. Gaboriau. The same skill in constructing a story is shown by both, as likewise the same ability to build up a superstructure of facts on a foundation which, sound enough in appearance, is shattered when the long-concealed touchstone of truth is at length applied to it."—*Brighton Herald.*

THE GILDED CLIQUE.
"Full of incident and instinct with life and action. Altogether this is a most fascinating book."—*Hampshire Advertiser.*

THE MYSTERY OF ORCIVAL.
"The Author keeps the interest of the reader at fever heat, and by a succession of unexpected turns and incidents, the drama is ultimately worked out to a very pleasant result. The ability displayed is unquestionable."—*Sheffield Independent.*

DOSSIER NO. 113.
"The plot is worked out with great skill, and from first to last the reader's interest is never allowed to flag."—*Dumbarton Herald.*

THE LITTLE OLD MAN OF BATIGNOLLES.

THE SLAVES OF PARIS. Two vols.
"Sensational, full of interest, cleverly conceived and wrought out with consummate skill."—*Oxford and Cambridge Journal.*

THE COUNT'S MILLIONS. Two vols.

INTRIGUES OF A FEMALE POISONER.

THE CATASTROPHE. Two vols.

Publishing in Monthly Volumes, 1s. each.

UNIFORM WITH GABORIAU'S SENSATIONAL NOVELS.

THE SENSATIONAL NOVELS
OF FORTUNÉ DU BOISGOBEY.

NOW READY.

THE OLD AGE OF LECOQ, THE DETECTIVE. Two vols.

TO BE FOLLOWED BY

THE THUMB STROKE.—SEALED LIPS.—THE GOLDEN TRESS.—SATAN'S COACH.—THE DETECTIVE'S EYE.

In Small Post 8vo, ornamental covers, 1s. each; in cloth, 1s. 6d.

VIZETELLY'S POPULAR FRENCH NOVELS.

TRANSLATIONS OF THE BEST EXAMPLES OF RECENT FRENCH FICTION OF AN UNOBJECTIONABLE CHARACTER.

" They are books that may be safely left lying about where the ladies of the family can pick them up and read them. The interest they create is happily not of the vicious sort at all."
— SHEFFIELD INDEPENDENT.

FROMONT THE YOUNGER & RISLER THE ELDER. By A. DAUDET.
"The series starts well with M. Alphonse Daudet's masterpiece."—*Athenæum*.
"A terrible story, powerful after a sledge-hammer fashion in some parts, and wonderfully tender, touching, and pathetic in others, the extraordinary popularity whereof may be inferred from the fact that this English version is said to be 'translated from the fiftieth French edition.'"—*Illustrated London News*.

SAMUEL BROHL AND PARTNER. By V. CHERBULIEZ.
"M. Cherbuliez's novels are read by everybody and offend nobody. They are excellent studies of character, well constructed, peopled with interesting men and women, and the style in which they are written is admirable."—*The Times*.
"Those who have read this singular story in the original need not be reminded of that supremely dramatic study of the man who lived two lives at once, even within himself. The reader's discovery of his double nature is one of the most cleverly managed of surprises, and Samuel Brohl's final dissolution of partnership with himself is a remarkable stroke of almost pathetic comedy."—*The Graphic*.

THE DRAMA OF THE RUE DE LA PAIX. By A. BELOT.
"A highly ingenious plot is developed in 'The Drama of the Rue de la Paix,' in which a decidedly interesting and thrilling narrative is told with great force and passion, relieved by sprightliness and tenderness."—*Illustrated London News*.

MAUGARS JUNIOR. By A. THEURIET.
"One of the most charming novelettes we have read for a long time."—*Literary World*.

WAYWARD DOSIA, & THE GENEROUS DIPLOMATIST.
By HENRY GRÉVILLE.

"As epigrammatic as anything Lord Beaconsfield has ever written."—*Hampshire Telegraph.*

A NEW LEASE OF LIFE, & SAVING A DAUGHTER'S DOWRY. By E. ABOUT.

"'A New Lease of Life' is an absorbing story, the interest of which is kept up the very end."—*Dublin Evening Mail.*

"The story, as a flight of brilliant and eccentric imagination, is unequalled in its peculiar way."—*The Graphic.*

COLOMBA, & CARMEN. By P. MÉRIMÉE.

"The freshness and raciness of 'Colomba' is quite cheering after the stereotyped three-volume novels with which our circulating libraries are crammed."—*Halifax Times.*

"'Carmen' will be welcomed by the lovers of the sprightly and tuneful opera the heroine of which Minnie Hauk made so popular. It is a bright and vivacious story."—*Life.*

A WOMAN'S DIARY, & THE LITTLE COUNTESS. By O. FEUILLET.

"Is wrought out with masterly skill and affords reading which, although of a slightly sensational kind, cannot be said to be hurtful either mentally or morally."—*Dumbarton Herald.*

BLUE-EYED META HOLDENIS, & A STROKE OF DIPLOMACY. By V. CHERBULIEZ.

"'Blue-eyed Meta Holdenis' is a delightful tale."—*Civil Service Gazette.*

"'A Stroke of Diplomacy' is a bright vivacious story pleasantly told."—*Hampshire Advertiser.*

THE GODSON OF A MARQUIS. By A. THEURIET.

"The rustic personages, the rural scenery and life in the forest country of Argonne, are painted with the hand of a master. From the beginning to the close the interest of the story never flags."—*Life.*

THE TOWER OF PERCEMONT AND MARIANNE. By GEORGE SAND.

"George Sand has a great name, and the 'Tower of Percemont' is not unworthy of it."—*Illustrated London News.*

THE LOW-BORN LOVER'S REVENGE. By V. CHERBULIEZ.

"'The Low-born Lover's Revenge' is one of M. Cherbuliez's many exquisitely written productions. The studies of human nature under various influences, especially in the cases of the unhappy heroine and her low-born lover, are wonderfully effective."—*Illustrated London News.*

THE NOTARY'S NOSE, AND OTHER AMUSING STORIES. By E. ABOUT.

"Crisp and bright, full of movement and interest."—*Brighton Herald.*

DOCTOR CLAUDE; OR, LOVE RENDERED DESPERATE. By H. MALOT. Two vols.

"We have to appeal to our very first flight of novelists to find anything so artistic in English romance as these books."—*Dublin Evening Mail.*

THE THREE RED KNIGHTS; OR, THE BROTHERS' VENGEANCE. By P. FÉVAL.

"The one thing that strikes us in these stories is the marvellous dramatic skill of the writers."—*Sheffield Independent.*

www.ingramcontent.com/pod-product-compliance
Lightning Source LLC
Chambersburg PA
CBHW022108300426
44117CB00007B/638